SALERNO

HUGH POND

Salerno

WHITE LION PUBLISHERS
London, New York, Sydney and Toronto

First published in the United Kingdom by
William Kimber and Co. Ltd., 1961

White Lion edition, 1974

ISBN 0 85617 128 X

Printed in Great Britain by
Biddles Ltd., Guildford, Surrey,
for White Lion Publishers Ltd.,
138 Park Lane, London W1Y 3DD

To

MY WIFE

MILA

Without whose long-suffering patience and
assistance this book would never have been
written.

PUBLISHER'S NOTE

THE Publishers would like to thank Canonico Professore Arturo Carucci of Salerno Cathedral for his very kind assistance in Salerno in the summer of 1960 and especially for having placed at their disposal the records of the battle written by himself and by his late father, Carlo Carucci, in 1943, when they were eye-witnesses of many of the events related in this book.

They also wish to thank Signora Lucia Apicella ('Mamma Lucia') of Cava de' Tirreni for having given so freely of her time in relating the work which she carried out after the war and which is the subject of the epilogue in this volume.

To Dr. Pasquale Vuilleumier of Ravello they are indebted for invaluable guidance and help while collecting, on behalf of Major Pond, material for the Italian side of the story.

PREFACE

THE military term D-Day has become very firmly fixed in the minds of the general public with the 6th June, 1944, and the opening of the Second Front in Europe. But there were hundreds of other D-Days in the Second World War, for operations both large and small which are equally important to the thousands of soldiers who fought in them from Norway to New Guinea and from Arnhem to Guadalcanal.

September 9th, 1943, was a particularly important D-Day for thousands of American and British troops who formed the 5th Army which made the first large-scale opposed landing on the European Continent. From this operation and subsequent ones, such as Anzio, many lessons of great value were learnt and put into practice at *Overlord*.

Salerno was operationally coded *Avalanche*, and some people have described it as an 'Avalanche of Errors', yet despite the near disaster which threatened in the first few days it was eventually successful and formed the prelude to the long and costly campaign up the length of Italy.

An individual's personal battle is always restricted to what he saw with his own eyes and heard with his own ears. One man's account of an action may be entirely different to that of another only a few hundred yards away, yet they all fit into a pattern which eventually makes the picture clear. Even so, exact timings and even specific days, are often confused, and moments of acute danger or anxiety lasting only a short time are magnified in the memory into actions out of proportion to the facts. Confusion, chaos and near catastrophe have all emerged during my discussions with those who were there, but the ultimate story is one of bravery and doggedness not only on the Allied side but also on the part of the Germans.

I have spoken to, and been in correspondence with, hundreds of soldiers who served in the Battle of Salerno, not only British but also American, German and Italian. They all have important pieces of the story to tell and it has been fascinating comparing the different accounts.

One thing upon which nearly everybody agrees is that it was the Navy which made final victory in this operation possible. The incessant and overpowering weight of naval shells harried and smashed the German forces wherever they formed for attack, and without the battleships *Avalanche* would have been turned into another Dunkirk. This is made plain in all personal accounts and all histories written by both sides. It was a fine example of co-operation and co-ordination between the Services, and it is unfortunate that Field-Marshal Lord Alexander should go against this general verdict and refuse to admit that naval shelling had been the deciding element.

When Admiral of the Fleet Lord Cunningham of Hyndhope came to write his Despatches he reported his conclusion that the Navy had been the deciding factor. Alex disagreed with this view, and publication of these Despatches was delayed for many months until the final version contained only a watered-down version of the account that hardly does justice to the part played by the American and Royal Navies.

From the German viewpoint the battle was extremely well fought, particularly by the 16th Panzer Division, who, against overwhelming odds, inflicted heavy casualties on 5th Army and very nearly swept them off their small beachhead. It is therefore the more regrettable that in recent German military histories the writers have seen fit to inject unnecessary half-truths as an excuse for defeat. The history of the 16th Panzer Division, published in 1958, claims that on D-Day the Allies landed six complete divisions. This is entirely incorrect as only three Allied divisions were landed. There is also mention of British parachutists fighting in Battipaglia, yet not a single British airborne unit was involved in the Salerno landings. Lieutenant-General Wilhelm Schmalz, in an account of the battle, reports that at Salerno on 9th September there was but one solitary company of infantry and a battery of six guns. This may well have been true of Salerno town, but the impression it gives is that this small force was responsible for the entire bay. German reinforcements travelling overland were much quicker to arrive on the scene of battle than those of the Allies, and at one time the balance of power was strongly in the Germans' favour. One gets the unfortunate feeling that German historians are rewriting history and covering up mistakes, ensuring that the present generation of German youth will have the 'correct viewpoint' put to them.

General Mark Clark emerges as a somewhat controversial figure

..d his performance is extremely interesting, particularly in view
of subsequent operations at Anzio and Cassino.

It is incredible that when he first contemplated the possibility
of evacuating the American bridgehead he did not take either
of his corps commanders nor other generals into his confidence. One
senior British officer, not at Salerno, described him:

> He had tremendous energy and enthusiasm and drove himself every
> bit as hard as he drove his troops. He was as straight as he knew how,
> and never went back on anything he said or undertook. His American
> troops admired his drive, but I doubt if they liked him much as a man.
> Tactically and strategically Mark Clark was like most of his col-
> leagues. He believed in attacking all along the front without much
> regard for the ground etcetera. He had no finesse—for him war was
> a matter of bludgeons rather than rapiers.

General Clark described his Salerno battle in *Calculated Risk* and
has recently said that nothing has since emerged to add to the
story as he saw it then.

I would like to acknowledge the tremendous help I have received
from hundreds of soldiers, sailors and airmen, from America and
Germany as well as from Britain. Particularly I am grateful for
the time given up with interviews and correspondence to the
following: Admiral of the Fleet Lord Cunningham of Hyndhope;
Lieutenant-General Sir Richard McCreery; Admiral Sir Geoffrey
Oliver; Major-General Sir Robert Laycock; Major-General John
Whitfield; Major-General L. O. Lyne; Major-General D. A.
Kendrew; Major-General Fred Walker, *USA*; Lieutenant-General
Wilhelm Schmalz; Captain E. G. D. Pounds, *RM*; Captain John
Parson, *RM*; Major Herbert Scheftel, *USAF*; Major Herbert
Duppenbecker; Major Günter Schmitz; Captain Christopher
Bulteel; Major Michael Crichton-Stuart; Lieutenant Colonel
Mervyn Griffith-Jones; Mr. Michael Aston; Mr. W. Hickman;
Mr. J. Whitmore; Mr. John Redfern; and countless others too
numerous to list, but most especially to all those soldiers who took
the trouble to write out their personal reminiscences and send
them to me.

I must also acknowledge the ungrudging help and advice given
me by the staff of the Imperial War Museum Library and Photo-
graphic Sections, and to the staff of the War Office Library and
to General Services Administration, Washington.

CONTENTS

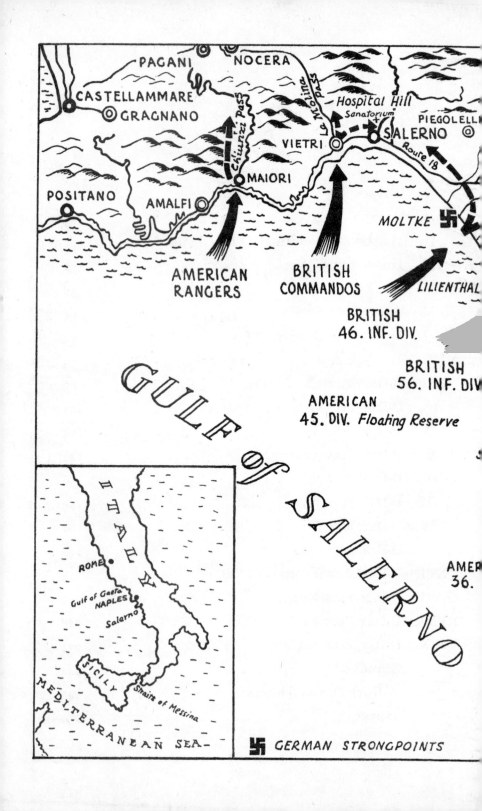

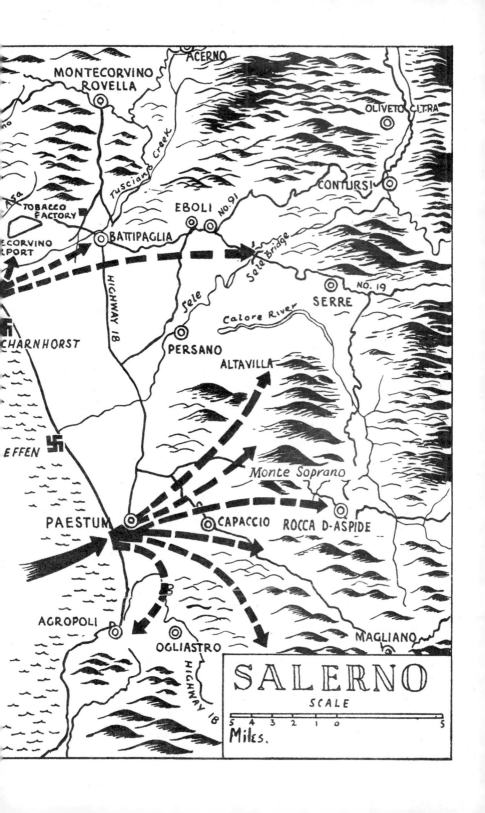

LIST OF ILLUSTRATIONS

Between pages 120 and 121

Chapter I

SALERNO—D-DAY MINUS ONE

8th September, 1943

ARTURO CARUCCI rinsed his thin hands in a china bowl of fresh water, dried them slowly and methodically, one finger at a time, on a white towel, while he looked thoughtfully in a small mirror above his washstand. Passing a brush over his black hair, he turned and went into his sparsely furnished sitting-room to await the arrival of a dinner guest.

He was Chaplain of the Sanatorium Giovanni da Procida, which sat squarely on a peak known as the Laughing Hill, overlooking the gulf and town of Salerno. Standing at the window, fingering a rosary, his eyes gazed lovingly but sadly at the green valley, patterned with vineyards, olive groves and tomato fields, and at the pink and white houses of the peasants whose years of labour had made the area lush and productive. His mind wandered over the events of the past few weeks. With some difficulty he opened the window which was warped and bent; the wall plaster was a crisscross of wide cracks, a result of Allied bombing which had been more or less continuous since the end of June. He wondered if that night would bring another flock of planes; he presumed that it would, as it was the time of the full moon and the roads, railways and bridges would stand out brightly as though on a lantern slide seen through the bomb-sights of the planes.

His heart was full of forebodings about the future, not only for Salerno but the whole of Italy. A hundred and sixty-nine weeks had gone by since the beginning of the war for his country, but there still seemed no end to it all.

There came a tap at the door; a nursing sister ushered in his guest, Lieutenant Aldo Pasquale Gatti. They greeted each other with the usual Italian warmth and almost immediately sat down at a small linen-covered table. The time being only six o'clock in the afternoon, Carucci apologised for the early repast.

15

"You must forgive the early hour of our meal, but with all this bombing we like to eat early, and at least have full stomachs for the nights we spend in the shelters."

Gatti had a long journey ahead of him to rejoin his wife in Piedmont. Picking up his knife and fork, he attacked his meal with relish, but after a few mouthfuls lowered his hands to ask: "Why aren't you eating?"

Receiving no reply from his host, he insisted: "Come on, hurry up with your food; we shall then listen to the wireless and take a walk in the park. It's such a lovely evening."

The priest broke out in voluble explanation. "I'll tell you why. I feel that grave things are about to happen. I sense it in my bones. We hear strange rumours that the Italian Government is considering making an armistice with the British. Yet we are bombed continuously; even this poor hospital is not left alone. In Salerno the English and American aeroplanes have dropped bombs everywhere except on the harbour. Why should they leave it alone? Yesterday German E-Boats cleared the harbour and destroyed the mole with torpedoes. Many of the sailors have been drafted into shore units, and even now engineers are blowing up dock installations and bridges. Again yesterday, the German troops held anti-invasion exercises on the beach, the plan of which, I hear, was a counter-attack on an enemy force which had landed at 4.30 a.m. north of the River Tusciano and captured the airfield at Montecorvino. What does it all mean?"

"How can you, a priest, know about such things? How can these rumours be true?"

"I can only tell you what I hear, and what I feel in my heart and in my bones. It is all very depressing."

It was an unsatisfactory meal for both host and guest. Soon Carucci switched on a small wireless set to break the embarrassing silence.

From Radio Roma came the strained high-pitched voice of an announcer, shouting defiance at the Allies and repeating an item from the German News Agency. "If Churchill and Roosevelt are awaiting, as is rumoured, the surrender of Italy, they might as well await Father Christmas."

And he added: "The Italian Government, despite propaganda to the contrary, is determined to fight to the bitter end."

The lieutenant nodded knowingly. "There, that settles the rumours once and for all."

Little did any of them realise how near was the bitter end!

The radio news seemed to slightly cheer the atmosphere and the chaplain told Gatti of the trouble they had been having with refugees who were pouring out of Salerno and Battipaglia following the heavy Allied raids, how in most of the coastal towns and settlements the majority of the officials had deserted their posts, leaving only the priests to guide and direct the people. He recalled that on that very morning at exactly 1100 hours a single-engined aeroplane had flown low over Salerno, its red, white and blue circles showing clearly; yet for some strange reason no anti-aircraft guns had opened up on it.

The flow of their conversation was interrupted by an authoritative voice on the radio, which announced that Marshal Badoglio, the Head of the Italian Government, was about to make an important statement. Instinctively they looked at their watches: it was 1945 hours precisely.

With a voice full of emotion, the marshal spoke: "The Italian Government, realising the impossibility of continuing the unequal struggle against the overwhelming power of the United Nations and to avoid further bloodshed, has asked for an armistice from General Eisenhower. This request has been granted. The Italian Armed Forces will therefore cease hostilities against the forces of the United Nations, wherever they may be." He went on to say that the Italian people would be kept informed by radio and, if necessary, leaflets, but his latter words were lost to the majority of his listeners. Carucci and Gatti looked in amazement at each other. They did not know whether to laugh or cry. Hurriedly they rushed out of the hospital buildings and ran across the park to a huge tunnel where the nurses and patients were already settled in for the night. As they gave the news, smiles lit up the faces of the men and women, whilst the sick troops, mostly suffering from tuberculosis, raised a small cheer. Gatti was the only one not to join in the congratulations. He warned them it was not an occasion for rejoicing: their enthusiasm was out of place, as the Germans would certainly resist these peace moves. Italy was likely to be plunged even deeper into war. Despite his gloomy forebodings, some of the people decided to leave the tunnel and return to their homes; the majority, however—several hundred—decided to stay put.

These words, entered daily in a diary by Arturo Carucci in a careful, monastic hand, kept a faithful record of events preceding the Allied invasion and of the days of battle to come.

Meanwhile, in Salerno, the news spread like lightning. Normally at this hour the town was deserted, as most of the inhabitants took their bedding and went into the hills to avoid the bombing. But on this night there was no thought of retreating into the country. The citizens poured into the battered streets; hundreds went into the churches asking that the *Te Deum* should be sung and the bells rung. But most of the priests urged caution, saying that an armistice did not necessarily bring peace, and that they should return to the air-raid shelters or their homes.

A few miles away in the small town of Olevano, north of Battipaglia, high up in the mountains, Carlo Carucci, a schoolmaster, father of the Sanatorium chaplain, was recording in a diary his inner feelings in this hour of crisis. His countrymen had been beaten on land, at sea and in the air by the English and he cursed Mussolini and his followers who had brought his land into such an abject state. His second thoughts were of his wife, who, even at that moment, was praying at the Chapel of the *Madonna del Soccorso*— the Madonna of Help. Calling the maid, he told her to run and tell his wife the news. The girl ran down the cobbled streets. She went through the heavy wooden door; in the excitement she crossed herself hurriedly, forgetting to dip her fingers in the bowl of holy water. The priest was standing in the pulpit, trying to instil faith and hope into his congregation. The women's heads, covered in black veils, and the bare heads of the men turned in amazement at the interruption, whilst the girl sidled up to her mistress. Soon the small church was full of whispering, as the momentous information was passed from mouth to mouth; they believed their prayers had been at long last answered: "It is a miracle performed by the Madonna!" There were tears, there was laughter; so much so that the priest had to rap on the pulpit.

"You are not in the market place," he admonished. "If you want to give thanks to God and the Madonna, let it be with dignity and peace."

A group of men in an *osteria* raised their glasses. The eldest remarked that the first thing he would do would be to change the name of the school. Since the coming of Fascism it had been called 'Costanzo Ciano'—a name hated by all—and he proposed that it should be renamed 'Giovanni Amendola', after a famous anti-Fascist and one of the regime's first victims.

Having absorbed the news, Carlo Carucci sat down again to his diary and wrote:

The Ministry of Education has ordered examinations to be held on September 16th. This will now be possible. Although I am old and have often thought of retirement, I should now like to teach for at least another year at the institute, to have the pleasure of speaking freely after the fall of tyranny, and to tell the youngsters that they should protect freedom as they do the pupils of their eyes. They should fear bondage which degrades, breaks all energy and takes away initiative, lowers and vilifies the spirit, prostitutes the soul, the heart and even the body.

But his school would not be open on 16th September.

*   *   *   *   *

In German military headquarters, after Badoglio's speech, which had been anticipated and prepared for, wireless messages were flashed to all subordinate commands with the code word *Fall Achse*, closely followed to field units by another code word *Ernte einbringen* —bring in the harvest—meaning that all Italian troops in the neighbourhood should immediately be disarmed.

At Frascati, the headquarters of Commander-in-Chief South, Field-Marshal Albert Kesselring was calmly putting into operation his plans for the disarming of the Italian forces in his area. In the morning a hundred and thirty B-17s with a bomb-load of 389 tons had raided his headquarters while he was in the middle of a planning conference. He had missed death by yards when a bomb landed near the glass veranda of his office, but the accuracy of the attack left much to be desired as the vital communications centre was only out of action for six hours. In his memoirs Kesselring accuses the king and Badoglio of "permitting this attack" and he cites as evidence the fact that fire brigades from Rome and *ARP* units were already at the entrances to the town, "sure evidence of foreknowledge of the attack". But this is extremely unlikely, as Eisenhower had refused to divulge his intentions in any shape or form, which was probably all to the good, as the Italians had vastly over-estimated Allied strength in the Central Mediterranean. The German field-marshal also accuses the Italians of giving away his positions, when a shot-down bomber was found to have a detailed plan of the Frascati headquarters.

Kesselring had been placed in a most invidious position by his Italian colleagues, most of whom had continued to assure him up till the last minute that there was no question of the Italians calling off the war and making a separate peace with the Allies. Kesselring's views, that the situation was nothing like as serious as was thought, brought down a heap of invective on his head from the Fuehrer, who complained that "that fellow Kesselring is too honest for those born traitors down there". In the event, Kesselring was proved wrong, and his faith in the Italians certainly made Hitler mistrust him. In fact, it is almost certain that Admiral Canaris, the head of the German *Abwehr* or Military Intelligence, was, for reasons of his own, supplying Kesselring with deliberately false information on this vital point.

In the early evening of 8th September Kesselring received a telephone call from General Jodl, who asked if the radio announcement about Italy's surrender was correct. As Kesselring had heard nothing about it, he arranged to make enquiries amongst the Italians. General Roatta, Commander-in-Chief of the Italian Army, who was at that very moment conferring with Generals Westphal and Toussaint, claimed that the whole thing was a hoax. Later that night Roatta rang Kesselring to assure him that he had not deliberately tried to hoodwink him but had himself been kept in the dark.

The Italian army in the Rome area laid down their arms, and in the majority of cases could hardly disguise their delight. Thousands of troops hastily disappeared from their barracks, and within a few hours were lost in the mass of civilians.

Kesselring immediately ordered the release of all the Fascist leaders who had been imprisoned after the deposing of Mussolini. He invited Marshal Count Cavallero, the former Italian Chief of Staff and a friend of his, to his headquarters as his personal guest. Whilst there, Cavallero shot himself and it was immediately alleged that Kesselring had given orders for him to be killed. Kesselring denied this at the time and continued to do so all his life, always insisting that, as Cavallero had been a party to a plot against Mussolini, he could not face a trip to Germany, where he would have had to stand up to these allegations from the Duce himself.

But in other parts of Italy the armistice was not so well received nor complied with quite so unresistingly. In the Salerno area, the 222nd Italian Coast Division was under command of General Don Ferrante Gonzaga. A descendant of an old Italian family with a tradition for military service, he had fought in the First World War and had been awarded many medals for valour. The first he knew of the armistice was when it was announced over the radio. He immediately gave orders to all his units to concentrate and to oppose any German attempts to disarm them. At the same time, true to his traditions of loyalty, he sent a clearly worded message to the General

Commanding the 16th Panzer Grenadier Division that all collaboration had ceased. Shortly afterwards a German armed party under the command of Major von Alvensleben arrived at the HQ of the 222nd Division and disarmed most of the staff, but could not find General Gonzaga. Von Alvensleben demanded to be taken to him; he found him at his desk, surrounded by a few staff officers, and ordered him to lay down his arms or join forces with the German Army. This the general obstinately refused to do, declaring that he would remain loyal to the legal government at all costs. The discussion, which had started amicably, quickly became more heated, and finally the German Major ordered Gonzaga to hand over his personal arms. Von Alvensleben went forward to relieve him of his pistol.

The General stepped backwards, trying to get the weapon out of its holster, shouting: "A Gonzaga never lays down his arms", and calling for his by then non-existent staff officers. Immediately from a group of German soldiers came a swift burst of Schmeisser fire. Hit in the head, the general collapsed and died. Von Alvensleben later declared his admiration for the Italian: "He died as a great soldier."

Gonzaga was later posthumously awarded the Gold Medal for Valour by the Italian Government.

Elsewhere, the Germans were equally quick to react to the code word *Ernte einbringen* and soon surrounded many of the Italian units before they could take offensive action. Major Herbert Duppenbecker, commander of the 1st Panzer Grenadier Battalion, 79th Regiment of the 16th Panzer Division, hastily sent a detachment to take over an important bridge across the River Sele to prevent the Italians wrecking it, only to find that another German unit had already done the necessary work. The problem was what to do with the hundreds of Italian soldiers, who would be an encumbrance in the event of battle. It was decided to send them back to their homes and the majority left cheerfully, only too keen to get out of the danger area. In one artillery position the Commanding Officer did ensure that the guns could not be used by the Germans by ordering his men to remove and bury the breech-blocks. But in most other cases coast guns and even machine-guns were left intact with the ammunition as a present to the Germans.

Duppenbecker, with an armed force in lorries, then drove to the other Italian positions. He was surprised to find how the news had spread and how the Italian soldiers had managed to get civilian clothes from the farmers in the neighbourhood. They had thrown their weapons in heaps and run away from their commanders. Duppenbecker, however, did meet some very bewildered Italian officers, who were standing around depressed and downcast. It was clearly apparent that they were more amazed over the armistice than were the Germans. One officer had shot himself, and two young lieutenants asked to join Duppenbecker's battalion. They wanted to have German uniforms and be allowed to fight, but were turned down. One of them, however, joined a German front-line unit, where he fought as a private soldier and was killed.

In other parts of Italy soldiers were arrested in mass and deported to Germany for forced labour. Some units, which put up a show of resistance, were allowed to demobilise themselves and go home.

At Supreme Headquarters, as reports poured in that Operation *Harvest* was working smoothly, there were sighs of relief and none more heartfelt than from Field-Marshal Keitel, Chief of Staff of the German Army, who had recently declared: "The only Italian Army that cannot betray us is the one that does not exist."

Italy had been in the war on Hitler's side for 1,184 days. Her armed forces had gone into battle after Mussolini's stab in the back to France, and her fighting abilities had been parodied and turned into rude jokes by Allied soldiers all over the Middle East. Badly directed and led by senior officers whose hearts were not in the war, her morale had dropped lower and lower, until the armistice delivered the *coup de grâce* from which it will take many years for Italian soldiers to recover.

Despite the excitement of the armistice and the work involved in disarming and dismissing their former Allies, this was the least of the German High Command's worries, for an invasion fleet had already been sighted by aircraft on the previous day and it was only a question of a few hours before the Allies would make a second landing on the Italian mainland.

*   *   *   *   *

South of Naples in the beautiful Gulf of Salerno, the 8th of September, 1943, began like any other day. The sun rose into a cloudless sky and the temperature climbed swiftly. After a leisurely breakfast, Major Herbert Duppenbecker attended to some papers and then went out in the sidecar of a motor-cycle on a tour of his battalion positions, which were situated near the village of Paestum—the ancient Poseidonia of the Sybarites—and spread over a distance of some nine miles to the mouth of the River Sele. Under his command he had approximately six hundred combatant troops, organised into three Panzer Grenadier companies (infantry), one heavy support company and an anti-aircraft company. Ever since taking over these positions Duppenbecker had worried about them. His troops were very thin on the ground and he remembered his instructors at an army college telling him that a battalion should never occupy a front of more than a thousand metres. Yet here he was ordered to defend nine miles of easily assaultable coast. Only the previous day he had conducted a defence exercise over the ground and he knew that he had done all he could to defend the area with the available forces—but he wished he had at least twice the numbers spread over the same stretch.

At 1100 hours exactly a lone single-engined plane flew over the beach, and Duppenbecker chuckled to himself as he thought of the nickname the local Italians had given it: *O'Ciccio ferroviere*—Ciccio the railwayman—as it had a habit of coming over regularly to strafe the railway. The plane, the red, white and blue circles of the Royal Air Force clearly distinguishable on its wings, circled lazily in the sky, but not a single flak gun opened up on it. Having presumably completed its non-apparent task, it flew off south the way it had come.

Duppenbecker returned to his headquarters to be given a radio message which had been received from 16th Panzer Division Headquarters, with the information that an enemy fleet was sailing up the coast. All air observation posts were ordered to keep a close watch, but as it was still not apparent whether the enemy intended to land at Salerno or further north at Naples, the orders were just to wait and see. At 1515 hours another message came in: *Powerful fleet of about 100 ships 50 kilometres from the coast.*

1540 hours. The code word *Orkan* was flashed to all formations. It meant that troops should get themselves to a state of battle readiness. The German Command had a system of code words for various eventualities. *Wind* indicated a small Commando-type landing; *Sturm* a medium-sized assault; and *Orkan*—Hurricane—a major landing.

In all the units messages were passed on to sub-units whilst officers and men scurried around arranging final details. Duppenbecker, on his motorcycle combination, set off once more along the coast roads and across the dunes to visit every detachment and every strong-point. Frequently he would stop his vehicle to climb to the top of the dunes and, with binoculars, would scan the horizon in the hope of seeing something of the reported fleet. But he could only see the waves of the Tyrrhenian Sea lapping gently on the sun-browned beaches of the scimitar-shaped Salerno Bay. Hannibal had been beaten near here when his troops had become soft through tasting the flesh-pots of the south. Would the English succeed where the great Hannibal had failed?

Duppenbecker had been part of the military machine that had been feverishly active ever since the Germans had first suspected that the Salerno bay might be used as an invasion point. The 16th Panzer Division, reinforced with other units, had carried out mock anti-invasion exercises designed to repel an enemy force that had supposedly landed in the Vesuvius-Agropoli area.

The curve of the gulf was divided into three sections under command of three separate combat groups. Colonel Dornemann, with the 16th Reconnaissance Section and attached units, controlled the area north and north-west of Salerno. Colonel Stempel, with the 64th Panzer Grenadiers, 2nd Engineers, 16th Panzer Grenadiers, 3rd Panzer Regiment and 3rd Artillery Regiment, was responsible for the sector between Salerno and the River Sele. Colonel Doering, with the 79th Panzer Grenadiers and attached troops, manned the defences in front of Paestum. In his History of the 16th Panzer Division, Wolfgang Werthen writes:

The terrain was reasonably favourable. It was dominated by a chain of steep mountains. One disadvantage was that counter-attacks would have to be mounted in full view of a landing fleet in the gulf; furthermore, the hilly country to the south made the organisation and advance of units very difficult. A further disadvantage was that the troops, who to date had fought in France and Russia, were unfamiliar with this type of ground and the equipment was, to some extent, unsuitable for the existing conditions.

To enable the defenders to attack any invaders at the crucial moment of landing, strong-points were built close to the coast and manned by infantry platoons and heavy artillery combined. These strong-points were constructed of reinforced concrete and defended by wire. The centre strong-point named *Moltke* was near Cioffi; *Lilienthal* north-west of Baracca; *Scharnhorst* near Spineta; and *Schlieffen* at the mouth of the River Sele. Observer squads and radio stations were established at other intermediate points: anti-aircraft guns were distributed between the strong-points and were sited in positions where they could be used in a dual role. Numerous minefields were laid to hamper the enemy.

The troops, despite their hard work on the defences, found time for leisure activities. The days were unbearably hot and at midday many soldiers hurried to the beach for a swim, whilst in the early hours parties would go foraging for the ripe, dark-blue grapes, tomatoes and lemons which grew abundantly in the fields and groves. Sundays were always off-duty days when battalions arranged football matches, concerts and film shows.

The morale of these troops was high. They had confidence in themselves and in their officers. Like any other army, however, they also had their petty squabbles and irritating incidents.

In the 2nd Panzer Pioneer Company, Lieutenant Gunter Schmitz that very day had been laughing over an acrimonious signal from a neighbouring unit, complaining that a wagon-load of potatoes had been pinched by his men. Schmitz had offered them in exchange a load of oranges and grapes, but this was not accepted as there were plenty in the fields to be had for the picking. By this time most of the potatoes had already been eaten and enjoyed, and it occurred to Schmitz, despite the humour of the situation, that a wagon-load of grenades would shortly be more valuable than potatoes.

Meanwhile, having completed the tour of his battalion, Duppenbecker retraced his steps back to the farmhouse, where he found all was quiet, and settled down to await events.

During the evening there came the sound of a huge explosion from Salerno, followed by a tall pillar of fire. The German garrison had demolished the ammunition dump and a firework display ensued that lasted for some time. This had been done without warning and many Italian civilians were killed as the result. Most of the Salerno garrison then pulled out into the hills, leaving a few tanks only in Via Indipendenza.

All along the semicircle of Salerno bay German infantry got into their foxholes and lookouts scanned the sea continuously. A few miles back in the hills artillery regiments made their final preparations and tank units moved to their tactical positions. Silence fell all over the country; only the occasional cough of a sentry hidden in the shadows, or the rattle of a machine-gun bolt being rammed home, disturbed the peace.

In the villages scattered amongst the foothills most of the Italian civilians, unaware of the approaching fleet, were preparing to spend their last night in the caves, tunnels and shelters. Mothers tucked their children more firmly into the blankets and the husbands smoked a last cigarette before turning in. In thousands of minds there was only one thought: peace had come—tomorrow life would begin again.

But there was to be little sleep for those whose lives were centred around the Salerno Gulf. High above them, coming from bases in North Africa and Sicily, flew wave upon wave of huge bombers, some marked with the roundels of the Royal Air Force and others with the five-pointed star of the United States Air Force. Keen-eyed navigators plotted their routes whilst pilots stared down at the boot of Italy, waiting for their target to come into sight. As soon as they could see the Island of Capri in the distance and the faint glimmer of Vesuvius, they would know it was almost time to press the bomb buttons and release their loads of high explosive.

Below them, in tight formation, steaming through narrow passages cut through the minefields, was an armada of four hundred and fifty ships of different cuts and rigs, all shapes and sizes, loaded with men and weapons of war under orders to assault the beaches at Salerno and to move to capture the vital port of Naples with the additional hope of trapping the German Army to the south and hastening the end of the war in Italy. Operation *Avalanche* was within a few hours of being launched—and it was well named, for it was the biggest and heaviest seaborne attack ever attempted and would be accompanied by a huge avalanche of shells and bombs, the equal of which had not been seen since the barrage of El Alamein, which had turned the tide of the war in the favour of the Allies.

The German *Orkan* was about to meet the Allied *Avalanche*.

CHAPTER II

THE INVASION ARMADA:

D-Day Minus One

AT sea, still fifteen to twenty miles offshore, 100,000 British and 69,000 American troops were mostly in a state of jubilation. On many of the *LCIs*, *LSTs*, *LCTs* and transports, men were cheering, having organised sing-songs, telling jokes and—where the ration had not been consumed—passing around bottles of beer and North African wine. A spirit of utmost exhilaration had conquered them all, for at 1920 hours a *BBC* newsreader had announced an armistice with Italy. Many troops thought the war was now over.

Earlier General Eisenhower had spoken from Radio Algiers:

"The Italian Government has surrendered its armed forces unconditionally and I, as Commander-in-Chief, have granted them military armistice terms which have been approved by the Governments of Britain, the United States and the Soviet Union; thus I am acting in the interests of the United Nations. The Italian Government has bound itself to abide by these terms without reservation. The armistice was signed by my representative and the representative of Marshal Badoglio and comes into effect immediately. Hostilities will cease at once and the Italians can now have the assistance and support of the United Nations to expel the German oppressors from Italian soil."

As the *BBC* message ended, for several seconds officers and men alike stood looking at the silent loudspeakers, hardly believing their ears. Spontaneous cheering then broke out on all the bigger ships. Men clasped each other and danced around the metal decks. British officers grabbed the last of their bottles of gin and whisky and went off to celebrate with the ships' officers. On several American transports highly emotional troops asked the padres to say prayers of thanks. From the larger vessels launches shot out and circled the smaller craft, passing on the news, to be greeted by a fresh surge of cheering wherever they went. Relief was audible and physical. Colonel B. L. Morton, a Pioneer officer of the 46th Division, recorded:

> The bow had been tautly strung for action and was now relaxed, and the delay caused by the psychological readjustment may have cost the assault a good start.

Senior officers hastened to undo the mischief by going themselves to the microphones to warn the men that the Italians were not the enemy: the Germans were still active and would put up a savage resistance; but, as Admiral of the Fleet Lord Cunningham wrote in his official despatches, *many took no heed of these warnings and viewed the proceedings with a sense of complacency.*

Commodore Geoffrey Oliver, R.N., and General Sir Richard McCreery were standing together on the bridge of *HMS Hilary* when they heard the news. They were as surprised as anyone else, and very worried about its effect on the troops. Orders were immediately sent out by boat and by lamp to all units, confirming that the operation was to go ahead as planned.

Brigadier L. O. Lyne, commander of 169 (Queen's) Brigade, had only just sent the following message to all his troops:

> Tomorrow the eyes of the world will be upon us, for tomorrow we strike a really vital blow to knock Italy out of the war. It is right and proper that the Brigade, which was one of the last to leave France three years ago, should have the honour to be one of the first to return to Europe. The success of our operation depends upon the coolness and steadfast determination of every single one of us to accomplish the task set and reach our objectives, whatever the opposition. I have every confidence that all ranks of this Brigade group will play their part with fortitude and courage and that complete success will crown our efforts: Good luck and God speed!

He hastily followed this up with another personal message warning the men they could expect plenty of opposition from the Germans. Sergeant Frank Hayward, a signal sergeant in the 2/7th Queens, recalls that many of his comrades thought they would sail merrily into Naples harbour and land as Cook's tourists!

Soldiers from Surrey villages shouted: "The Eyeties have jagged it in!"—"It's all over bar the shouting!" Whilst the issue of a rum ration a short time before added to the general exhilaration, and Brigadier Lyne's matter-of-fact message only penetrated into a few of the wiser heads.

Even on an *LCT* carrying men of the 3rd Battalion Coldstream Guards, hardy veterans of the desert, the same feeling enveloped the troops. The drink ration was hastily issued and swallowed and it was generally decided that they would land unopposed; with no Germans for miles around, all they had to do was march to Naples. The younger and more virile members of the regiment speculated on the creature comforts that could be expected, and one young officer bemoaned the fact that he had left his dinner jacket in Africa!

After several uncomfortable days aboard an *LCI*, an officer of the Grenadier Guards was delighted to find a reason for a party:

"I grabbed a bottle of sherry which I had been saving to give me courage on the following morning and took it to the bridge and with the Captain and Number One we celebrated the downfall of Italy."

On the headquarters ship, *USS Ancon*, General Mark Clark, the Commander of 5th Army, and his staff, with Vice-Admiral Henry Kent Hewitt, *USN*, listened gravely to the broadcast. Clark expanded the information slightly by saying that the Italians would not allow the Germans to take over the coastal defences and would not maintain the road and rail traffic. But even he seems to have been over-optimistic, and although expressing some doubts that the Italians would be unable to enforce the terms, he concluded that "at best we could steam into Naples harbour unopposed; at worst, we could have a hell of a fight". As an afterthought in his memoirs he wrote:

Anyway, we were on our way and, at last, I had my first battle command!

Down below, in a ward room of the *Ancon*, a group of *RAF* officers, including Group Captain Jack Millar, were unconcernedly playing bridge, and at another table nearby Captain Herbert Scheftel, *USAF*, was concentrating on the rolling of poker dice; the general feeling was that no great opposition would be encountered in view of the Italian surrender.

James Cooper, war correspondent of the *Sunday Express* aboard a warship, recalled:

The Paymaster, Commander Holmes, idly switched on the radio and we heard a woman say "An armistice has been granted; hostilities have ceased". I heard cheering on deck, everyone had heard of the Italian surrender. Some sailors asked for a prayer from the padre, others for an order to splice the mainbrace, but they got neither. The bearded commander, J. H. Ruck-Keene, shook his head and, going to the ship's loud hailer, broadcast: "Do not relax at all."

Aboard the *LST* carrying the 16th Battalion Durham Light Infantry the boys had a sing-song, and although their officers assured them that the enemy would still be on the beaches, the idea persisted that the nearest Germans were in Naples. Colonel John Preston, commanding the battalion, remembers:

> I did not expect to enter the harbour garlanded with flowers. I imagined a number of Italian soldiers wandering about without arms, but also the occasional one who had not packed up having a shot at us. I had always warned my men that Italians were apt to be treacherous. I also thought the Germans would react quickly, but not as quickly as they did! However, I think the troops were pleased and thought it would be a "piece of cake".

On another of the *DLI* ships the Battalion Padre George Meek held a service thanking God for the Italian armistice.

The 179th Regimental Combat Team at sea further out as floating reserve for the whole of 5th Army also burst into cheers, as staff officers were knowledgeably forecasting: "The Krauts will only be able to muster 30,000 troops maximum."

Two hundred men of the 2nd Battalion Scots Guards, crammed inside a hot noisy *LCI*, had had enough of the blue Mediterranean sea. The first news they had of the armistice was when signal lights started blinking from blacked-out ships all around them. Major Michael Crichton-Stuart, standing on deck, heard a little Navy signaller shouting:

"Crikey, Italy's surrendered!"

He could hear faint cheering from the surrounding craft. Inevitable optimism ensued; the company piper was instructed to hurry up and compose *The Scots Guards' March through Naples*. But soberer thoughts soon followed and it was generally decided that the Germans would not let them land easily. The biggest toast was drunk to the health of Lieutenant Archie Elliot of Right Flank, who celebrated his twenty-first birthday within sight of the Salerno hills.

A man of the Royal Northumberland Fusiliers was reading a pamphlet on how to behave in Italy, when he heard the news and someone nearby muttered: "See Naples and live, eh!"

A soldier leaned over his shoulder to ask: "What do you say in that lingo to ask for beer?" Another queried: "How d'you say: I'd like a nice girl of about eighteen?"

A few miles farther north the convoy of ships carrying the Commando force and the *US* Rangers heard the startling news and even those blackened-faced warriors paused in their stride to wonder if they would have an unopposed landing.

One wag shouted out: "The Mayor of Salerno in his cocked hat will be there to greet us on the beach with bottles of vino!"

But Captain John Parsons, who was to win an *MC* in the forthcoming battle, remembers that they all decided that this was dangerous thinking and continued with their battle preparations. Brigadier Robert 'Lucky' Laycock—soon to be Chief of Combined Operations—who led the Commando brigade, was aboard the *Prince Albert*. A naval commander asked if in the circumstances the initial barrage should be scrubbed.

"Not on your life," replied Laycock. "There are still plenty of Germans there."

And so the pent-up feelings of the invading troops relaxed and under the bright stars floating on an oily calm sea the majority of soldiers approached the coast under a sort of analgesic spell, accentuated by lookouts reporting the flashes from the smoking peak of Vesuvius in technical jargon, the twinkling lights of Positano and the napthalene flares of the Amalfi sardine fishermen. Forthright Admiral Samuel Morison in his hard-hitting history wrote that *one should have been sitting in the stern sheets of a rowing barge singing* O Sole Mio.

The effect of the armistice announcement on the troops was a psychological blunder of the first order.

CHAPTER III

THE ARMISTICE NEGOTIATIONS

BEHIND the scenes armistice negotiations had been dragging on since 17th August, when the Italian General Castellano presented himself to Sir Samuel Hoare at the British Embassy in Madrid with the offer that if the Allies would land on the Italian mainland the Italian government and people would join them in the fight against the Germans and accept the unconditional surrender terms. Unknown to Marshal Badoglio was the fact that on 7th August an invasion had already been decided upon and it had been settled that Salerno was the northernmost point at which the attack could be launched; it was at the limit of fighter range from Sicily. At a subsequent meeting between Castellano and the British Ambassador it was stated that Marshal Badoglio could not accept the surrender terms until the main invasion had taken place, and that if the bulk of Italian forces was to join the Allies, then the landing must be in the Rome area. There was even talk of the British and Americans using thirty divisions in such an operation, which shows how vastly the Italians overestimated Allied strength.

From reports and records it appears that General Eisenhower then became worried that no armistice would be signed and he offered to fly an American Airborne Division to Rome, if the Italian Army could guarantee to hold the airfields and stop the anti-aircraft fire. The armistice would have to be signed and announced just before the drop. Marshal Badoglio and the King of Italy agreed; the actual document was signed in Sicily on 3rd September, just ten hours after the 8th Army had crossed the Straits of Messina to land on the toe of Italy.

In the next few days hurried arrangements were made to prepare the 82nd *US* Airborne Division for the flight to Rome. Brigadier Maxwell D. Taylor, Deputy Divisional Commander, went on a daring mission by *MTB* up the Tiber into the Eternal City to personally check the arrangements. He reported back to Eisenhower with the code words *Situation innocuous*, which meant the situation was in fact unfavourable and advised against dropping the airborne

32

division. At much the same time Marshal Badoglio, who was getting cold feet, sent a plaintive message to the Commander-in-Chief. He unknowingly confirmed Maxwell Taylor's appreciation of the position and said it was therefore impossible for him to accept the armistice before the seaborne assault. Eisenhower, at once suspicious that the cunning old marshal was trying to wriggle out of the pact, sent back an immediate terse signal:

> I intend to broadcast the existence of the armistice at the hour planned. If you or any of your armed forces fail to co-operate as previously agreed, I will publish to the world the full record of this affair. Today is X-Day and I expect you to do your part.

General Eisenhower broadcast at 1830 hours and then sat back at Supreme Headquarters in Algiers in a tense and expectant atmosphere to wait for the Italian marshal to keep his word. Three-quarters of an hour later Badoglio spoke. Breathing sighs of relief, senior officers switched their attention to the invasion only a few hours ahead.

It is interesting to consider why it was so important that the armistice be announced prior to the actual landing. Admiral Samuel Morison writes:

> In justice to the Italians the armistice had to be announced before we landed on their soil . . .

But why "in justice"? Badoglio had already told Ike that he was unable to control the airfields or his army. That view had been confirmed by Maxwell Taylor, and Badoglio had demanded the invasion first and the armistice second. Field-Marshal Lord Alexander in his official despatches was of the opinion that:

> The news of the Italian armistice could not be kept from the troops, who were even then heading up the Gulf of Salerno, nor was it honourable or advisable not to inform them that the Italians were pledged to fight on our side.

If Badoglio had been able to keep his side of the bargain this would have been quite correct, but he was incapable of controlling the situation; the Germans, already alerted—and it is most probable that the information had been leaked to them from a high Italian source—had virtually taken over. Badoglio did not want the armistice before the landing. Could it be that Eisenhower thought that the world at large would be tremendously impressed by the fall of the Italians? Did he seriously imagine that German morale in Italy would collapse when their weak and failing partner threw in the sponge?

It is possible that Eisenhower overestimated the strength and power of the Italian Armed Forces and was frightened that they would be able to sway the balance against the invasion force. The real reason, however, is that Eisenhower was not his own master in the matter, but had to obey orders from the President in Washington and the Prime Minister in London. These two statesmen were determined to make much propaganda capital out of the Italian defection; they had high hopes of its effect against the Germans. Nothing was to be allowed to stand in the way of this great coup. As a result, the launching of the invasion of the Italian mainland nearly foundered as it slid down the slipway over rollers of optimism and the 'It's all over bar the shouting' attitude induced into the troops by the early armistice announcement.

It was a psychological blunder of great significance. The initial assault came very near being flung back into the sea; and there was no fleet of little boats to take them twenty-odd miles back to an island fortress. An evacuation from Salerno Bay would have involved a retreat of several days across seas into which the Germans would have launched every available U-Boat, whilst the Luftwaffe in a supreme effort would have pounded the withdrawing ships for several days.

However, the invasion was on the point of being launched and, like lemmings rushing to their fate, there was no holding the Allied troops. It had to go on. D-Days and H-Hours, plusses and minuses, had been marked on calendars, maps and charts. There were objectives to be achieved and targets to be hit; the biggest seaborne assault machine ever produced up to that time was about to be tested on what Winston Churchill inaccurately termed "the soft under-belly of Europe".

*   *   *   *   *

And now to the reason why and the plans for this assault.

There are those like Major-General J. F. C. Fuller who were of the opinion that the war in Italy

> Was strategically the most useless campaign of the whole war: it prolonged the war; wrecked Italy; and wasted thousands of American and British lives.

This opinion was shared by many other people. Even that great and loyal officer Field-Marshal Alexander, later in the campaign, was forced to ask: "Who is containing whom?"

·But by the summer of 1943 a vast strategic re-think by the war leaders had to take place. The 8th and 1st Armies had cleared the Afrika Korps and the Italian Army out of North Africa. Sicily had been conquered and vital bases from which Southern Europe could be bombed, threatened or actually assaulted, had been obtained. The Mediterranean had been classed as of minor importance because the vital Washington Conference in May, 1943, had decided that the next major move in the war would be the attack across the Channel to France in the summer of 1944. The importance of Italy was on the wane. In the meantime, however, something had to be done, as in the words of Winston Churchill "we must fight the Germans somewhere; we can't merely sit and watch the Russians". And in Moscow and at every conference Uncle Joe Stalin was banging the table with insistence, claiming that America and Britain were not doing their share.

Churchill was keen enough to have a go at Italy, but the Americans were not; they were convinced that the British were trying to wriggle out of the Normandy operation. The Chief of the Imperial General Staff, General Sir Alan Brooke, recorded in his diary on July 5th:

USA looks at present like trying to close Mediterranean theatre if they can after Sicily. We must wait and see how Sicily operations go and what I can do at next Chiefs of Staff meeting.

Yet a surprise ally in the shape of General George C. Marshall, the American Chief of Army Staff, who had always been opposed to Churchill's concentric strategy, agreed that if too much material was not taken away for the build-up of *Overlord*—the planned invasion of France—then the successful ending of the Sicilian campaign could be quickly followed by an attack on the Italian mainland. Moreover, he was in favour of a bold seaborne assault in the Naples area, which delighted Churchill so much that he produced another of his great descriptive phrases: "Why crawl up the leg like a harvest bug from the ankle upwards? Let us rather strike at the knee."

The expected advantages to be reaped from an invasion of Italy could be summed up as follows:

(1) To capitalize on the Italian surrender.
(2) Keep German divisions from France and the Russian front.
(3) Provide airfields for attacks on the heart of Germany, France and the Balkans.
(4) Give the Allies complete control of the Mediterranean.

The surprise agreement by the American Chiefs of Staff went only so far; they were not prepared to change their minds over the logistical support that had already been timetabled, and Eisenhower, Alexander and London were all told that they would have to make do with the men, supplies, ships and aeroplanes they already had. Stimson, the American Secretary of State for War, was a believer in the 'all eggs in one basket' principle. On a visit to Britain in July to inspect American troops, he called on General Frederick Morgan, the chief cross-Channel planner—*COSSAC*—and, according to war historian Arthur Bryant, *secured from him, or at any rate supposed he had secured, an admission that grave delays in the invasion programme might be caused by 'getting too deep into commitments in the Mediterranean'.* This he passed on to the Prime Minister, who became impassioned and ended by having a flaming row with Stimson, giving the latter the erroneous impression that he was anti-Normandy invasion.

General Sir Frederick Morgan says that this is basically correct, and that he did say that he had to have back the forces and material ordered for *Overlord*. The troops and crews all had to be re-trained from desert warfare and non-amphibious operations. There is no doubt that this backing up of the American viewpoint did not endear Morgan to Churchill, and in the planning ahead, where Morgan tried to keep an even balance between the Allied opinions, he frequently fell foul of the Prime Minister.

Admiral of the Fleet Lord Cunningham has since commented:

> There was too much over-insurance in the Mediterranean landings. In London they were making too much fuss about getting boats back in time for re-training and equipment. We could have got them back in plenty of time.

However, by 19th August tempers had cooled and minds changed. Eisenhower received confirmation that *Avalanche* was on. Basic agreement had been reached at Quebec between the Prime Minister, the President and the Combined Chiefs of Staff.

The haggling over the ships and the planes still continued. Eisenhower on 28th July requested the Chiefs of Staff that the 8th

Army Air Force in Britain should lend him a hundred and forty B-17s for six weeks. He received a firm *No*. Following heavy Luftwaffe raids on August 17th/18th on Bizerta, where the invasion craft were concentrated, the Supreme Commander sent another urgent cable to the Combined Chiefs of Staff, asking permission to retain three squadrons of Liberators earmarked for return to Britain. His plea was perfectly reasonable: he just did not have enough bombers to keep the enemy airfields out of action for the days preceding the invasion. Again the Combined Chiefs of Staff rejected his request. This refusal infuriated Admiral Sir Andrew Cunningham, Commander-in-Chief Mediterranean, who, in a message to the Admiralty, wrote:

> I believe that we can and shall succeed, but only if we go flat out. If we whittle away our resources now to build up *Overlord*, our chances of success will be greatly reduced, and if *Avalanche* fails *Overlord* may be still-born.

In the end, with the inevitable delay caused to the planners, who never knew from day to day the forces available to them, the Supreme Commander was reluctantly allowed to retain three squadrons of Wellington heavy bombers and certain assault landing craft. Ten large troopers were also later returned from Britain.

The Commanders of all three Services were appalled by the attitude of the Combined Chiefs of Staff. Having agreed that the Italian invasion should go ahead, they were now endangering the plan before it was ever launched by demanding the return of vital war supplies that would be lying idle in Britain until the following June, and for want of planes and ships *Avalanche* might well have failed, with the consequent loss of material and men for *Overlord*. Admiral Morison comments pithily:

> Thirty *LCTs* which were retained had been ordered to Scapa Flow for the singularly inappropriate use of handling torpedo nets.

CHAPTER IV

THE PLAN

A BRAND-NEW army was formed for the Salerno assault. This was the 5th Army, commanded by Lieutenant-General Mark Clark, a tall, gangling American with a flamboyant air and a team of hand-picked public-relations officers who recorded his moves and kept reporters informed of every detail. For him it was his first action—and it proved to be a baptismal fire of a particularly unpleasant nature.

General Eisenhower was Supreme Commander in the Mediterranean. By August 1st the basic organisation of Operation *Avalanche* had been settled. This plan was based on a previous one coded *Buttress*, which had been in preparation for an attack on the Gulf of Gioia on the toe of Italy. The terrain was very similar to that at Salerno and much the same sized forces and number of ships had been arranged, the three Service commanders being General Sir Harold Alexander, Admiral of the Fleet Sir Andrew Cunningham and Air Marshal Sir Arthur Tedder.

The ground forces were organised into the 5th Army, divided into two corps: the United States VI Corps under Major General E. J. 'Mike' Dawley, with the 36th and 45th Divisions for the initial assault and the 3rd and 34th in reserve; the British X Corps under Lieutenant-General Sir Richard McCreery, made up of 46th (Oak Tree) and 56th (Black Cat) Divisions.

Under Admiral Cunningham were all the amphibious forces, which included the Western Naval Task Force commanded by Vice-Admiral H. Kent Hewitt, *USN*, with ships from the *US* Navy, the Royal Navy and the Dutch and Polish Navies. It comprised the Northern Attack Force, mostly from the Royal Navy under Commodore G. N. Oliver, *RN*; the Southern Attack Force, mainly American and commanded by Rear-Admiral John L. Hall, *USN*; and a smaller force on the northern flank in support of a group of British Commandos and United States Rangers, under Rear-Admiral L. Connolly, *USN*. This officer, though senior to Commodore Oliver, volunteered to serve under him, having signalled Cunningham:

The Plan

I can't keep out of this—can I take my coat off for the battle? In addition, there was a diversion group commanded by Captain C. L. Andrew, *USN*, which did important work in the surrounding waters. A grand total of four hundred and fifty vessels was involved.

The Allied air forces could put into action a total of 3,127 aircraft of all types made up as follows:

> 461 heavy bombers
> 162 medium night bombers
> 703 medium and light day bombers
> 1,395 fighters and fighter bombers
> 406 transport aircraft.

General Alexander was told to go ahead with planning, but with the multifarious duties of the three Allied Services in the Mediterranean, the headquarters were widely dispersed and there was a distinct lack of liaison between them. Planning conferences meant that the commanders had to spend hours travelling by plane to places as far distant as Oran, Alexandria, and Algiers; Mostaganem, site of Clark's planning *HQ*, was very much out of touch. General Alexander found it impossible to submit a fairly definite plan to the Supreme Commander until 30th August, only ten days before D-Day, and even then, owing to the refusal of the Combined Chiefs of Staff in Washington to agree over requests to keep shipping and planes in the Mediterranean, the plan was full of holes and gaps, some of which were still being filled as the vessels sailed towards Italy.

For several months the various staffs had been working hard, producing plans for the invasion of Italy with the clockwork regularity of conjurors pulling rabbits out of top hats. They had schemes for almost every contingency, from small Commando-type landings in the Greek Islands to grandiose projects for the capture of Naples. The Mediterranean was a veritable planners' paradise and they took full advantage of it. By the time Alexander got down to considering objectives, the field had been reduced to three possibilities. The first was north of Naples; the second the Gulf of Naples itself; and the third the Gulf of Salerno. The reason for the choice of this part of Italy, halfway up the leg, was the prime necessity for obtaining at the earliest possible date a port capable of handling the vast traffic accompanying the invading force. Naples was the only port capable of carrying out this task.

Let us take them in turn.

The ground immediately north of the great port of Naples had been carefully considered and there were many in favour of a landing in this area. The country is open and flat and well suited to troops who had been trained for desert warfare. The American Air Force planners, enthusiastic about the idea, claimed they would be able to give good air support. The Navy was ill-disposed towards it from the outset, as it felt that the waters off the Gulf of Gaeta were less protected than in the Bay of Salerno. Clark was confident that the Army and the Air Force would be able to win the Navy round to their way of thinking, but when he got in touch with Air Marshal Sir Arthur Tedder, the latter flatly turned the plan down with the firm opinion that proper fighter support could not be given so far north.

A direct assault on Naples was almost immediately ruled out on the grounds that the sea approaches were heavily mined and the coastal batteries too strong.

This left Salerno. The main object of the operation was to capture the port of Naples and overpower the German forces to the south. It was optimistically forecast that Naples would fall on the third day. The beaches along the thirty-six mile curve of Salerno Bay were ideal for an assault landing. There were no shoals or river-mouth ridges to impede the boats and the sand shelved gently and evenly. But the coastal plain behind the beaches—largely reclaimed land—was narrow, and in some places almost non-existent, dominated by the mountains from which a beachhead could be observed and pounded by artillery. The only exit from this plain was through two narrow passes, which could easily be held by light, strongly entrenched forces.

The nearest air bases for our fighters, apart from carrier-based planes, were in Sicily, which meant that Spitfires fitted with ninety-gallon wing tanks would be able to remain over the area for a maximum of twenty minutes, an operation which called for tremendous co-ordination to be effective. For the first three days the ground troops would have the support of a hundred and twenty Seafires of the Fleet Air Arm, operating from five Royal Navy carriers under the command of Rear-Admiral Sir Philip Vian.

Hectically the preparations went ahead, but there were many details to be ironed out and so many last-minute amendments regarding ship loading, detailed plans and fire support, that it is not surprising that junior commanders were still poring over messages while they sat in the ships, by which time it was often too late to do anything about them. One of Commodore Oliver's staff officers recalled that an American launch one day delivered a vast sack containing amendments; they were so aghast that it was hidden away and lost! The naval orders alone, in orange *Top Secret* covers, were over two inches thick.

One of the most surprising decisions about the assault was General Clark's insistence that there should be no preliminary softening up of the defences by a naval bombardment. He held that it was better to have a silent approach, which would give the troops the advantage of tactical surprise—an admirable idea, if one has been able to formulate the plans in secret and advance to the start line unobserved. In the event, however, the Luftwaffe had no uncertainty about what was afoot, as was proved by their heavy air raids on the North African ports where the fleets were forming up. In two eighty-plane sorties by Ju–88s on Bizerta they sank one infantry landing craft and damaged three other vessels, killed twenty-two men and wounded two hundred and fifteen. During one of these attacks Lieutenant-General Sir Brian Horrocks, Commander of X British Corps, was wounded by a spent anti-aircraft shell and had to be replaced by McCreery, who took over a ready-made plan which he thought was too ambitious. He would have preferred a shorter bridgehead concentrated round Salerno. His views were shared by Brigadier Calvert Jones, *CRA* 56th Division, who after a conference drew McCreery aside, saying:

"This plan just isn't on, you know."

McCreery commented: "We have no choice now but to go on with it."

Admiral Morison, the *US* naval historian, had some biting comments to make:

Of all decisions about *Avalanche*, the most unfortunate was the Army Command's insistence on no preliminary gun-fire support in order to gain tactical surprise. Admiral Hewitt argued against this in vain. He pointed out that the Germans knew something was on, as evidenced by their August raids on Bizerta; that any officer with a pair of dividers could figure out that the Gulf of Salerno was the northernmost practicable landing-place for the Allies; that reconnaissance planes would snoop the convoys; in short, that it was fantastic to assume we could obtain tactical surprise. He was right in every particular. Implicit in the denial was the fear that preliminary bombardment would attract German forces to Salerno. But on 6th September the Germans had already sent the 16th Panzer Division into the Salerno plain. The enemy had several days in which to set up 88-mm. and other guns, cut down trees, build strong-points, site the Italians' Breda machine-guns and field-pieces on the beaches and their exits, bring up tanks, and cram nearby airfields with their planes. As it turned out, a good selective shoot on strong-points on the edge of the Salerno plain, for a day or two before D-Day, would have rendered the landings much less arduous.

Many other British and American commanders, with far more active service experience than Clark, did their best to change his mind and failed.

Behind all this thinking was also the feeling that if the Italians carried out their part of the armistice the coastal batteries would be largely manned by their troops and we could not, in all fairness, shoot at them. The only let-out in this ban was the proviso that if the coastal batteries opened up, Allied ships could then return the fire.

General Clark had originally planned to make use of the 82nd American Airborne Division led by Major General Matthew B. Ridgway in a daring drop on the plain north-west of Salerno and south-east of Mount Vesuvius, where they were supposed to block the movement of German divisions coming down from Rome and Naples to reinforce the defenders. They were also supposed to seize the northern ends of the two narrow passes leading from Salerno. Luckily this plan was vetoed by all the Air Force experts. Undeterred, Clark then proposed another drop even farther away, across the River Volturno north-west of Naples, to blow up bridges and delay enemy reinforcements. This would have placed the airborne troops forty miles away from the 5th Army. Initially, the only man to object was Ridgway, who had reason enough, having had half of his division dropped in the sea and widely scattered in Sicily. Tedder and Spaatz were very keen on the idea; Ridgway eventually agreed. Although this plan was not put into operation owing to the diversion of the division for the projected drop on Rome, which was cancelled in its turn after the Italians admitted their inability to control the situation, it is interesting to speculate on what might have been the fate of these units.

Few airborne operations in Europe in the last war, apart from the Normandy landings and the crossing of the Rhine, were successful, mainly due to the fact that higher commanders never appreciated the limitations of the lightly equipped parachute and glider soldiers. These units were formed as shock troops to be used in surprise situations where they could cause chaos for a limited period of time against a moderately equipped enemy. It was impossible for them to hold out against heavily armoured formations, nor were they designed for this task. An integral condition for any airborne operation should always be that the troops be relieved as quickly as possible, preferably within a maximum of forty-eight hours. It was the wildest optimism, characteristic of Clark, and a complete lack of experience of airborne operations, which persuaded the planners that the 5th Army would capture Naples and join up with the 82nd Airborne Division on the Volturno two, or even three, days later. Without a doubt, and admittedly with hindsight, the Volturno River would have been turned into another Arnhem and those troops lost for the vital part they were to play in Normandy.

Even worse things might have befallen the parachutists if they had dropped on Rome. This plan was originally the brain child of Admiral of the Fleet Sir Andrew Cunningham and General Bedell-Smith, Eisenhower's Chief of Staff. It is not at all clear how an admiral became mixed up in an airborne plan, but he was convinced then—and still is today—that he could have sent a stream of gunboats up the Tiber to keep the parachutists supplied until the arrival of the 5th Army. The survivors of the 82nd Airborne Division should be thankful that Badoglio was a pessimist and not an optimist.

On 23rd August, two weeks before D-Day, there was a last-minute change in the command of this division. Major-General H. A. Freeman-Attwood was removed overnight from his command and replaced by Major-General John Hawkesworth. The reasons were hushed up at the time, but General Freeman-Attwood was flown to Algiers and put on a boat for England, where he was arrested on arrival at the War Office. In a letter to his wife from North Africa he had written *I hope I shall be drinking a bottle of champagne somewhere in Italy on our wedding day.* This had been picked up by a zealous censor and the writer swiftly removed from his command. At this period there had been several breaches of security and the British Army was determined to stamp it out. It was unfortunate for Freeman-Attwood that this slight breach was picked on to provide an example to others.

Throughout all the planning stages great emphasis had been placed on security. Not until a late date were battalion commanders told that the objective was Salerno; in most regiments the officers and troops were not told until they were at sea. General Alexander in his official despatches refuses to believe that the Germans had previous definite information that the landings were to be at Salerno. Yet there were several serious breaches of security. Colonel John Preston, commanding 16 *DLI*, recalls that the headquarters of the 46th Infantry Division, while still at Bizerta, issued an administrative order containing the names of places in and around Salerno. This document was given the widest circulation, with the result that many orderly room clerks were able to pass on tit-bits to their pals.

Commodore Oliver in his despatches wrote:

> So far as I can ascertain, no leakage of information took place at Tripoli, with which port I was principally concerned in the final stage. It was reported to me, however, that certain airborne soldiers returned from Sicily, and met with on shore by seamen from Force 'N', professed to know full well that the destination of the expedition was 'Naples'.
>
> I have it, also on hearsay, that 'Naples' as the destination of *Avalanche* was common knowledge among military officers and other ranks in Sicily before the expedition sailed.
>
> These matters naturally could not be followed up at the time owing to the need for secrecy and the departure of the expedition.
>
> That no surprise was in fact achieved and that the enemy were ready waiting for us on the shore does not necessarily prove that security broke down. It needed little foresight to deduce our destination.

Italian civilians in Salerno had been discussing the possibility of an invasion for several weeks before. They based their information on the pattern of bombing raids on the marshalling yards at Battipaglia, Eboli and Salerno itself, where the docks, however, were mainly left unmolested. "When will the landing be?" was a current conversational phrase in the early days of September.

Lieutenant-Colonel B. L. Morton of the 46th Division Pioneers wrote: *security had been bad, and what had been discussed so freely in Bizerta had no doubt helped the Germans in making their dispositions.* This general opinion is backed by Eric Linklater in his book *The Campaign in Italy*:

> Our destination was top secret, but in spite of that a Chinese cook on a water boat shouted in farewell, "See you in Naples".

* * * * *

Major Herbert Duppenbecker, commander of the 1st Panzer Grenadier Battalion 79th Regiment of 16th Panzer Division, recalls most clearly that during the morning of 8th September he received the following radio message: *Air reconnaissance reports that an enemy flotilla is approaching the Gulf of Salerno.* This is more than confirmed by the *History of the Oxfordshire and Buckinghamshire Light Infantry*, where it is stated that an officer after the war was told by the general commanding the 16th Panzer Division that they had had three clear days' warning.

General Alexander bases his opinion on the fact that only thin German forces were covering the beaches at Salerno. But the German High Command had no need to concentrate several divisions in the area. Their reserves were tactically placed near Naples ready to go anywhere, and, as was later proved, they were able to reinforce with astonishing rapidity. Weeks before, Kesselring had already summed up the situation that Salerno was "indeed a uniquely suitable place to land. . . ."

At this stage the German Army in Italy consisted of eighteen divisions including five Panzer divisions. Field-Marshal Kesselring, that doughty warrior and then Commander-in-Chief South, controlled eight divisions organized into two corps—XIV Corps North and LXXVI Corps South—with the following units:

16th Panzer Division in the Gulf of Salerno.
15th Panzer Division near Naples, refitting with the Hermann Goering Division.
1st Parachute Division at Apulia.
26th Panzer Division without armour in Calabria.
2nd Parachute Division and 3rd Panzer Grenadier Division near Rome.
29th Panzer Grenadier Division and 26th Panzer Division facing Montgomery in Calabria, with reserves back of Salerno.
Under command was XI Flieger Corps.

On the immediate Salerno front there were probably 20,000 troops.

There were another eight and a half divisions in the North of Italy, under command of the Desert Fox, Erwin Rommel. But Rommel had convinced Hitler that it was useless to fight in the south and the German High Command had already virtually written off Army Command South. Kesselring had argued this point with the Fuehrer, claiming that Allied possession of the Apulian air bases would mean much stronger bombing attacks on Southern Germany. But Hitler had made up his mind and was immovable. He did not even order Kesselring to abandon the area and retreat northwards. He just left the troops to their fate! Yet, as will be seen, a mere two divisions sent by Rommel would have turned the battle in favour of the Germans and the 5th Army would have been pushed back into the sea.

Despite this situation between Kesselring and Hitler, German morale remained high. The treachery of the Italians had been expected and they did not consider it any loss. In fact, owing to the hasty evacuation made by the Italian Army in Sicily and the south, the Germans were at least able to take over the whole of the front, albeit thinly in places, confident that troops would not throw up the sponge at the first shot.

* * * * *

Time was running out. The Hermanns, the Fritzs and the Rudolfs settled into their trenches and manned their guns determinedly, whilst forty miles off on a calm sea the Allied troops still hummed their songs, anticipating the pleasures of Italy. Few of them had had any battle experience. The 56th British Infantry Division, with the exception of the 201st Guards Brigade, had been in action for a few days fighting around Enfidaville in Tunisia, but had not particularly shone. The 46th British Infantry Division had experienced some unlucky engagements in the same area, whilst the American 36th Division was completely inexperienced, having only recently come from the States. They were to be the first *US* troops to land on European soil and the eyes of America were on them.

Just about the same time, the convoy commanders in sight of Capri passed orders to the helmsmen to change course. Until now, they had been sailing due north, in the hope that the Germans would be fooled into thinking an attack was imminent in the Naples area. The new course was set for the Salerno Gulf.

Slowly the outlines of grey ships of all shapes and sizes faded in the gathering gloom; the vessels were blacked out, most of them being illuminated only with blue lights. Officers of the watch kept a careful eye to their stations, and regularly altered course according to their marked charts. This part of the invasion was strictly the sphere of the Navy; the soldiers could only hope that the sailors would get them to the various anchorages on time.

In the vast hangars of the aircraft carriers sweating mechanics worked over the engines of the fighter planes, loading them with ammunition and petrol. Anti-aircraft gun crews with their flash masks sat tense at the controls, waiting for more bombers to come into the attack. In the gun turrets every detail was being checked, and below sea level the shells and cases were prepared for the lifts. The troops sat around, idle and relaxed. Some were reading the pamphlets issued by Allied headquarters, telling them how to behave in Italy and the customs of the country. Others wrote letters home, many expressing the view that they would be home for Christmas, with the war safely behind them. Men checked their rifles and Bren guns, or cleaned grenades and armed them with detonators.

There came a drone of aircraft engines approaching from landward and suddenly the flotilla of ships was illuminated by millions of candle power, as the leading bomber dropped a parachute flare. The night sky was perforated with the brilliant colour of thousands of tracer bullets, as Oerlikons and multi-barrelled Pom-poms and machine-guns opened up on the marauders. The clatter and rattle of the weapons mixed and mingled with the explosion of bombs. It was 2100 hours. Slightly to the north, the vessels carrying and supporting the Commandos and Rangers came under heavy attack. *HMS Ledbury* scored a direct hit on one bomber, which crashed in flames in the sea; another caught fire and, its height gradually diminishing, limped back to the shore. These attacks continued for about two hours, but in spite of their intensity only one ship, *LST 375*, was hit—and that was with a dud. The mistake of the German pilots was to concentrate on the larger capital ships, which were more than capable of fending for themselves. *HMS Delhi*, fitted out as an anti-aircraft ship, was kept busy in these final hours, as she circled the anchorage sending up an impressive weight of shells.

At 2320 hours a ship's look-out sighted the first of the close inshore reference vessels flashing the letter 'W' with its lamp, and gradually the separate convoys took up their stations in the allotted positions. As the vessels reached the 100-fathom line about twelve miles off shore, anchor chains rattled and the ships swung gently round on their moorings. Minesweepers moved out from the main fleet and with their paravanes out slowly and deliberately cleared clear channels through the dense minefields.

The watchers at sea saw German searchlights begin to range the beaches and the water; many troops inexperienced in these matters were convinced that they had been sighted and picked up in the beams, in spite of being twelve miles off shore. From time to time vast orange flames shot into the night sky and explosions drifted across the water as the Germans hastily demolished ammunition dumps and vital parts of the Salerno dock installations. It was obvious that the enemy knew something was afoot and that surprise had been lost. There was still time for General Mark Clark to change his mind and ask the Navy for a preliminary bombardment to soften up the defences, but he would not change his opinion; he was solidly stuck with the idea of a silent surprise landing. Naval gunners in their turrets, longing for targets, cursed their commanders for not letting them have a go; there were those who had been with Monty's 8th Army when it crossed the Messina Straits, who recalled the vast bombardment that he had laid on the beaches, with the subsequent result, when resistance was proved negligible, that he was accused of wielding a sledge-hammer to crack a nut. Yet here was exactly the reverse situation: Mark Clark was trying to break a boulder using the equivalent of a drum-stick.

For the moment the offensive was left to the North-West African Air Force, which came over in their hundreds in an effort to destroy all communications and block the entrances and exits into the area; B-25s at Avellino, Auletta and Potenza; Wellingtons at Fornia, Gaeta, Battipaglia and Eboli. Ever since June the Allied air forces had paid particular attention to Salerno and the surrounding area by day and night. Clouds of smoke and dust, flame and explosion filled the coastal plain. The railway line to Naples and the marshalling yards at Battipaglia had been prominent targets. The electricity supply had soon been cut off and the warning sirens silenced. A new warning in the shape of three single gun shots had been instituted, the 'All clear' being a lone shot. Factories, hospitals, shops and houses, all had suffered from these attacks. The population had mainly deserted the towns to live in the smaller hill villages. The roads and lanes were continually full of streams of refugees transporting their household goods on carts, perambulators and farm implements as they searched for haven. In the midst of raids, screaming women would rush deranged into the streets and fall on their knees, eyes and hands pointing up to the sky as if praying to the pilots, shouting *"Basta! Basta!"*—enough, enough. But it was not enough. Bridges were still standing, railways still operating. Fresh German and Italian anti-aircraft guns had been brought into the area, but they could not halt the tide of destruction. German headquarters, located in the heart of Salerno in the Hotel Montestella, had been finally destroyed, but not before a large portion of the residential district had been flattened. The Umberto Barracks, deserted by troops, were wiped out, and the vegetable market, the slaughter-house and the Sanatorium—despite its enormous red crosses—were all damaged.

The civic authorities had fled the city and the only people to remain were the priests, headed by the old Archbishop Monsignor Nicola Monterisi, who went about their tasks of burying the dead and comforting the bereaved with bravery and singleness of purpose.

On the demolished walls of houses survivors had chalked messages for those who came searching, often giving lists of killed and the new address of the survivors. On the corner of the Corso Vittoria, a disillusioned Italian with a bucket of whitewash had tried to scrub out *Viva Mussolini* and replaced it with the equivalent of short four-letter words, describing what he thought of Mussolini, Hitler, Churchill, Roosevelt and Stalin, a feeling that was echoed by all these peasants who had never wanted any part whatever in a war not of their choosing.

Yet down on the beaches on the night of 8th September, and away from the urban areas, all was strangely quiet. The moon, risen from behind the mountains, fitfully gleamed in the criss-cross water of the canals which divided the numerous orchards and the fields of tomatoes and melons. The earth, which had absorbed the sun's heat during the day, gave it up to the cool breezes.

Major Duppenbecker was chatting with his adjutant and orderly officer in the small fruit garden of his farm headquarters. Little lanterns twinkled where men scribbled on pads what many of them thought were their last messages home. They had been watching the distant bombing raids of Salerno and Battipaglia and wondering when the first air attacks would be launched at them. At regular intervals the bell of a field telephone set tinkled, as outstations on the fringe of the beaches and on the dunes reported "Situation quiet". A murmur of oscillation came from the headphones of a wireless set, and occasionally Duppenbecker gave the operator instructions to signal "Nothing to report" to divisional headquarters. The officers were talking about the old days at Stalingrad, when their division had been the first to reach the Volga. They were regretting the loss of Colonel-General Hubem, who had commanded them in Russia, and was commander of the XIV Panzer Corps stationed nearby. The morale of these Germans was high. They had a tradition born during the holocaust of Stalingrad, which had survived reorganisation and reinforcement. Between the officers and men there was a genuine trust and a spirit of true comradeship. Almost everybody knew everyone. They knew they could depend on each other. They had experienced many forms of war, and as Duppenbecker wrote in his diary, *we old fighters had experienced and gone through so many situations that it was not easy to upset us.*

Throughout the whole of the 16th Panzer Division the scene was the same, with mixed feelings of tenseness, expectation and confidence.

On the outskirts of Battipaglia was stationed the 11th Panzer Grenadier Tank Battalion, equipped with armoured cars. Its commander, twenty-five-year-old Captain Eberhard Spetzler, had moved his troops of armoured cars out of the built-up area during the night, to avoid the bombs which had half destroyed the town, blocking many of the roads and making movement difficult. He had finalised his plans, being at a moment's notice to move his armoured vehicles into a counter-attack wherever it was needed.

* * * * *

This was the situation at midnight on 8th September, 1943. The largest, to date, combined operation of World War II was poised in flight about to stoop on to the Italian mainland. In London and Washington the war leaders waited impatiently for the news of the landings, and none more impatient than General Mark Clark, aboard the American Flagship *Ancon*. High up on the bridge of the warship, he stood with Vice-Admiral H. Kent Hewitt, the naval commander, watching the sailors put into effect the result of the planning. This was the Navy's important task: to get the Army to the right beaches on time. As Mark Clark later recorded:

There was nothing we could do but wait.

CHAPTER V

D-DAY: 9TH SEPTEMBER, 1943

A WARNING bell jangled loudly inside the tin walls of a submarine lying in a few fathoms of water just off the Salerno beaches. The captain ordered: "Periscope up!" and, gripping the handles with both hands, scanned the sea and the shore, trying to pierce the darkness. All seemed quiet. Having glanced at his watch, he gave orders for *HM* Submarine *Shakespeare* to surface.

As the conning-tower emerged from the depths of a ring of foam and hissing water, a keen-eyed German sentry of the 1st Battalion 79th Panzer Grenadier Regiment saw its vague shape through the blackness. He hastily turned the handle of his field telephone and reported to battalion headquarters:

"No, I cannot be sure what it was. But there certainly was something."

From German strong-points warnings flashed back: "Sounds of engines out to sea"—"Shadows amongst the waves". But nothing definite; only misty pictures, hazy variations in light and shade. Was it just nerves? Or had it really been an enemy vessel that had come inshore and then gone? An hour went by; the sentries visibly relaxed. Not yet—but soon.

Shakespeare had been operating in the Salerno waters since 29th August, and not without considerable excitement. On the previous morning she had radioed the fleet that she had sunk an enemy U-Boat and seen two others in the area. It was this vessel which had reported the presence of mines in the Gulf. Her job now was to act as beacon light and guide all the landing craft into their correct beaches. An officer supervised the erection of a green light on the conning-tower that shone steadily out to sea, where hundreds of helmsmen were waiting anxiously for it.

With a twelve-mile trip ahead of the assault craft, the first flight were swung overboard and dropped down the davits on to the calm waters. On board the *Prince Albert* bells rang and lights flashed calling the Commandos up from the mess decks, where they had been waiting. With corked faces and the backs of their hands blacked, they sat looking like extras in a nigger minstrel show. Their rubber-soled boots made hardly a sound on the steel-plated decks. Each man bore an enormous variety of gear, weighing on an average over half a hundredweight. Personal armament consisted of either a rifle or a Tommy-gun; one or two grenades stuffed in the pockets of the camouflage smocks, an anti-tank mine tied round the neck, spare magazines for Brens and sub-machine-guns. Others carried prepared demolition charges, looking like cheeses tied to their persons. The 3-inch mortar team and the machine-gun teams were burdened with heavy loads, well in excess of one hundredweight each. Brigadier 'Lucky' Laycock, the young leader of the Commando Brigade, was called from his cabin about midnight. Like hundreds of others, he struggled into his clothes and equipment before going up on deck to see what was afoot. In some hurry, he stepped out of his cabin, treading on the head of a sleeping matelot who had found a vacant strip of floor on the overloaded craft. A stream of abuse followed the brigadier up the gangway, and he was very pleased not to have to go back and face the man again!

On another vessel Lieutenant Colonel John Whitfield, *CO* of the 2/5 Battalion of The Queen's, was resisting with determination the plan of an officious sailor, who wanted to get all the infantry into the assault craft hours before it was necessary. Whitfield was a little tired of the sea, and had already been horrified at the Navy's noisy habit of sounding sirens loudly every time they got into position or were about to move. He was convinced that every German for miles around had been kept wide awake by the hooting of the ships. The naval officer pointed out that as long as the troops were at sea they came under naval orders. Whitfield agreed, but retorted that the moment they landed they were under his command, and he did not want a battalion of sea-sick wraiths to stagger up the beach looking for somewhere to lie down. In the end, as is usual in petty service squabbles, they compromised: the troops only sat in the craft for fifteen minutes, arriving at the rendezvous ten minutes early. Hundreds of *LCA*s were lowered and, with gurgling swirling foam behind them, went to their stations in the forming-up area.

Meanwhile, tiny scout landing craft were edging their way shorewards quietly to take up positions in front of the landing beaches. They anchored a few hundred yards off the coast and then shone the appropriate coloured lights directly out to sea, where they were picked up by the assault-craft convoys.

Commanding the scout craft off the American beaches—*Red, Green, Yellow* and *Blue*—were mostly very young officers or ensigns, on whose shoulders lay a heavy responsibility, as it was of vital importance that they be located in the exact spot. They had sailed through mined waters, leading the minesweepers on the correct path. Ensign George Anderson, *USN*, only recently graduated from officers' school, took in his boat to a point 400 yards off *Red* beach and at 0230 hours started blinking a red light. Nearby, Lieutenant Grady Holloway, *USN*, took up position in front of *Green* beach by taking a fix on the ancient medieval watchtower at Paestum, which could be seen standing up dimly through the dark. Along the thirty-six-mile stretch of the Salerno Gulf boats and men were silently performing similar hazardous tasks. Many of the craft were so close inshore that they could distinguish German lorries moving, hear an occasional shout and see the odd flicker of light, as a negligent German sentry lit a cigarette. Yet close as they were—and they had to sit there for hours—not one was discovered. The sailors had orders to wear rope-soled or rubber shoes, all hatches and doorways were carefully opened and closed, and not a chink of light was allowed to escape.

Tank-landing craft *Number 637* housed a group of troops from 9th Battalion Royal Fusiliers, cheerful cockneys of London's own regiment. Fusilier Bill Turner sat in a sheltered part of the ship, filing away at a handful of bullets which he was hoping would eventually fit into an old French pistol that he had acquired in North Africa. It had been an uncomfortable journey for these landlubbers. The vast hold of the ship was crammed with vehicles of all shapes and sizes. Up at the blunt bow, almost touching the huge ramp, was an enormous Matador lorry complete with trailer and loaded with massive rolls of wire mesh intended for laying a temporary road up the beach. Behind it was a white scout car, with a large metal roller on the front, crewed by Royal Engineers and loaded with bangalore torpedoes and Teller mines.

A giant Sapper Sergeant found great pleasure in telling all around him: "If a spark hits that lot, you'll be helped on your way to hell!"

Filling the rest of the space were three Bren carriers, bearing the 3-inch mortar crews of the battalion, and several command jeeps, one of which belonged to 'Handle Bar Harry', nickname of the commanding officer, Lieutenant-Colonel Ted Hillersden.

To keep the party spirit going, a matelot wandered around small groups of sea-sick Fusiliers, waggling a piece of pork fat on the end of a string and shouting: "Bring it up in the 'oggin, boys. Don't spread it round the deck!"

Other troops of the same battalion travelled on the Polish ship *SS Sobieski*, from whose mast flew an enormous homemade regimental flag. When the time came they clambered down nets into assault craft that bobbed gently alongside the hull. Men cursed as they slipped or as pieces of equipment got caught in the netting. Thirty-five men to each vessel; on one of these a young sixteen-year-old Navy boy was quietly crying from a bad attack of nerves. Fusilier Albert Fitzgerald, the *CO*'s batman, sat nearby trying to cheer him, and finally managed to coax a smile from his pale face.

The columns of assault craft steadily approached the beaches, the helmsmen keeping station by the red lights in the stern of each vessel. The roar of their engines intermingled with exploding mines and the crash of bombs from planes, which had now switched to shore targets. But from the supporting battleships came not a shot, not a sound. On shore the Germans were getting edgy; they knew it could not be long. They held their fire and awaited the orders. In the northern sector, the American Rangers under Colonel Bill Darby, and the British Commandos under 'Lucky' Laycock, were fast approaching Maiori and Vietri. Their object was to capture the high ground overlooking Salerno and deny it to the German artillery observers. They were also to take and hold the narrow passes leading into the Naples plain.

At 0135 hours a battery of coastal guns opened up on the craft carrying the Commando force; Commodore Oliver aboard *HMS Hilary* noted in his log: *It was realised that any prospect of even local surprise had been lost.* In the south, however, the Germans remained quiet and the American ships could still not get permission to open up.

The troops, thoroughly bewildered by this sudden barrage from the shore, following the Armistice announcement, just could not make up their minds what it was all about. Some Coldstream Guardsmen, still aboard their parent ship, decided that either the Italian communications had broken down or the gunners were too idle to unload their guns. This led to remarks such as: "Who's got the bugle? Blow the cease-fire for them!"—"Poor bloody Eyeties, can't even get their cease-fire orders right!" and "Lazy bastards, I suppose they think it's easier to fire rather than unload."

The first hostile shells from the coastal batteries, taken over from the Italians by the 16th Panzer Division a few hours beforehand, struck well on target with some losses. The American tank-landing ship *Number 357*, carrying Rangers, received a direct hit, killing many of the troops and crew, as well as holing the vessel in several places. The Navy was at last relieved of their 'No fire' order. *USS Biscayne* immediately set off a smoke screen, whilst guns of the British destroyers *HMS Brecon* and *Blankney* were soon belching forth clouds of smoke and rocking to the recoil; firing from 5,300 yards, they quickly ranged on the battery and silenced it. Other guns opened up from behind the beaches, shortly to be assaulted by the 56th and 46th British Divisions, but the Navy gladly took on these targets as they appeared. Yet it was not easy locating them; they were largely using flashless ammunition, which made it very difficult for the observers, but wherever one was spotted it was soon put out of action by the deadly accuracy of the Royal Navy gunners.

H-Hour was only a short time ahead. No alterations could now be made to the plan; the dice was cast and the players were about to learn in whose favour it was loaded.

*   *   *   *   *

The military plan had been rushed through all its stages. Commanders frequently did not know from one day to another what troops and equipment they would have in the order of battle. General Alexander in his despatches wrote:

> It is fair to say that few operations of war of this magnitude have been so distinguished by the speed with which they were mounted and the shortness of time between the decision to undertake the invasion and its launching.

Commodore Oliver in his despatches remarked:

> By superhuman efforts on the part of all concerned, and under conditions in which I hope a combined operation will never again have to be concerted, orders were ready for issue by 29th August . . .

Yet it is remarkable, in view of instructions that never got to their destination, amendments that were being handed out even as troops were disembarking, and the profusion of detail points that were never understood, that there were so few major errors. The last-minute decision of General Eisenhower to remove the 82nd *US* Airborne Division from the 5th Army meant that the original plan was short of a complete division.

Mark Clark had divided the thirty-six mile curve of the Salerno Gulf into two sections. The northern half—where the hills came down very much closer to the beaches and which included the port of Salerno, Montecorvino airfield and the important rail centre of Battipaglia—was allocated to the British X Corps, under command of Lieutenant-General Sir Richard McCreery. The southern half was to be assaulted by the inexperienced troops of the American VI Corps under command of Major-General Ernest K. Dawley, who planned to use the untried 36th Texas (National Guard) Division in the attack, with two regimental combat teams of the 45th 'Thunderbirds' Division, veterans of the Sicily campaign, in floating reserve, ready to land as and where needed.

It is interesting to note that, whereas the British corps was headed by commanders who had complete confidence in each other, in the American corps there was nothing like the same feeling. General Clark had been offered for the landing the 36th or 34th Division, the latter alone having had battle experience. On the strength of having known Major-General Fred Walker before the war and having recommended him for the command he was now holding, Clarke chose the 36th Division.

Just prior to this operation the *US* War Department asked Eisenhower to accept VI Corps under command of Major-General E. K. Dawley. Clark in his memoirs comments:

> I was not well acquainted with Dawley, but I did know that General McNair thought very highly of him and I placed a great deal of confidence in McNair's sound judgment. I talked to Ike about Dawley, and he was far from enthusiastic, although he reluctantly concurred when I said I recommended replying affirmatively to the War Department.

With Ike not enthusiastic for Dawley, and Clark having urged his appointment against the Supreme Commander's advice, it is not surprising that Eisenhower, Clark and Dawley were soon at loggerheads.

The gently shelving beaches were ideal for an amphibious landing. Evenly intersected with small rivers, from the map the area had a look of a chequer-board with a pattern of minor roads, streams, canals and dykes. It was mostly reclaimed land and very fertile. The local peasants had good cause to bless Mussolini for the good work that he had carried out in this zone. There were few villages in the coastal plain, as the inhabitants had discovered years before the virulent mosquitoes which spread malaria and infested the low ground. They worked in the fields by day, retiring to their squalid hill hamlets at night. A variety of crops were grown, including

tobacco, fruit, walnuts, olives, oranges, lemons, melons and tomatoes, which were mainly exported fresh to Naples or canned in
local factories. Dotted along the edge of the sand stood numerous
conical stone watchtowers, eroded and decayed, erected centuries
before to warn the locals of the approach of marauding Saracens.
At the southernmost tip of the invasion area was the ancient town
of Paestum. Founded by the Sybarites in 600 B.C. as Poseidonia, the
city of Neptune, it contains the remains of two wonderful Doric
temples, probably the most beautiful in the whole of Italy. But
the next visitors to Neptune's Temple would not be interested in its
history nor in its beauty: they were to use it as a shelter and as a
hospital.

* * * * *

The order of battle for the landings, from north to south, was:
the American Rangers, whose task was to dominate the mountains
of the Sorrento peninsula on the northern flank of the landings;
the British Commandos, who were to land at Vietri and capture
the passes through to Naples; the 46th British Infantry Division,
who had two tasks—the capture of Salerno town and the establish-
ment of a bridgehead; 56th London Division, with the task of seizing
Battipaglia, a vital communications centre, and Montecorvino
airfield; then came the gap between the British and American
sectors; and finally the 36th US Infantry Division with orders to
capture main roads and push out to contact Montgomery's 8th
Army; in floating reserve were two regimental combat teams from
the American 45th 'Thunderbird' Division.

All the troops had been trained in North Africa and had carried
out limited invasion exercises. The 46th Division was under Major-
General 'Ginger' Hawkesworth, known to his troops as 'The
little man with the big stick' from his habit of carrying a five-foot
thumb stick in the manner of the late Lord Baden-Powell. He
assumed that initially there would be only light enemy opposition,
but that probably in a couple of days the Germans would gather
strength for a large counter-attack, by which time he thought he
would have achieved his objectives and be strongly entrenched.
His orders from McCreery were to seize a beachhead between the
small Picentino and Asa rivers, covering about a one-mile length
of the coast opposite the village of Pontecagnano. The second phase
of· the attack would be to consolidate, in conjunction with the
Commandos, the capture of the two vital passes leading to the Naples
plain. General Hawkesworth decided on a one-brigade attack,
landing on two beaches known as *Red* and *Green*. He chose the 128th

Brigade, consisting of three battalions of the Royal Hampshire Regiment, and gave them the task of destroying all immediate enemy opposition and capturing the hills overlooking the Salerno road. Behind them he placed the 138th Brigade, made up of the 6th Battalion Lincolnshire Regiment, 2/4th Battalion King's Own Yorkshire Light Infantry and the 6th Battalion York & Lancaster Regiment, who were to capture Salerno and link up with the Commandos. In divisional reserve was the 139th Brigade (2/5th Battalion Leicestershire Regiment, 5th Battalion Sherwood Foresters and 16th Battalion Durham Light Infantry).

The divisional password was *Mailed Fist*, with the reply, taken from the divisional sign: *Hearts of Oak*.

To their right the 56th London Division, under command of Major-General Douglas A. H. Graham, had been given two vital tasks. The first was to seize Montecorvino Airfield, only a short way inland, and then the important road and rail junction at Battipaglia. The airfield was Objective Number One in the whole of the assault plan. It was badly needed to supply fighter support for the operation as, until it was captured, the bulk of the fighter aircraft would have to fly up from Sicily. It was optimistically forecast that it would be taken early on D-Day and four squadrons of Spitfires would be able to give full-time close support to the troops.

General Graham decided to attack with two brigades and placed the 169th Brigade, with two battalions abreast, on the two *Sugar* beaches; the 167th Brigade on a similar plan on two beaches coded *Roger*. The 201st Guards Brigade was in reserve ready to go in wherever the need was greatest.

This division had by far the hardest task and was to be involved in the most vicious fighting.

The scene was set. The minesweepers had done magnificent work in carving out clear lanes, but the job allotted to them had been too large for the time available and as a result many loose mines were still floating around the support areas, which were meant to be cleared for destroyers.

On the mainland, General von Veitinghoff, commanding the 10th German Army, had ordered the 26th Panzer Division opposing the British 8th Army in the south to break contact and hasten northwards to strengthen the 16th Panzer Division, which, for the moment, was all alone and thinly spread on the ground. The 8th Army had crossed the Messina Straits and landed in Italy on 3rd September; on D-Day they were 150 miles from Salerno. To

General Wilhelm Schmalz, commander of the Hermann Goering Panzer Division located in the Caserta area, north of Naples and about fifty miles from Salerno, went orders to attack and destroy the enemy forces landing at Salerno. Units marched through the defile leading to the Gulf; at Nocera they collected a Recce Unit which had been forced out of Salerno, and by the evening they had come under heavy naval gunfire and were in action against Commandos and Rangers along the Pagani-Maiori road, on Monte Sant'Angelo and near Campinola. General Schmalz soon realised he was up against very tough and experienced troops.

Front-line units had earlier received a morale-raising declaration from Field-Marshal Kesselring:

> The invading enemy in the area Naples–Salerno and southwards must be completely annihilated and, in addition, thrown into the sea. Only by so doing can we obtain a decisive change of the situation in the Italian area. I require ruthless employment of all the might of the three Army units. The British and Americans must realise that they are hopelessly lost against the concentrated German might.

*　　*　　*　　*　　*

At 0315 hours the guns of the Royal Navy in the British northern sector let off a strong barrage for a fifteen-minute softening-up programme on the beach defences. But in the south the supporting naval guns remained silent, reluctantly obeying the Army Commander's instructions. General Fred Walker, aboard Admiral John L. Hall's Flagship *USS Samuel Chase*, was busy studying the latest air photographs of the beaches and the surrounding high ground. He could not find any fixed or organised defences near his sector. There was one three-gun artillery battery opposite the beaches, but he had been assured by Intelligence that this was Italian, obsolete and unmanned. He did not anticipate that any troops of the 16th Panzer Division would be in the area in any strength; and in view of the fact that the British had already decided on a short bombardment in the north, he thought this might mislead the Germans to believe that the main attack was being launched there, allowing him to slip in unobserved. Accordingly, he did not ask the Navy for fire support. Since the war, General Walker has admitted that this was a tactical error and it would have been good psychologically for the troops and a great encouragement to the first assault waves.

0320 hours. The first troops began to land in the extreme north on the Sorrento peninsula at Maiori without any opposition. They were American Rangers under Lieutenant Colonel Bill Darby, who were to operate independently on the flank of the British Sector. A steeply shelving gravel beach allowed the large ships to come in very close to the shore and soon *LCIs* were landing stores almost like a peacetime manœuvre. These dogged shock troops pushed on to dig positions overlooking the vital Chiunzi Pass, which was one of the two passes leading to Naples. From here they dominated the roads and railway running from Salerno to Naples. Three hours later all supplies and equipment were ashore; the troops were congratulating themselves on a 'cushy' operation.

0330 hours. The assault craft of the Commando force neared the small port of Vietri just north of Salerno; it stood at the mouth of the Molina defile, the second pass to Naples. The guns of *HMS Blackmore* roared out to silence a noisy shore battery with quick success. The troops crouched low within the thin steel walls of their vessels and watched the heavy shells of the Navy bursting in huge flashes of orange fire on the beach, sending up huge spurts of rock and sand; occasionally one would land on a house, some of which went up in flames or collapsed under the weight of shells. No response came from the German defences. The first wave of Number 2 Army Commando went ashore, headed by Lieutenant-Colonel Jack Churchill, a fabulous figure, a cross between a military genius and a mad mullah, who encouraged his men with brief four-letter words. They landed on the small sheltered beach almost before the Germans knew they were there. When a storm of machine-gun bullets began hitting the sand, the men were already across the dunes and into a battery which, after a short hand-to-hand struggle, gave up, the first disconsolate prisoners being herded back to the beach. Without a pause, the troops rushed a German barracks, where they found evidence of a hasty evacuation, and as one Commando remembers, "There was shit all over the place, discarded weapons and papers".

Colonel Jack Churchill later discovered in a wrecked office an abandoned operations order, giving a detailed and accurate fore-cast of how and where the Commandos would land. If only the Germans there had carried out their task, they could have made it difficult, if not impossible, for the Commando assault to succeed.

Behind the Army Commandos at 0400 hours came the 41st Royal Marine Commando. By this time, the enemy was wide awake and reacting with ferocity. It was still dark, but a faint glimmer of light was brightening the eastern sky. The German gunners were mainly concentrating on the fleet and leaving the beaches alone. Captain

John Parsons, *RM*, brought his troop in to shore in two *LCIs* and calmly directed the craft to moor alongside a mole, where the Marines trooped off as if alighting from a pleasure steamer. A single burst of machine-gun fire ripped the air; one of the Section commanders, Sergeant Maddocks, was hit in the leg as he stepped ashore. The immediate silence surrounding them was uncanny. Yet at a distance came the roar and flash of heavy enemy 88 mms. and from behind the Commandos the more mature sound of destroyers and cruisers, firing broadsides at every possible target. Brigadier 'Lucky' Laycock came in behind the Marines with his brigade headquarters; by then a German counter-attack, launched from behind Vietri, had found a clear run through to the Marina beach. As the staff with their batmen and a few signallers bumped an enemy patrol, firing at close quarters broke out.

Laycock rounded the corner of a crumbled building, to find himself three feet away from a German with a levelled rifle. Laycock fired his pistol and missed; the German fired and missed.

"We both turned and ran," recalls Laycock.

Still in the half light, a burly Marine came charging behind the Brigadier, yelling "Get down, get down!"—and pushed him roughly to the ground; then, using Laycock's buttocks as a barrel rest, he continued firing his rifle at the enemy.

Up forward, Lieutenant-Colonel Bruce Lumsden, *CO* of the 41st Royal Marine Commando, with two troops under Major J. M. Edwards, completed the capture of Vietri, their first objective, where even as the battle swelled civilians were running in and out of their houses to put up shutters and lock up animals, glancing fearfully over their shoulders at the Commandos with shouts of "*Presto, presto.*" The Royal Marine Commando then, joining in one force, rushed for La Molina Pass, the vital route to Naples, and were soon in positions dominating the road and railway. There they dug in, determined to stay until the main force arrived, which was expected before the end of the day.

Back on the beach at Marina, German mortars and guns switched their attention to the assault craft and launches bringing in reinforcements, ammunition and other supplies. The situation soon became noisy and fraught with danger. Several craft received direct hits, whilst the beach parties clearing the supplies were shot up with machine-guns. Somehow panic started; *LCIs* began to close their doors and pull off, heading back to the *LSI Prince Albert*. En route they shouted to other vessels that the beach had been retaken by the Germans and it was impossible to go there. Supplies badly needed by the Commandos were stopped at a crucial moment; it was not until a few hours later that the beach was reopened. Brigadier Laycock received an irate message from Major-General Hawkesworth: *At all costs you must retake Marina beach.* To this Laycock replied: *This is impossible. I have never lost it.*

As a result of this lack of control the Commandos never received greatcoats, razors, personal kit and other important supplies, and had to exist without them for many days.

There was undoubtedly a misappreciation of the situation by naval officers on the spot, who became confused by the heavy shelling and by the proximity of enemy forces.

The report by Commander Stratford Dennis, *RN*, Commanding *HMS Prince Charles,* who was in charge of subsidiary landings, reads:

> At 0810 hours the following signal was received from *Prince Albert*: *Beach retaken by Germans. Impossible to land Commando stores. Request instructions.* Followed at 0812 hours by the signal: LCT *and* LCI *sunk on beach.* No further communication was received from the beach. An officer of *Prince Albert* flotilla stated that on reaching the beach at 0645 hours he found it occupied by the enemy.

Captain John Parsons, *RM* Troop Commander, advanced swiftly inland with the object of capturing the La Molina Pass. With still no action on this front, all his men were wondering if the landing really was going to be unopposed and the Italians had managed to control the Germans. From intensive study of air photographs, they had learnt their route by heart, but on reaching a path leading into a gully, they found it blocked by a landslide, probably caused by a nearby bomb burst. Suddenly out of the shadows stepped a man; every Commando rifle, pistol and tommy-gun jerked, itchy fingers on triggers, in his direction. As it turned out to be a friendly local youth, they asked him the way in broken Italian; he volunteered to guide them personally. With a certain amount of suspicion they followed him up a steep winding path, which eventually brought them to the road. But the detour round the landslide had cost valuable time and the glimmer of light in the east was fast spreading over the sky. Parsons's troops had to reach the main Naples–Salerno road and seal it off from the north to prevent enemy movement from that direction; they were still a thousand yards short of the point where they were to block the pass. Parsons, running at the head of his troops, almost silent on their rubber boots and beginning to look a little incongruous with their blackened skins, shot round a bend in the road to find himself face to face with a Tiger tank at a distance of ten yards. The Commandos stopped and gaped at a German sitting half out of the turret: the Jerry gaped back. First to react was the tank gunner: he let go a burst of machine-gun fire that sent the Commandos scattering into a deep drain at the side of the road, where they found comparative safety, as the gunner could not depress his weapon sufficiently to get them in his sights. Some of the tank crew, who had been behind the vehicle, came creeping out of cover in an attempt to climb on to it, and in spite of the British Tommy-gun fire, one of them managed to leap into the turret. The Marines rushed forward in sudden attack: clambering on top of the tank, a corporal lifted the hatch cover, tossed in a grenade and slammed it shut. There came a dull roar followed by a flash of flame; in a few seconds the tank was a blazing inferno with bullets, shells and signal flares exploding and shooting into the air.

Hardly pausing in their stride, the Marines rushed onwards to the road, where they came under heavy automatic fire. Soon locating the source of trouble, Parsons asked his *CO*, Colonel Bruce Lumsden, for 3-inch mortar support, but was told to get on without it. On their right was a steep railway embankment cut into the side of an escarpment; from there the ground rose even more precipitously. This was the only way to assault the enemy; Lieutenant Walker at the head of a section went off in a right-flanking movement up the embankment. Most of the attack was over open ground and Parsons and the rest of the troop watched the German gunners get the group into their sights. Walker was wounded in the back half-way up the embankment and several men fell with him, but the threat had been sufficient to frighten the enemy, who hastily pulled out. There was a scurry of Germans running down the road. One man, too interested in the material things of life, stopped to load a few personal belongings on a pram and was shot by a Marine; on hands and knees, he continued pulling along the pram and the Marines sportingly gave up the hunt.

By the time the sun was climbing in the sky the Commandos were able to signal back to their headquarters ship: *All objectives captured.*

Once again Commando troops had proved their value. Their training had taught them to rush on swiftly without waiting for support and assistance, and the British Commandos and the American Rangers had literally jostled the defenders out of Vietri and Maiori.

Chapter VI

THE BRITISH SECTOR: D-DAY

MEANWHILE, on the other beaches to the south the main landings in the British Sector were proceeding according to plan. The long columns of assault-boats were steady on their courses; six minutes before H-Hour a rocket landing craft launched with a fantastic roar and a meteoric extravaganza 790 simultaneous 3-inch rockets onto *Green* Beach. Troops in the craft, their heads ringing from the blast, turned in awe to watch. Many were so close in that they were smothered with dirt, stones and pieces of metal, whilst the beach ahead disappeared in an earthquake of terror that demolished or decimated everything in its path. The main purpose of this rocket carpet was to destroy all mines, providing a clear path for both infantry and vehicles.

The rocket craft, nicknamed 'Hedgerows', were in use for the first time at Salerno. They had been invented and designed back in Britain and were to be built on to the assault vessels; only two weeks before the landings a ship had arrived from the United Kingdom with all the parts and pieces of equipment. Unfortunately somebody back in England had forgotten to send the blueprints, and apart from one sailor, who had vaguely seen an experimental rocket ship, nobody had much idea about how they should be put together. However, the Navy set to with a will and soon rigged the contraption on several *LCA*s, converting them to 'Rocket Landing Craft'—or *LCR*s. It was wisely decided to carry out one test firing; this was done on 29th August in Bizerta Bay in a Force 8 gale. Salvos of only twenty-four bombs were fired to see the effect. The results were immediately apparent. There were fantastic explosions. *LCR 446* nearly turned turtle, became waterlogged and shortly sank in fifteen fathoms; *LCR 403*, in almost as bad a state, barely made harbour. Various modifications were carried out as quickly as possible, but it was with some trepidation that the crews approached D-Day and the use of these vessels in action.

The crew of *LCR 403*, under the command of Sub-Lieutenant A. Tod, *RN*, spent a large part of their journey to Salerno painting the

hull of their craft with a rough coating of red lead paint in an effort to seal an undiscoverable leak. This vessel was lowered from the ocean tug *USS Nauset* at 1240 hours. Finding he had only twenty minutes in which to make the rendezvous, Tod rang the engine-room for 4,000 revolutions, although this was at the risk of cracking the big end. En route the craft nearly collided with a reference vessel, which, for some reason, was moving slowly astern; the sterns of the two vessels actually touched. At 0315 hours destroyers opened fire and *LCR 403* moved in to within forty yards of *Red* Beach. At 0324 hours the *LCR* opposite *Green* Beach launched her rockets. Six minutes later Tod gave the fire order and his rockets screamed away, whilst he put the engines hard astern to prevent the vessel from grounding. The fantastic explosion sent a small tidal wave back from the beach; the whole craft was showered with dirt, stones and pieces of metal. Germans were seen emerging from the ruins staggering and dazed, wandering aimlessly around.

Unfortunately, the rocket craft supposed to be opposite *Green* Beach was almost half a mile off target and the murderous bombs fell on *Amber* Beach. Orders had been issued by Admiral Connolly and General Hawkesworth that the troops must follow the rockets even if they fell off target, as it was thought imperative for the landing zones to be cleared of mines. Thus the first waves of the 56th Division went ashore on the wrong beach.

Having completed their task, the officers of *LCR 403* inspected the equipment and found that all girder beams had parted and most of the electric cables fractured from the force of the explosion. Frantically the crew worked to repair the damage; within forty minutes the craft was again ready for action. At 0405 hours the Beach Master on *Green* Beach, where the rocket craft's bombs had gone wide of the target, could be heard on the wireless saying that, owing to 'S' mines still uncovered, no further troops should land there. Sub-Lieutenant Tod offered the services of his vessel to blast a lane, but was shortly told that he was not required, the reason being put forward that it was too dangerous for the troops.

On *Amber* Beach a scene of unutterable confusion soon ensued. Troops of the 46th Division were mixed with others of the 56th Division; soldiers and sub-units wandered around lost and confused. To make matters worse, after the Sappers had cleared safe lanes, all vehicles and heavier weapons were landed on the correct beach and often did not join up with their units until the evening, or, in some cases, until the following day; and many were blown up by a battery of 88 mm. guns which had been left intact just behind *Green* Beach.

The boats containing 8th Battalion Royal Fusiliers—their objective was the high ground north-east of Eboli, fifteen miles inland—were headed for *Roger* Beach. Regimental Sergeant-Major Pat Murphy stood gazing over the blunt nose of an *LCA* which bobbed and waltzed in the wake of another identical craft ahead. When they had first started, he had told all troops to keep their heads down, but with the activity going on around them it was impossible to enforce the order; the soldiers lined the steel plated walls and watched with wonder. As they neared the coastline, *RSM* Murphy could see huge mounds of earth being flung into the air where the shells and rockets landed. Slowly the barrage began to lift, concentrating on targets further inland. Way ahead of them, earlier assault craft had disgorged their occupants; under a constant chatter of machine-gun fire Sappers patiently prodded for mines and laid white tapes as they slowly made their way up the beach. German shells were landing around the lines of assault craft, but only a few appeared to be hit.

The beach loomed up. There was a heavy crunch and the *LCA* stopped with a grinding jerk. The ramp was swiftly lowered by the sailors; with a shouted order, every soldier was on his feet running into waist-deep water, holding weapons above his head and struggling to get legs moving through the waves. With a group of men, *RSM* Murphy ran up the gently shelving beach and flung himself down, with bursting lungs, behind a small mound of earth. Around them hung the fog of war. The acrid smell of cordite and smoke was everywhere. They could see a few beach huts, some burning or leaning drunkenly on sagging walls; strong-points and trenches, a mass of twisted rubble where heavy naval guns had pounded them into nothingness; and back at the water's edge, troops still streaming ashore and empty assault craft manœuvring for return to parent vessels. Already wounded men were being carried back to the boats for evacuation to the hospital ships. Officers and *NCOs* were shouting orders and trying to get sub-units marshalled for the advance.

In another battalion vessel was 'Popular' Tom McQuade, the Post Corporal—Popular because of the letters he delivered and also his duties as Master of Ceremonies at battalion dances. As the ramps were lowered, he dashed into three feet of water; in front of him, diminutive Fusilier Micky Fineman, an East End

Jew and the unit wag, fell headlong in the sea, disappearing from sight. McQuade reached into the water and dragged him to the surface.

Choking and spluttering, the irrepressible Fineman, looking mournfully at a ruined wrist-watch, gasped out: "Anybody vant to buy a vatch?"

There was a burst of laughter; tension relaxed and the group continued its charge ashore.

Bullets from German strong-points were whipping up the sand, while Regimental Policeman Lance-Corporal Bill Whitby, standing at the water's edge, calmly directed the men to rendezvous points. Seeing McQuade, he went towards him to ask in a worried voice: "Hey, Mac! My stamps have got wet and stuck together; do you think I'll be able to use them on my letters?"

McQuade, perpetually bothered by all ranks for postal information, was shocked that anyone could think of so unimportant a point at such a time; in a flabbergasted voice, he yelled back: "Of course you bloody well can! Don't keep me gassing on this ruddy beach."

The troops followed the white tapes denoting clear paths through the sand, bitterly recalling that they had been told the beaches were clear. Those in the know reported that a low flying photo-reconnaissance aircraft a few days before had taken a picture of a German soldier and his signorina using one of the beaches as a lovers' lane.

"Must have been a mirage," muttered a sapper as he carefully dug around a mine.

A Petty Officer, harassed but efficient, stood at the top of another craft's ramp, waving his arms and shouting: "Get off, everybody, quick! For Christ's sake get a move on; I've got umpteen more trips like this to make!"

Shells were falling; the wounded lay in the sand, some of them vaguely trying to crawl to safety, others scratching shallow foxholes with their hands. Sergeant George Buffell, the Battalion Signals Sergeant, with a group of operators, was ordered to dig in only a few yards up the beach, as the rifle companies had made no progress and the exit lanes were jammed full of men and vehicles. Naval beachmasters tried vainly to organise order out of chaos, but as fast as they cleared one exit, more vehicles and men were disgorged from the ships to create fresh traffic blocks.

LCT 637, carrying men of the 9th Battalion Royal Fusiliers, received several direct hits from 88-mm. guns. Fusilier Bill Turner was thinking of the Royal Engineers' vehicle in the middle of the ship and waiting for its dangerous cargo to explode. Several ships nearby had been struck and were blazing merrily; he and his comrades felt like sitting ducks waiting for the end. Wounded troops were groaning or suffering in silence, whilst one young lad, horror-stricken by the death and destruction around him, sat clenching and unclenching his fists in a paroxysm of nerves, crying quietly: "Oh Mum, I want Mum!"

With a bump that made everyone think they had hit a mine the craft beached. The drivers, already in their vehicles, were warming up the engines and waiting for the word go. First off was the huge Matador lorry, which ran off the side of the ramp and stuck, jamming the exit. Sailors cursed and officers roared, but the giant lorry would not be budged. As the skipper ordered engines full astern, the lorry dropped off into the water. The helmsman swung the wheel, bringing the *LCT* in once again.

The Germans, who must have been watching this performance, concentrated on the vessel, and as the ramp went down for a second time bullets came straight through the opening. It was nearly daylight; the mast had been shot away, the engine-room had received a direct hit, putting one screw out of action. The sailors manning the anti-aircraft guns had all had their backs peppered with minute pieces of shrapnel. But before the vehicles could unload, a naval launch came shooting alongside and a very angry red-faced officer screamed abuse at the captain, telling him he had come into the wrong beach. An embarrassed crew reversed once more out to sea and headed back to the main convoy, where the dead and wounded were unloaded. Turner and his chums vaguely hoped that they would be unloaded, too, but the ship was turned and with the sun just rising they went in to the correct beach. This time it seemed just like a peacetime pleasure trip. No shells, no bombs or machine-gun bullets. They even had time to shake hands with the matelots before clambering into a Bren carrier and going off on to dry sand. As Turner drove along, he suddenly remembered the French pistol stuck in his belt and realised that, if they met any Jerries, it would be quite useless. He had not found time to file down any more bullets.

'B' Company of the 9th Battalion Royal Fusiliers reached the assault area immediately north of the 8th Battalion, and were ordered to lie half in and half out of the water, whilst sappers crawled carefully forward pushing lengths of Bangalore torpedoes up the beach. The torpedoes exploded with a shattering roar; the men charged along the thin drain-like craters they made. Even so, the first man ashore trod on a mine and had his leg blown off. German machine-guns had fixed lines firing across the sand, but luckily these had been set too high and the men were able to double under the bullets. As Lance Corporal Harold Lampard, a wireless operator, marched forward for about a hundred yards to a rendezvous near a farmhouse, a ship in the bay was hit in its armoury. He suddenly saw the large vessel erupt into an enormous firework display, lighting up the surrounding area and hastening the dawn, which was fast approaching.

Other troops of the battalion landed at 0345 hours to find a German rocket battery ranging the beach. A naval forward observation officer signalled its location to the headquarters ship. Soon the Fusiliers saw the gladdening sight of a destroyer steaming close inshore at a rate of knots, turn broadside and let fly at the guns. *The shells almost parted our hair*, wrote a Fusilier, *but that was the last of the rockets and it was the first of many occasions when our pals in the Navy were to help us out of sticky positions.* A machine-gun nest, located on the flank of this beach, had remained untouched by the barrage, and a platoon, led by Lieutenant David Lewis, a red-haired Welsh rugby player, charged with grenades and bayonets to take twenty-five prisoners of war, but at the cost of Lewis's life.

An officer of brigade headquarters went ashore at 0400 hours. The first thing his foot touched on land felt like a body *which did not exactly give him courage.* The beach, the wrong one, was utter chaos. Officers and troops were milling around, just like Hampstead Heath on Bank Holiday Monday. Groups stood studying aerial photographs under shaded torches, trying vainly to find familiar landmarks, until it was eventually realised they were miles off target. The Commanding Officer of the 9th Fusiliers crouched over his wireless set, still wearing a soft hat, shouting orders and trying to get his widely spread battalion under control.

His batman, Fusilier Albert Fitzgerald, heard him angrily shouting: "Christ, we must be a mile off our axis!"

A lone dive bomber came over and added the scream of its dive to the rattle and explosion of the nearer positions. Destroyers, answering urgent calls for support, were racing like greyhounds through waters as yet largely uncleared of mines. A large white house was particularly strongly held, but a destroyer silenced it with two salvos. Radio operators received confused reports of bayonet assaults and often heard the screams of men burnt by flame-throwers. Groups of German prisoners were herded back towards the sea, many of them to be killed by their own guns which were now fully awake and registering on the beaches. Subsequent waves of craft brought in mobile barrage balloons, and there followed the extraordinary sight of these monstrous clumsy beasts being trundled off the ramps, tethered to barrows pushed by *RAF* ground personnel.

The forward companies, held up by local defences, were broken up by the fire into individual groups and were trying to capture batteries and strong-points. Headquarters of the 9th Battalion Royal Fusiliers moved up a lane and settled into a ditch. Close by Albert Fitzgerald lay a dying man with most of his stomach shot away; seeing the Padre nearby, Fitzgerald called him over, and the chaplain lay down in the muddy ditch beside the dying soldier to comfort him for the few remaining moments of his life. As he expired, four frightened German soldiers stuck their heads through the hedge and politely asked if they could be made prisoners. They were rudely welcomed by a shell which landed close by, killing two of them outright.

RSM George Hollings—later to be commissioned in the field and the only regular soldier of this Territorial battalion—lay in a four-foot drain so far untouched by shot or shell. Deciding their haven was all too close to other targets, he ordered the men with him to disperse to other ditches in pairs. Last to move, he had only gone ten yards when a terrifying scream forced him to the ground. Looking back, he saw the drain blown to smithereens.

To the left of the Royal Fusiliers was the 169th (Queen's) Brigade. Brigadier Lewis Lyne had decided to attack with two battalions up. His main task was to capture Montecorvino Airfield and consolidate in the hills immediately to the east, denying them to the enemy. With Lyne was the American war correspondent Henry Knickerbocker, who kept him regaled with stories of his adventurous life all over Europe, interviews with Hitler and Mussolini and pre-war life in European capitals. He had also proved himself adept at helping with the washing-up and mixing cocktails in the temporary officers' mess aboard the *LSI*.

The 2/5th Battalion Queen's went ashore at 0410 hours. They had a dry landing; as Lieutenant-Colonel John Whitfield stepped off his boat, the *RSM*, all correct and properly dressed, saluted, shouting: "Straight up ahead, sir!"

The Battalion 'Orders Group' ran along a white-taped lane for a hundred yards to enter an area of flood water, which came up to their chests. Runners who had been carrying bicycles threw them away in disgust and signallers pushed wireless sets on barrows under the water. Whitfield could not find his position, as the floods had obscured many landmarks and they floundered around, trying to keep a straight path. Eventually they clambered on to a dyke which stuck a few inches out of the water.

In the half-light Whitfield shouted out: "George, are you there?"

From fifty yards away, loud and clear came the reply of Major George Lane, one of the company commanders: "Sir!"

Repeating his shout—"John, are you there?"—Whitfield received an identical reply from the left flank. He ordered his men to keep straight ahead in the hope that they would find a known landmark. The Luftwaffe came to their aid by dropping an enormous parachute flare; some hundreds of yards away, they all immediately recognised a prominent house. Soon the battalion was in an organised body, accounting for dead, wounded and missing.

The 2/7th Queen's under Lieutenant-Colonel Allen 'Chippy' Block found their beach a shambles, with movement restricted by troops lying down under vicious air-burst shells instead of getting off the shingle into better cover. Soon after, passing through the stringy sand grass of the dunes, they came under fire from a farmhouse; a platoon led by Lieutenant Peter Poyser brought it under Bren-gun attack and charged. When they got within fifty yards, the doors and windows opened and out came a dozen Germans with their hands up. The Queen's went forward to disarm them, but when they closed in the Germans dropped to the ground whilst a hidden Spandau opened fire on the Queen's, killing and wounding several men in the platoon, including the officer. Their enraged comrades stormed on to kill every German they could find.

By first light Brigadier Lyne was ashore, greeted with a report that all initial objectives had been reached. Henry Knickerbocker, who had been scribbling in his notebook, snapped it shut and, turning to the brigadier, asked:

"Well, General, what's the programme for today?"

"How could I tell him?" recalls Lyne. "I hadn't the faintest idea myself!"

Just offshore Lieutenant-Commander C. E. Hall, aboard *HMS Princess Astrid*, ordered members of the crew to clear up masses of ammunition, weapons and equipment left behind by the troops. During the passage he had erected a large sign in the troop decks: *Take your ammunition with you. You'll need it.* But the troops paid little heed and in his report Hall stated: *Despite this order it didn't help and in some cases up to fifty per cent of the gear was left behind by lazy troops.*

Tommy Burke, Company Sergeant Major of 'A' Company 2/7th Queen's, was wounded in the thigh by an exploding mine as he ran up the beach. He refused to be evacuated, cursing anyone who suggested it. With only a rough dressing to quench the flow of blood, he led his company through a minefield and carried on with the advance for five hours, in spite of increasing pain and loss of strength. For his gallantry and determination he was awarded an immediate Military Medal and evacuated after being given a direct order by his company commander.

The leading units eased themselves gradually into the head-high tobacco plantations, into the vineyards and the orchards. These were all infested with enemy snipers, who moved rapidly from one position to another, and in the close country where visibility was very limited the invading troops found it almost impossible to winkle them out. Company Sergeant-Major 'Tug' Wilson of 'C' Company, having received a very painful wound when he was shot through the nose by a sniper, was delighted to escort some prisoners back to Battalion headquarters on his way to the aid post for treatment.

The Commanding Officer, Lieutenant-Colonel Block, interrogating a couple, found them to be from the 64th Panzer Grenadier Regiment. One of the prisoners, a six-foot blond full of conceit and pride, lit a cigarette sneering at the *CO*. Objecting to his attitude, Block ordered Wilson to remove the offending cigarette and made it plain that if there was any further dumb insolence it was highly likely they would all be shot.

Captain C. W. Litton, Quartermaster of the 2/6th Queen's, in charge of a bunch of prisoners, left his batman to guard them while he went to find the whereabouts of the prisoner-of-war cage. On his return, he found the soldier looking very uncomfortable, with a rifle alternately levelled at the prisoners and at a hostile crowd of excited Italian civilians, who with drawn knives and clubs were threatening the Germans with all the enthusiasm of a local inquisition. With some little persuasion, they forced the Italians off and managed to drive away.

*   *   *   *   *

To the north in the 46th Division, whose main target was the capture of the port of Salerno, much the same pattern of fighting was being followed. The 128th Infantry Brigade was launched into the assault with the object of capturing the hills overlooking the Battipaglia–Salerno road and destroying all local defences.

The 2nd Battalion Royal Hampshire Regiment landed on a beach raked with accurate machine-gun fire on fixed lines, but that had been cleared of mines by a rocket ship—they were the first ashore there. It was unfortunately half a mile away from the correct beach and on the wrong side of the River Asa. In the darkness, and unfamiliar with the strange surroundings, they could do little apart from mopping up the immediate enemy strong-points and trenches as and where they revealed themselves. Lieutenant-Colonel S. J. Martin, the *CO*, decided to push on as best they could to try and get on to the correct axis and fit the battalion back into the planned pattern. Every hedgerow and every dyke concealed enemy platoons, tanks and machine-guns. The Hampshire casualties were heavy, but they gave more than they received. One company actually fought its way into the small town of Pontecagnano, where they were told to dig in and await the inevitable counter-attack. Other companies moved on to the hills overlooking the main road.

The 1/4th Battalion of the Hampshires, led by Lieutenant-Colonel R. Chandler, moved forward with determination, probably encouraged by the fact that news of the Italian armistice had not been broadcast to them and they were in a true fighting mood. The beaches on this northern flank were not so heavily defended, but they faced great hazards from mines, guns and a mobile railway battery which fired unceasingly at them.

In immediate reserve, as follow-through battalion, the 5th Hampshires were heavily shelled whilst still in their *LCA*s and as they got closer to the coast mortars and machine-gun bullets ranged accurately on them. Battalion headquarters ship had a jammed landing ramp, so that they all had to run down the remaining one on the starboard side. The beach was being hotly contested; they were forced to dig in not far from the water's edge and wait for the forward battalions to finish clearing the machine-gun nests. The edge of the beach became a mountain of equipment of all sorts, which the beach groups were incapable of moving into the planned store areas. The time came to move: the Commanding Officer ordered all the companies to cross the Asa to their correct positions. 'B' Company was told to advance up a narrow walled lane towards Magazzeno. Six hundred yards inland they were caught in a counter-attack, led by tanks which rumbled forward, their main armament and machine-guns chattering. Without any anti-tank weapons, the company tried to fight it out, but were overwhelmed. Men fell wounded and dead in the narrow roadway; the tanks advanced remorselessly, crushing the living as well as the dead with their wide steel tracks. The main portion of the British battalion had formed up just behind, but when it seemed likely that they too would be overrun, the attack fizzled out.

The battalion had been badly mauled. The lane known from then onwards as 'Hampshire Lane' was a scene of terrible carnage. In the ditch lay a line of crushed and mutilated bodies; by a wireless set was the dead operator, the lower half of his body flattened, and the earphones still broadcasting unacknowledged messages into his ears.

So the British X Corps was ashore in Fortress Europe, but, as in most military operations, not according to plan. The troops had been shocked out of their complacency and were now bestirring themselves to the realities of life. The Germans were in force and had no intention of handing over any real estate without hard and vicious fighting. A great metaphorical shake-up took place; like a dazed boxer with the points against him, the troops prepared to come up fighting in the second round.

CHAPTER VII

THE AMERICAN SECTOR: D-DAY

FOR the Americans in the south the immediate situation was possibly worse than in the British sector. Their main task was to protect the right flank of the bridgehead and to make contact as speedily as possible with Monty's 8th Army advancing slowly up from Calabria. Between the British and American sectors was a wide-open gap some ten miles wide, into which not a single Allied soldier was supposed to step. The planners had erased this area from their schemes owing to sand bars obstructing the mouth of the River Sele. The Germans were soon to discover this tactical error and make the most of it.

Not a gun fired along the whole of the American sector. The lines of assault craft silently approached the coast under the impression, fostered by their officers, that the enemy were unaware of their presence and the Italians had kindly packed their bags and gone, leaving great gaps in the beach defences. Admiral Hewitt had offered them rocket landing craft, but they had been refused.

With American precision, the leading craft hit land dead on 0330 hours, but before they even touched down the troops of the 16th Panzer Division had started firing mortars, machine-guns and 88-mm. cannons. Their illusion shattered, the men, still in their flat-bottomed boats listening to the British bombardment in the north, crouched, wondering now at the futility of approaching an enemy who was obviously only too well aware of what was afoot, without the support of guns.

Four beaches had been chosen for the landing by two regimental combat teams. No. 142 *RCT* under Lietenant Colonel John D. Forsythe was to land on *Red* and *Green* Beaches; 141 *RCT* under Colonel Richard J. Werner was destined for *Yellow* and *Blue* Beaches; 143 *RCT* was in reserve, to be landed later at the most convenient point. The D-Day plan was to advance to the railway 2,500 yards inshore, reorganise and push forward quickly to the hills ten miles inland. If this had worked, they would have been in control of a hundred square miles of Italian territory and the whole of the southern half of Salerno Bay.

Several official United States histories and unit records claim that as the first American stepped ashore, a loudspeaker blared out and an obviously German voice cried: "Come on in and surrender: we have you covered."

The rugged Texans yelled back obscenities and defiance and charged up the sand into action.

General Fred Walker denies that this ever happened: "None of my units have included any such incident in their reports. I have never heard it mentioned by my own personnel in connection with the Salerno operation."

Be that as it may, the Germans were certainly ready for the invaders. On all four beaches, machine-gun fire and mortar bombs met the troops as soon as they stepped ashore, and small parachute mortar flares illuminated the landing zones. On *Red* and *Green* beaches the fire was particularly heavy; both assault battalions of 142 *RCT* were pinned down by cleverly sited machine-guns, tanks and snipers, who poured a withering fire from behind the protecting mass of the medieval Paestum tower and several nearby buildings. In the dunes, detached parties of soldiers, often fighting without officers or *NCOs*, battled their way through entrenched positions in an effort to reach the railway, their first objective. Successive waves of craft ran into heavy shell and mortar fire; as the fresh troops landed they found, all too frequently, that the initial formations had not even got off the sand.

There were several cases of individual bravery. T/Sergeant 'Ugly' Gonzales discovered an 88-mm. cannon firing point-blank into the open doors of the landing craft. The weapon was defended by a platoon of Panzer Grenadiers, and as he crawled towards it, grenades in both hands, a tracer bullet set his pack on fire. He ripped it off where he lay and then, running a zig-zag course through a hail of bullets, tossed all his grenades into the pit, killing the crew and blowing up the ammunition. A Distinguished Service Cross was awarded to him.

Private John C. Jones, finding himself surrounded by a crowd of frightened leaderless men, collected fifty of the stragglers and guided them off the beach, destroying several machine-gun posts en route.

On the right flank, 141 *RCT* on *Yellow* and *Blue* beaches got clear of the shore, but most of them got pinned down by heavy mixed fire four hundred yards inland. Private James M. Logan of 1 Company 3/141st Regiment, finding himself all alone, advanced along an irrigation canal, to be faced by three Germans with fixed bayonets charging at him through a hole in a wall. With a burst from his carbine he shot them down. Discovering a machine-gun nest nearby from which the crew were retreating, he jumped into the pit, turned the gun on its former owners and sat down to wait for his unit to catch him up.

The 1st Battalion 141st Regimental Combat Team under Lieutenant-Colonel Carlos Smith successfully landed two waves. As the shooting intensified, however, the following boats were unable to land, and had to be switched farther north. There, opposite Paestum, the Germans were fighting from well-concealed and protected positions in the dunes and in the close cultivated flat area leading to the mountains. They had felled trees to enlarge their arcs of fire, and thick fences of barbed-wire blocked the exits. Heavy tanks, which had been driven into the backs of houses, were completely camouflaged. Others were hull down behind thick stone walls. With such confusion, it was a battle of individuals and groups who fought as and where they could. Following up the first two assault waves came the third, carrying vital heavy weapons, including three 75-mm. cannons. The first landing craft turned back for no apparent reason, the second hit a mine and drifted helplessly, adding to the chaos in the landing area, but the third managed to drop its ramp and the guns, under First Lieutenant Claire F. Carpenter, moved straight into action in the dunes. Within minutes they were supporting the infantry, having knocked out a tank and a machine-gun post. An 88-mm. shell, landing nearby, damaged the gun sight. Carpenter courageously ran to a nearby broken-down gun, collected a fresh sight and ran back to his own position. As he was adjusting it, another shell landed almost on top of them, killing his companion outright and severely wounding him.

Beachmasters were trying to sort out a fantastic muddle of vehicles and men which was piling up at the water's edge, and by 0415 hours frantic Navy officers were urging troops to "Get up and go". Offshore, hit and burning landing craft were drifting around and, to make matters worse, enemy aircraft were dropping flares and bombs on the incoming waves.

Army engineers worked under appalling conditions clearing minefields, laying wire mesh roads and dragging equipment off the shore. Anti-aircraft guns were unshipped and went into action on the beaches.

In the face of such bitter opposition, the Army commanders desperately tried to get in touch with the Navy to call on the heavy guns to blast a way through. A Navy forward observation officer, Ensign Alistair Semple, vainly twiddled the knobs of his radio set. The major ships were still far out to sea and out of range. In too many places soldiers, faced with fire for the first time in their lives, could only think of digging holes and crouching under the shells, instead of forcing a way through.

General Fred Walker, with part of his staff, landed on *Red* Beach at 0755 hours. On the way in he had seen a group of *LCM*s loaded with tanks and artillery moving aimlessly about, but with no radio contact he was powerless to give them any orders. As the nose of his vessel embedded itself in the sand, a Luftwaffe fighter shot down one of the anti-aircraft balloons, which fell blazing and hissing into the water. Advancing up the beach, he was pleased to see that in this area most of the troops had gone through and the follow-up troops, although under shell-fire, were determinedly moving inland.

The area was clear up to the railroad. As they passed a wrecked defence post, he was amused to hear German military commands coming through the speakers of two abandoned wirelesses. Divisional headquarters was set up in a tobacco warehouse at Casale Vannula and soon the commander was in contact with most units who, strangely enough, assured him that things were going more or less according to plan. Paestum had been captured and now the high ground beyond it had to be secured. Walker's main object at this time was to get possession of the north-west nose of Monte Soprano, in order to divide the German defences and prevent them from co-ordinating their attacks. By 1100 hours this was achieved, resulting in the subsequent enemy withdrawal from the southern half of the beachhead during the coming night.

Divisional headquarters was so far forward that it was attacked twice by groups of tanks during the morning. Luckily sufficient anti-tank guns were ashore by that time and, as the Panzers had gone in without infantry support, it was comparatively easy to destroy them.

General Walker is critical of the Navy for being too cautious in the earlier stages, when loaded assault vessels lay offshore, instead of coming in to beaches which were only being moderately shelled, with the result that badly needed tanks and artillery were delayed, in some cases for many hours. Similarly the failure of the Navy to respond quickly to calls for support resulted in many setbacks and casualties which could have been avoided.

In the south on part of the American sector the beaches were forced to close, all following waves being switched to the north.

The 36th Cavalry Reconnaissance Troops, with Shermans, arrived on *Yellow* Beach at 0700 hours and trundled off the *LCT*s, firing as they went. At 0800 hours four Panzer Mark IVs attacked through the dunes and were only stopped by two mobile 105-mms. which had just landed. Even so, farther south, two of these armoured vehicles did get through to the beach, but were frightened off by a light anti-aircraft gun, manned by men of the 531st Shore Engineers firing horizontally over open sights.

Private Manuel Gonzales of the 2nd Battalion 141 *RCT* ran towards a marauding tank and was hit by a burst in the legs. Before he could roll clear, the tracks crushed him into the sand. Another soldier, rushing in from a flank to toss a grenade into the turret, found himself caught in the mesh of a camouflage net and dragged along for several yards, before he could break loose.

On the whole, the scene was chaotic. Major Brinkenhoff, of an artillery battalion, was heard to remark in the midst of the fighting: "We've got them just where they want us!"

Adding to the confusion was the presence of considerable numbers of Luftwaffe fighters, which, unopposed except for anti-aircraft defence from the ships in the bay, were roaming up and down the beaches, cannons and machine-guns blazing, firing almost at random except for what they could see by the light of odd flares. The Allied air plan for fighter cover over the bridgehead was not due to go into action until 0830 hours. Up to then, the only land defences were a few barrage balloons floating at two hundred feet to stop the fighters diving too low. The Luftwaffe pilots revelled in this rare freedom. Operators aboard *HMS Hilary*, the old coal-burning ship, headquarters of Commodore Oliver, listened to intercepted radio conversations between Luftwaffe headquarters and the pilots. The planes were urged to attack the shipping rather than the troops, but many were frightened of the heavy ack-ack that met them every time they ventured over the convoys. Some, however, did attack the ships, and between 0417 and 0537 transports were under moderate bombing; *USS Nauset* was set on fire.

At that moment the Germans were supreme in the air and in the weight of armour they could put against the invaders. The Allied plan did not allow for any large number of tanks to go ashore in the early stages, and there was little the infantry could do against the marauding Tigers and Mark IVs with rifles and light anti-tank projectors.

The approach of dawn brought a sea mist which obscured the positions and offered some relief to the troops who were temporarily out of direct observation from the German artillery in the hills which Kesselring rightly called "God's gift to the gunners".

*   *   *   *   *

The troops of 16th Panzer Division under Major-General Sieckenius were by no means demoralised by the landings; preparations were being made for early counter-attacks, which had been planned and even practised. The 79th Panzer Regiment, commanded by Colonel von Doering, covered the territory from the River Sele right down to Agropoli. Thinly spread, its strength was based on a mobile defence able to move from one trouble point to another and on a series of strong-points supported by tanks and heavy guns. The 1/79th Regiment under Major Herbert Duppenbecker was responsible for the Sele down to Paestum; the 2/79th Regiment was settled in well-defended positions in the mountains on the Agropoli peninsula, from where it could command the Paestum–Ogliastro–Vallo di Lucania road against surprise attacks from the 8th Army. A strong-point was established by 1/79th Regiment south of the mouth of the River Sele, where they anticipated a strong Allied attack. The water had been heavily mined and a company of forty Panzer Grenadiers with six *LMG*s and a 7.5-cm. gun was stationed there. In close contact with the divisional strong-point which was sited on the north bank of the river, they were capable of mutual support. At Paestum another strong-point consisted of a full company of Panzer Grenadiers, plus mortars, anti-aircraft guns and field pieces. A third mobile group constantly patrolled a front of about five miles. Behind them were the batteries of field artillery, counter-attack battalions and several squadrons of tanks. The division's wheeled transport had been evacuated on the previous evening inland into the hills around Altavilla, overlooking Paestum, so that any immediate reprisal against the landing had to be carried out on foot; there was bound to be an element of luck in the placing of the reserves.

At exactly 0330 hours the strong-point at Paestum reported by telephone the approach of heavy engine noises from the sea, but nothing could be seen. The post near Paestum shortly afterwards reported that it was under heavy machine-gun fire from its left flank near the Paestum garrison. Duppenbecker tried to get through by phone and radio to its commander, but received no reply. He at once sent off a reserve company for a counter-attack at Paestum, which he feared had fallen in the first assault. By now most of the German beach positions were firing at the oncoming craft, which loomed out of the mist. A landing craft started nosing in towards the mouth of the Sele, but as a 7.5-cm. battery opened up, it swung away to the north. Still unable to contact the Paestum position, Duppenbecker called on the artillery to lay a heavy barrage on the beach in front; the shells landed in the middle of the 1st *US* Battalion 141 Regimental Combat Team as they fought their way slowly forward. Amidst the appalling noise of the guns of both sides and the rattle of automatic weapons it was impossible for the German commander to know if his heavy coastal guns were still firing or if they had been captured. The Germans were grateful to the different coloured Very lights fired by the Allies, which, although useful to the attacking troops, gave away their positions and were therefore of great value to the German gunners who were able to register on them. Shells had broken most of the defenders' telephone wires, and soon the various wireless frequencies were hopelessly jumbled, producing a mix-up of languages sounding like the Tower of Babel. The German officers had great fun with a German-speaking American, who kept calling them up with orders to move. His crudeness gave him away and the Germans, after leading him along, finally recommended him to "put his head in the lavatory".

Despite the breakdown in communications, German commanders were confident that their thorough plans for all eventualities would be carried out by the leaders of the front-line units. With the presumed capture of the Paestum defences, the plan was for the 2nd Battalion 79th Panzer Grenadiers with tanks to attack north-west from Agropoli towards Paestum and for 1/79th to attack south-east. The assaulting forces set off. As they approached Paestum, the sounds of battle diminished, and by the time they were within about a thousand yards of a strong-point, all resistance and attack appeared to have ceased. The sun was rising, and as the morning heat dissipated the fog from shore and sea the Germans were greeted with the sight of the vast armada of ships almost filling the Salerno Bay. If the situation had not been so serious, Duppenbecker felt *he could have remained there all day merely to watch these goings-on with admiration!* By this time it was obvious that the strong-point had been taken and the men of the 1/79th Regiment could clearly see their opponents' trenches and the might facing them. The aim of the counter-attack was to retake the position, but the necessity disappeared when it was found that it had been wiped out; the Germans withdrew into their prepared posts and issued new orders. One battery of 15-cm. guns was still firing at the landing craft and onto the beaches, but its effect was rather like a flea pounding against an elephant. It was eventually decided to order a cease-fire because it was attracting too much retaliation and, as a German officer commented:

"Moreover, the war would not be won with this battery alone, and we could perhaps use it to better purpose in another place!"

Strangely enough, the main feeling of these seasoned Wehrmacht troops was one of relief that they were fighting British and American troops instead of Russians, and could expect fair treatment.

"In Russia the worst fate of all was to be captured: better to die. But here in Italy the worst fate was to die."

As the first Italians bestirred themselves at dawn to venture out of their shelters, tunnels and caves, Arturo Carucci, the padre of the Mennola Sanatorium, went back to the hospital with some members of the staff and a few patients. After Mass they went into the park to gaze and wonder at the awe-inspiring sight in the gulf. For the time being the Sanatorium was a haven of peace in the midst of battle. They watched the fight flowing and saw the ant-like figures of soldiers running through the vineyards and orchards spread out in glorious panorama below them, whilst German tanks drove towards the coast along the roads through Salerno and towards Vietri.

Chapter VIII

D-DAY: ACCOUNT SO FAR

BY 0800 hours the corps commanders were reporting to General Mark Clark aboard the *Ancon* that, as far as they could tell, most of the initial objectives had been seized. Progress was not as good as had been expected the commanders being a bit optimistic in view of the number of the objectives for the first day still to be secured. Some difficulty was being experienced in getting naval shore fire control parties on dry land, and until these had been established it was impossible for the Navy to give all the support they had in their power.

Troops, vehicles and supplies continued to pour ashore. As the mist lifted, so were the guns of both sides able to size up the situation with greater clarity; the *LST*s were being swiftly unloaded, but several were badly damaged. *LST 386*, with a heavy pontoon causeway, struck a mine near the shore, which destroyed the pontoon and caused forty-three casualties. *LST 385* received three direct hits during her approach, yet her skipper, Lieutenant Jerome Brock, *USNR*, discharged all his vehicles and men, although he was fighting fires all over his ship and taking action against enemy machine-gunners. *LST 375* was going into *Red* Beach at 0715 hours when two direct hits set fire to some petrol and broke the lift cable, making it impossible for her to unload vehicles on the main deck. She pulled off the shore, as her crew worked frantically to repair the elevator; two hours later she came in again, but a direct hit from a bomb blew a large hole in her hull. Undeterred, she remained until all the transport she was carrying had been unloaded.

Immediate fire support for the troops was supplied by destroyers and *LCG*s (landing craft armed with 4.7-inch guns): the 46th Division had three destroyers and three *LCG*s as artillery support; the 56th Division three destroyers and four *LCG*s. In support of the corps front, the 15th Cruiser Squadron, commanded by Rear Admiral C. H. J. Harcourt, *RN*, in HMS *Mauritius*, together with *Uganda*, *Orion*, the monitor *Roberts* and the destroyers

Tartar and *Nubian*, arrived in the bay at 0630 hours. They were under Commodore Oliver's immediate command for use as and where needed. Unfortunately, communications with the land from these ships to their *FOO*s for most of D-Day were very ineffective; it was therefore left to the destroyers, who had a field day, *HMS Mendip* and *Brecon* with three small gunboats hardly stopped firing. So good was the German camouflage that it was difficult to locate many of the batteries, and although the guns would often stop after a destroyer's salvo, the 88 mms. being mobile would quickly shift to another area and recommence their barrage. Admiral Connolly, *USN*, earned himself a considerable reputation that day. He personally spotted a battery that was firing into transport shipping from a position south east of Salerno. Having tried unsuccessfully to raise a destroyer on the wireless, he ordered his flagship to go inshore. Twelve rounds from her 5-inch guns did the job and earned him the nickname 'Close-in-Connolly'.

In support of the 56th Division *HMS Blankney* pounded every German gun that opened up. A cry for help came from *Green* Beach, when it was wrongly reported to have been retaken by the Germans; *Blankney*, *Loyal* and *Laforey* steamed so close to the shore that they came under rifle fire and *Loyal* had a boiler knocked out by a lucky 88 mm. shell. *Laforey*, after hitting an ammunition dump, was straddled by the infuriated battery, receiving five direct hits, but she silenced the guns and retired out into the bay to effect repairs.

At dawn Allied planes appeared in the shape of Seafires from the carriers under command of Admiral Sir Philip Vian. The first flight came in as light was breaking and remained over the beaches until 0745 hours, when they were relieved by Spitfires, Lightnings and P-38s flown from Sicily. With the advent of Allied aircraft, the Luftwaffe more or less packed up, putting in only a few desultory hit-and-run attacks.

A Fleet Air Arm pilot from *HMS Unicorn*, who crash-landed in the middle of a minefield on *Red* beach, reported that he was flying with eight Seafires when they met thirty FW-190s, but the German fighters refused to engage and went off at high speed.

When the Sicily-based planes went 'home' at 1800 hours, the Seafires reappeared and took over until after dark. On D-Day Air Support Command flew from Sicily 700 sorties, and Vian's Seafires 250. The total for the Luftwaffe this day, mostly in the early hours before the appearance of Allied planes, was 82 fighter sorties and 26 in ground attack, mostly by Focke Wolf 190s. The Lightnings and Mustangs proved more than a match for them.

Vian's Seafires, operating from five 'Woolworth' carriers—
Unicorn, Battler, Attacker, Hunter and *Stalker*—soon ran into trouble
through lack of natural wind and an over-high accident rate. The
maximum speed of these carriers was seventeen knots; in the dead
calm which existed round Salerno, this was scarcely enough for
landing and take-off. Yet the vast majority of plane crashes was,
in the opinion of Admiral Cunningham, due to "insufficient
training". In the middle of the battle it was suggested that the
propellers of these aircraft should have five inches lopped off.
Although there was some argument over the effect this would have
on performance, the propellers were duly shortened, the accident
rate dropped and none of the pilots commented adversely about
performance.

In the earlier hours the fighter direction ship *HMS Palamares*
had difficulties directing aircraft to targets, owing to the thick mist,
and often sent them back to Sicily before time. The proximity of
the mountains considerably upset the naval radar system, whilst
enemy jamming was very successful. The Luftwaffe interceptors
also understood the British grid map reference system and were
able to tell exactly which targets were to be engaged.

*   *   *   *   *

On the 56th Division front in the centre some of the troops had
managed to keep going forward. The 7th Battalion Oxfordshire and
Buckinghamshire Light Infantry had gone in with the two Royal
Fusilier battalions and had assaulted an 88-mm. battery that had
been the cause of some hold-up. A wireless operator of 'B' Company
was staggered to hear a German voice broadcast in English on the
battalion network:

"Message for Major Montgomery, Oxfordshire and Buckinghamshire Light Infantry."

It was on a nearby beach that a German psychological war unit
caught many men unawares: screams came from a flank, with cries
of "Help! Help!"—but any who went to the rescue never returned.
Other broadcasts urged: "Lay down your arms; it's all over!" and
"Is this another Dunkirk? Look at all the ships behind you; they
have come to save as many of you as they can."

Major Peter Montgomery, leading 'B' Company, pushed on
towards the south, trying to expand the small beachhead. They
trudged through the marshy floods, each footstep an effort, the slimy
mud sucking and pulling at their sodden boots; the men cursed as
they slipped and fell heavily, their packs swinging them backwards.

Suddenly, an alert rifleman shouted: "Tanks! Get down!"

As one man the company slopped into the mud. Several Mark IVs, fitted with flame-throwers, appeared ahead trying to get round the marshy area and closer to the British troops. The tank gunners raked the ground with machine-guns; then from one, more impatient than the others, came an ominous whoosh, as a great streak of fire forty feet long of blazing pitch and petroleum shot ahead, like the tongue of a dragon flickering and stretching in an attempt to reach the prostrated troops. As the flaming mass fell on the mud, the stench of burning slime and the fumes rolled over the infantrymen, who pushed their faces into the earth to avoid the searing flame, alternatively cursing and praying for deliverance. At last from behind came the welcome crack of several 6-pounder anti-tank guns, that had just landed and gone straight into action. The German commander, seeing he was in difficult tank country with the possibility of becoming bellied in the mud, withdrew; the Ox and Bucks, somewhat shaken, continued their advance.

The battalion, hampered mainly by wandering snipers who ran from position to position, hidden in the olive groves and tobacco plants, slowly moved towards Santa Lucia, a tiny village east of Battipaglia. The village was deserted and undefended; the roads strewn with bomb debris and family belongings; the poor houses bespattered with shrapnel. Bren carriers went ahead along the narrow street, cautiously feeling their way around each corner. About half a mile past Santa Lucia, they were engaged by automatic fire and anti-tank guns; several carriers were knocked out immediately and the troops went to ground in the surrounding orchards. Here the battalion halted; without armour they could advance no further. They formed a defensive position round Farina Farm, about a mile short of Battipaglia, which fell after a brisk skirmish, and there they waited for the tanks to come up and help them forward.

The 6th Battalion York and Lancaster Regiment, under command of Lieutenant-Colonel Joe Kendrew, who was to win three *DSOs* during the Italian campaign, ground to a halt on *Red* Beach near Salerno at 0430 hours. Their immediate front was peaceful, but to their right, where the Hampshire Brigade had landed, the sand was pock-marked with a continual hail of bombs and shells. Nearby a dog fight between Tigers with 88 mm. guns and infantry was raging. At the double, the dour North Countrymen moved up the shingle through the grass-covered dunes into a maze of tomato fields and tobacco plantations. Spreading his unit in a rough all-round defence, Kendrew went back to the beach to hasten the battalion's transport. There his brigadier gave him a map reference on the Avellino road, just outside Salerno, where he was to form a defensive position and block the road. In his jeep with Major Eric Kearsley, some company guides and a signaller, he drove off at a smart pace into Salerno, which was now a no-man's-land: a few frightened civilians waved out of broken windows shouting *"Viva gli Inglesi"*, but the group was too busy watching the debris-littered road ahead for mines and booby-traps and avoiding gaping craters. Finding themselves in the middle of a group of houses quite unsuitable for local defence, Kendrew soon realised that his map was out of date. He ordered his driver to continue and kept a careful lookout for a suitable position; they drove with a fair amount of confidence in the belief that a reconnaissance screen was ahead of them. Coming upon an ideal place from where his companies could cover a road, rail and river intersection, he sent the jeep with the runners back to guide the battalion; he and Major Kearsley were left alone.

Shortly after the jeep had driven off, round a corner they heard a scream of brakes and a guttural shout of *"Halte!"* At the same time the roar of tracks approached from their rear and, as they both dived into a ditch, an armoured half-track shot past heading the way they had come. In a few minutes they heard it returning; hidden behind some bushes in the ditch, they saw the half-track—preceding it, covered by German guns, was their jeep and the guides.

Realising that they had been allowed to drive through an enemy road block, Kendrew decided to return on foot as best he could to warn the battalion. Kearsley asked if he could stay:

"I must try and do something for those poor devils."

Reluctantly Kendrew agreed and they parted. Leaving the road, the colonel squirmed his way through the dense plantations; as he rounded the bend, he saw a German road block with an 88-mm. gun in position across the road. Back at the battalion, he deployed them off the road and prepared to make a plan of attack. Orders were received to stay put. Some hours later Kendrew was sitting by the roadside with his medical officer, Doc Braham, eating grapes and regretting that he had allowed Major Kearsley to remain behind, when an *NCO* in charge of an anti-tank gun shouted: "Tanks coming!"

Kendrew rushed to the position and focused his binoculars on a half-track, seated on the front of which was a man waving an enormous white flag. To his utter amazement he recognised Eric Kearsley, but warned the gunner to keep the vehicle in his sights in case of tricks. Yet it was no deception: Kearsley single-handed had rounded up the Germans manning the road block, captured the half-track, the 88-mm. gun, and retaken the jeep with its crew.

After Kendrew had left him, Kearsley had eased his way towards the enemy, staying hidden just out of sight. Some time later a lone German left his position heading up the road; Kearsley waited for him to pass and then crept up with his pistol. The private gave in without struggle. Over a period of a couple of hours the rest of the half-track crew did the same; Kearsley captured them one by one, until he finally marched the whole bunch up the road and persuaded the one remaining German to give in. For this exploit, Kearsley was awarded the *DSO*, but within twenty-four hours he was captured and spent the rest of the war in a camp in Germany.

* * * * *

Confused messages were now being sent back to headquarter ships. At corps and the two divisional headquarters the general impression was that all was going well. Major-General D. A. H. Graham decided to get his reserve brigade ashore and ordered the 3rd Battalion Coldstream Guards and the 6th Battalion of the Grenadiers to land. Their *LST*s and *LCA*s drummed steadily towards the coast through a maze of battered ships and drifting craft. Several times fighters swarmed down, machine-guns blazing, but the pilots, wary of getting caught in the anti-aircraft screen, sacrificed accuracy for height and did not succeed in doing much damage. As the doors of a craft carrying men of the Coldstream slowly lowered, the first sight to meet their eyes was a Bluejacket nonchalantly waving a huge flag at the water's edge, shouting: "This way to Naples, boys!"

Lieutenant Christopher Bulteel of the Coldstream Guards was standing at the blunt prow of his craft, a bottle of gin in each hand, peering through the remains of a smoke-screen laid by a destroyer which had bounced the assault craft like corks in its wake, as it manœuvred dangerously in and out of the assorted vessels. The ramp went down; the first Guardsmen to set foot on European soil since the Dunkirk fiasco went ashore. As the leading Guardsmen ran up the beach, there came a vicious rattle of anti-aircraft guns from the ships; looking up, they saw a flight of four fighters spattering the shingle with neat lines of bullets. Bulteel dropped on his belly, both bottles of gin shattering on the pebbles.

"Messerschmitts!" shouted the skipper, as he screamed to his gunners to open up.

"Mustangs!" retorted the mate, but the guns let fly; a chunk of fuselage fell from a plane and it flew out to sea in a slowly descending spiral of smoke, until it disappeared beneath the waves. On the very edge of the beach a battery of 25-pounder field guns was firing inland, the crews cursing as their weapons shifted in the loose pebbly sand.

Orderly files of Guardsmen, thankful for a dry and unopposed landing, moved off in step through the sparse grass of the dunes into a maze of dykes and flooded fields. Two things which seemed of equal importance flashed in Lieutenant Bulteel's mind: "Italy and dry feet." The beach was a hive of activity: sailors signalling out to the ships trying to delay any further flights of men and materials; Sappers laying immense rolls of metal netting, making rough roads for vehicles to plough their way through the sand; men with mine detectors and others with pointed sticks probing for mines and unreeling white tapes to denote clear paths; bulldozers and tractors heaving at stuck vehicles; a few small groups of ragged prisoners-of-war; Italians protesting at being mixed up with the Germans. In the dunes were slit trenches, some occupied by dead bodies of defenders, others already taken over by British infantry setting up machine-gun posts. They reached a metalled road, and moving into the orchards, found themselves in a zone of flat country, largely smothered with brown muddy water. Small square fields of corn and grass, hedgerows dotted with Lombardy poplars, oleander trees and the occasional small squat house with yellow walls and red roof, damaged and deserted. Dead cows and goats littered the area, whilst the warmth slowly filled their bellies with gas and hordes of flies gathered for a gigantic banquet of rotten meat. The Guards were ordered to mark time, while new plans were made out for the disordered front. Soon Tommy cookers were flickering with their pungent odour and mess tins of water were boiling for the inevitable brew-up. Men wandered around with inverted steel helmets picking ripe apples from the trees; others buried their faces in slices of melon picked from vines. Apart from the rattle of war all around, they too found it moderately quiet on their front.

Very few vehicles, apart from reconnaissance jeeps, had landed, and many of the troops started scrounging around to find transport to ease the loads on their backs. The padre of the Coldstream Guards, whose job kept him moving continually round the unit, came upon a lonely and abandoned fat chestnut pony, and decided that this was just what he wanted. Although he searched the stables and surrounding buildings of the farm where he found the beast, he could not trace a saddle or a bridle; when he tried riding it bare back, he soon discovered that it knew only one speed, and that was a gallop. A Guardsman then told him that one of the company commanders had found a magnificent figured-leather saddle and a silver-mounted bridle, including a pair of enormous deadly Mexican-type spurs. The padre and the major met to do business, but the argument soon came to a deadlock. The padre maintained that, as he had the pony, he should be presented with the saddlery; the major stubbornly insisted that, as he had the harness, he should have the pony to bear it. The colonel (Sir Terence Falkiner) was called in to arbitrate; he decided in favour of the chaplain. His only proviso was that the spurs should be confiscated, as the padre, an amateur horseman, would have disembowelled the poor animal. From then on the chaplain carried out his priestly duties on horseback. Despite being tossed on many occasions, much to the amusement of the troops, who felt that a dog collar and horses did not go together, he became a common sight going his rounds, until he was killed when visiting a forward company.

Not far from the Guards, a furious argument was raging between a beach group commander and an *NCO* in charge of a sergeants' mess. A piano had suddenly appeared on the ramp of a landing craft, having been included under the heading *Essential Assault Stores*. The naval officer, who wanted to throw the instrument into the sea, was roundly berating the *NCO*, who had been threatened with torture by his *RSM* if the sergeants' mess piano did not arrive in good condition. The argument ended when the *NCO* hastily summoned some gunners, who rushed it up the beach while the naval officer's attention was distracted.

Private initiative and creature comforts were very much in evidence; one unit came ashore with chickens, geese and turkeys in crates lashed to jeep bonnets. One three-tonner had a monster sow in a crate, which was being fatted up for an officers' mess dinner and was destined to be the major course in a banquet to be held in Naples after its capture.

By 1030 hours diesel Sherman tanks of the Royal Scots Greys were grinding ashore to go to the support of the 56th Division. As the doors of an *LCT* opened, an 88-mm. shell shot through the entrance, setting fire to the leading vehicle. A frightened trooper, slightly wounded, screamed out:

"For Christ's sake, shut the bloody door!"

Another *LCT* of 'A' Squadron, commanded by Major Stewart, was hit five times and had to be abandoned out of control. Yet most of the tank landing craft came in unmolested. Within ten minutes of beaching, eight of these Shermans in support of the 167th Brigade had become bogged down in the soft soil and bulldozers were urgently called up to help extricate them. All the officers, including a brigadier, dug and strained; within two hours the tanks were running again. Armour was urgently needed, but the ground was quite unsuitable. The tank crews had been used to the wide-open spaces of the North African desert; it was some days before they became accustomed to the close country and lack of space in which to manœuvre.

The 8th Battalion Royal Fusiliers, halted some way inland, had been attacked by flame-throwing Mark IVs and a complete platoon had been burned to death. The Greys were asked to go forward to deal with the trouble. Captain Sir M. O. Williams ordered a troop to take a wide sweep round to the left behind the Germans, avoiding a head-on clash. The tanks set off along a rough lane and came out slightly to the rear of the small hamlet of Porta di Ferro. The leading Sherman, having sighted a Mark IV at 500 yards, knocked it out with the first round of its 75-mm. cannon; rounding a corner, it came face to face with a flame-thrower, but before the cascade of liquid could be fired another shell pierced its hull, killing all the occupants.

John Whitfield, Commanding Officer of 2/5th Queen's, surprised to find that all his units had arrived at their objectives, established his headquarters in a partially wrecked agricultural college and then set off on foot back to the beach to urge forward the transport which should have arrived. With his batman he walked along a narrow lane, where, to his utter amazement, he met a body of troops marching in step with a sergeant shouting: "Lip righ, lip righ!" Forced off the track into a ditch, they realised that elements of the 201st Guards Brigade had landed and were intent on marching to their objectives; not looking left or right, they would have made an easy target for a marauding plane. At the water's edge a Beachmaster directed Whitfield to his vehicles, and they were soon driving towards the battalion. Mounting a Bren carrier, the colonel ordered the driver to go round the company positions; he sat precariously, shouting directions from the top of a mound of swaying blankets. At a crossroads they saw a crashed Mercedes saloon and, advancing cautiously towards it, found a dead driver and a mass of abandoned papers. Proceeding farther, they rounded a bend to be faced with a huge Tiger tank.

"Tread on the gas," bawled Whitfield, as the driver pivoted the carrier, revving madly to stop the tracks spinning.

The tank gunner opened up with his machine-gun at the back of the retreating vehicle, the bullets peppering the blankets; Whitfield felt like a fairground target.

Back at battalion headquarters, the colonel learned that many of the troops were short of cigarettes, having had them ruined by sea-water. Whitfield, a non-smoker, had at one time tried to ban smoking during exercises, but, discovering it produced an appalling effect on morale, he determined that the troops would always have a liberal supply. Before leaving North Africa, he had bought five thousand and loaded them into his jeep. He told his batman to fetch the parcel, but was told that it had been stolen: the culprit, much to his sorrow, was never discovered!

Brigadier Lewis Lyne, Commander of the 169th Brigade, was content that they had achieved all they set out to do and issued orders for further advance to be delayed until later in the evening, although they had not secured the airfield at Montecorvino, nor the road beyond it.

With the Queen's battalions of the 169th Brigade was 'C' Squadron Royal Scots Greys, whose first task was to support the capture of the airfield. Their vessels arrived half an hour late and the infantry were impatient to assault. The 2/6th Queen's under Lieutenant-Colonel Keighley were reported in position just short of the airfield and the tanks went at full speed to join them. The Queen's were temporarily held up by dug-in infantry of the 2nd Battalion 10th Panzer Grenadier Regiment, and several light anti-aircraft guns converted to a ground role. Tank support was badly needed to help them across the open ground to their objective. One platoon were exulting over having shot down an enemy bomber as it raced along the runway in a vain effort to escape. A section of *MMG*s of the Cheshire Regiment mounted their guns on the edge of the field and shot up two Me-109s as they tried to get airborne.

Supported by the Shermans of the Scots Greys, the troops pushed across the airfield in a series of swift short rushes, one section giving covering fire as they leapfrogged along. Several planes were burning, ammunition erupting. From the deep shadows of a crashed bomber, a tank gun exploded viciously at the Shermans, but one of the latter with a lucky shot set the tank and plane on fire. They finally reached the far side of the field and had hardly settled in when the Germans unexpectedly launched a tank-and-infantry counter-attack from the south.

This attack was made by the 2nd Company 16th Panzer Pioneer Battalion under command of Lieutenant Gunter Schmitz. They drove across the airfield in armoured cars and half-track troop-carriers supported by mortars and machine-guns, but just as they were about to come into close contact with the Queen's, they received the surprising order to withdraw and prepare an attack on another position near Battipaglia. Schmitz and his men were furious, as the battle was going in their favour and they could not understand the reason for this change of plan. As they drove back, they were attacked by two Lightnings; the German unit opened up with every weapon it had, succeeding in hitting both aircraft.

Lieutenant Fitzgeorge Parker, troop commander of the Greys, did not realise that the assault had been halted and called urgently for more armoured support, but was informed that one troop had been almost completely destroyed and others were blocked by an overturned carrier. Parker, thinking that the Germans would soon discover his tank force to be only four strong, knew that in the event of an attack he would not stand a chance. He then found that the infantry had withdrawn, without telling him, and he was com-pletely out on a limb. In order to fool the enemy, he kept his tanks changing positions hoping they would think he had at least a squad-ron force; eventually he was ordered to retire. Trying to turn away from enemy fire which still came from the far side of the airfield, the Sherman commanded by Sergeant Rich received a hit in its differential. Another tank rushed to its aid and under a hail of bullets they endeavoured without success to fix a tow rope. There was nothing to be done but for the remaining three to retire; on driving back into their own lines they had the galling experience of being shot up by their own troops, luckily only with Bren guns, and there were no casualties. Parker received a Military Cross for his exploits. His troop leaguered in a farmyard for repairs and maintenance, much amused by the antics of a flock of bomb-happy hens, which jumped two feet off the ground every time a gun went off.

Company Quartermaster Sergeant Harry Nelson of the 8th Royal Fusiliers with 'B' Echelon, a group of cooks and storemen, came into the beaches in a later wave and settled down in an orchard brewing up, waiting for vehicles to arrive. Almost the first person he saw was an Italian soldier ambling down a road with a portable radio, accompanying an orchestra in a Neapolitan song. Grinning happily, he serenaded the Fusiliers, who, coming to the conclusion that he had pinched the radio, relieved him of the burden and sent him scurrying back to the beach with a sharp kick in his pants.

In a farmyard where they settled with battalion headquarters the cockneys were disturbed by the cows screaming in agony, as they had not been milked for many hours and their udders were bursting with the pressure. Nelson and several others, most of whom had never seen a cow milked, set to with a will and soon had mess tins and steel helmets overflowing with warm creamy liquid.

Supporting the 46th Division were armoured vehicles of the 46th Reconnaissance Regiment, who had landed early in the morning and with a group of Royal Engineers acting as Infantry had driven through Salerno to join the Commando Force. After dropping the Sappers at Commando headquarters, the armoured cars moved slowly up the Vietri Defile and actually drove into Cava de' Tirreni. Progress through all the villages was somewhat hampered by joyful civilians, who fêted the troops with flowers, fruit, vino, and plenty of close-contact kissing and hugging. In the main street of Cava, the Piazza San Francesco, they were halted by the crowds; an officer had to stand on a vehicle and through a translator address the citizens assuring them: "The *Inglesi* are here to stay."

Feeling rather foolish, the troops stood by their vehicles, keeping a sharp lookout northwards for any sign of the enemy. Suddenly a group of Italians came forcing their way through the crowd to present the unit with a very frightened German soldier, obviously not very well treated by his captors who had proved their manliness by kicking and striking him. The prisoner volunteered the information that only one and a half miles farther north was a formation of twenty-five tanks and five hundred infantry ready to advance at any minute. A hurried consultation, and the recce unit decided to leave the town and report back to division. Within a few moments there was a roar of engines; from the northern end of town a fresh group of tanks and lorries drove in. The Italians hastily turned about, cheering what they thought was a fresh detachment of Allied troops. Their cheers died to silence as they recognised Germans. A short but swift engagement was fought by the retiring British during which a few civilians were wounded. Soon a half-track came back into the main street and an English prisoner was ordered to dismount. With an escort, he went to German headquarters in Via Indipendenza. An enquiring Italian, who spoke to him, learnt he had been born in Newcastle. He was tall and blond; when interrogated, he refused to give any information other than rank, name and number. Full of admiration, the Italians pressed round to listen and watch, as the German guards searched him. They took everything, apart from his cigarettes, which he offered with a smile to those around.

In Salerno town the remaining inhabitants hid in their houses awaiting the arrival of Allied troops. Luckily for them the Navy, presuming that troops were already there, did not fire on the buildings yet in fact the town for most of the day was occupied by small bodies of Germans, in tanks and armoured cars, which clattered the streets trying to intercept Allied soldiers. During the morning some shots had been fired from a house in Via Monti, aimed at the Piazza Luciani, where two German tanks and a group of infantry were stationed. Two Germans were killed and five wounded. The German tanks went into action and soon set the building on fire, following up with an assault of infantry who captured several British soldiers and about twenty civilians. The German officer was convinced that the civilians had been working hand in glove with the English troops and, threatening to shoot them all in reprisal, hustled them off to the town hall. A woman, whose husband had been captured, ran screaming to the Church of the Annunziata, asking the priest, Don Aniello Vicinanza, to go to the German commandant to secure their release. At once the priest in his black cassock followed her; he strode determinedly into the headquarters, brushing aside a sentry who barred his way. Outside in the street men and women went on their knees praying for the release of the hostages. Inside Don Aniello faced a Panzer major, who was determined to teach the locals a lesson. Pleading and gesticulating, the priest finally offered himself as a guarantee to the future behaviour of the inhabitants of his town. The German relented; the civilians were released with the warning that any further assistance rendered to the Allies would be heavily punished.

But the feeling of new-found freedom was quickly getting into the volatile blood of some Italians. Just a mile or two up a valley north of Salerno in the village of Fratte, where the Germans were preparing to defend the bridge, a young Italian, heedless of caution and encouraged by the belief that he would not be understood, shouted out in bravado: "Lousy Nazi bastards!"

Unfortunately for him, one of the Germans knew Italian; he casually pulled the pin from a stick grenade and tossed it into the crowd. The youth who hurled the abuse fell dead, and several round him were wounded.

95

Battipaglia was the target of the Fusilier Battalion. Lieutenant Colonel Ted Hillersden had pushed his men hard to get there. So successful had his drive been that they entered the town under only slight opposition to take up positions facing northwards. But they did not know at that time that both their flanks were exposed, the 8th Royal Fusiliers and the 7th Ox and Bucks having met much firmer resistance, and they were stuck out like a spearhead into enemy territory. The town was in an awful mess. Bomb craters littered the streets; railways had been wrecked so that the lines and sleepers stuck into the air like monstrous growths. Freight trucks and passenger carriages lay burning and exploding. As some of the troops moved into partially wrecked houses and shops, the irrepressible humour of the cockneys came bursting out. Several men were seen ambling around in long black overcoats and dark trilby hats, looking like street bookies. Some, entering a tailor's shop, even donned civilian suits and went round shouting:

"Ice cream, come and get it!"

Many chaps tasting wine for the first time thought it was red vinegar. One man announced he was going to start a brothel, but his chief problem was to find any ladies. A London Irishman named Kelly, sporting a pair of jack-boots pinched from a German store, was haggling with Fusilier Bill Turner over the price. But Kelly would not sell. Turner wandered disconsolately round a house, looking at the discarded possessions, and finally came upon a rosary with a gold cross, which he put in his pocket as a memento.

Lance-Corporal Harold Lampard, a signaller of 'B' Company, helped in the search of several signal-boxes and buildings at a level crossing, where they were attacked by an armoured car which, however, faced with a burst of Bren and rifle fire, decided to retreat back through the town.

Corporal Fred Hawthorn of 'A' Company 9th Fusiliers had volunteered with a group to storm a farmhouse. On arriving inside, they found the only inhabitant to be an elderly lady who had refused to leave her home for Germans or British, and was quite convinced she was about to be killed. A few bars of chocolate and encouraging words—"Don't worry, old dear! Go and hide in the cellar," and "Watch out the Guards don't rape you!"—and they were off out of it. Just then a shell landed by the farm gate, wiping out a group of Fusiliers. A haystack not a hundred yards away had suddenly split in two and a self-propelled 88-mm. gun emerged, firing as it disappeared.

The 9th Fusiliers dug in and prepared for a counter-attack.

With the 8th Fusiliers, Signal Sergeant Buffell had marvelled at the greenness of the countryside after so long in the desert and had enjoyed picking fruit from the trees. The battalion had hit resistance almost from the moment of landing. Very early on, attacked by three Tiger tanks and a Mark IV Special, they had gone to cover in the hedges and ditches without an anti-tank weapon between them. The tanks slowly advanced; it looked as if they would be driven back. Just as the order was about to be given to retire, three lorries towing 6-pounders came into the area. The Commanding Officer, Lieutenant-Colonel 'Fanny' Bellassis, had just jumped out of a ditch to tell them where to go, when three shells in quick succession came screaming in to wreck all three guns and lorries. Bellassis was wounded in the head, but refused to go for medical treatment. Yet the appearance of the anti-tank guns made the Germans extremely cautious, giving time for the first troops of the Royal Scots Greys Shermans to put in an appearance. The Shermans deployed and half an hour later the troop sergeant drove back with the news:

"We caught the Jerries with their trousers down."

A cry for help from a wounded soldier was answered by Buffell, who ran forward to a trench to see *RSM* Murphy turning the man over: he was by now quite dead. It was Davis, one of Buffell's young signallers, who had amused them for hours with impersonations of Donald Duck. *RSM* Richard Murphy had only shortly before ordered Davis to carry a message to a forward company. The young soldier had crawled along a ditch and then had appeared to lay down, despite the *RSM's* shouts to get a move on. Murphy had hurried forward to give him some words of encouragement, and found him dead with a neat bullet wound through the back of his head. Buffell and some of his lads dug a grave; they found Padre Jarvis, who came and read the burial service, undeterred by a German fighter that swooped down nearby, its machine-guns blazing.

The forward companies of this battalion had been caught in the open country by a troop of German flame-throwing tanks. Many men had been horribly burned to death; others, their skin scorched and blackened, and blinded, had been led back to the sea. Several hours later, *CQMS* Harry Nelson, going forward with a cooked meal, arrived in an area where he saw many dim red lights glowing. Thinking that men were smoking, he yelled:

"Put those bloody cigarettes out; you'll have shells landing all over us."

An *NCO* stepped out of the dark to tell him that it was the remains of the flame-thrower fires which were still smouldering; only then did Nelson notice the horrible smell of scorched earth and human flesh.

RSM Richard Murphy did what he could to help the men who were dying of burns and got a small amount of pleasure from the fact that the German tanks that had carried out the fearful attack had all been knocked out by the Royal Scots Greys. An enemy commander was rescued by Fusiliers from his burning vehicle; his skin had been baked black and most of his uniform burnt from him: yet he still lived, screaming in agony. A British doctor did his best, but mercifully the man died shortly afterwards; a Fusilier was heard to remark: "As you reap by the sword, so shall you perish by the sword."

The *RSM* and a party of men later returned to bury the dead, both British and German, but found it hard to identify bodies, as Italians had crept out of their hideouts, stripped them of all clothing and boots, and disappeared back into the holes.

At Montecorvino airfield other German units had launched a series of tank-infantry assaults, and in some places had overrun the Queen's. One company on the right flank was mostly taken prisoner; they had no anti-tank guns and only twenty men survived. The Germans then switched to the left in a similar attack, but ran into the fire of two 6-pounders, which fought them off, knocking out three tanks, one at three-hundred yards' range. Corporal Collins, in command of a gun, had all his crew killed one by one, but continued to operate it alone, until those nearby saw a shell blow him and the gun sky high. Despite heavy casualties, John Whitfield decided to try to push on, so as to capture the main road beyond the airfield.

As they advanced in the dusk, a company commander called him on the wireless: "There is a German vehicle some way ahead of us. Is it in accordance with your wishes that I fire at it?"

Whitfield, somewhat amazed by the request and the language in which it was couched, replied: "It is certainly in accordance with my wishes."

A few seconds later an explosion and a splash of flame showed that the target had been hit.

There followed an enormous German artillery barrage that swamped the area. The company went to ground and the situation, when Whitfield got there was very confused. German tanks were charging around in the dark, whilst groups of British and Germans often passed each other, believing they were friendly parties.

Back at battalion headquarters, Whitfield ordered the vehicles and jeeps into a nearby farmyard to get as much cover as they could. When they got there, the driver of an *RASC* ambulance reversed through a gateway and crashed into what he thought was a wall. Alighting to ascertain the damage, he was horrified to find he had rammed a German tank; what was more, from certain sounds in the farmhouse it was obvious that the crew were stirring. A German came rushing out and jumped on the back of the soldier, who threw him to the ground, smashed his face in with a rifle butt, and shot him. Stunned and shocked, the *RASC* driver stood looking for a few moments at the dead man, and then ran around yelling: "I've shot a German, I've shot a German dead!"

Whitfield shouted to him that that was the object of the operation, and it would be a good thing if he went out and shot some more.

From the sounds of engines starting up all round, it soon became clear that battalion headquarters had settled down in the middle of an enemy tank leaguer. Another horrified soldier was walking from group to group confiding: "D'you know, I actually peed against one of those tanks thinking it was British. Blimey!"

Whitfield's group consisted of only about eight men; he ordered them to move slightly back, avoiding the roads, and get out of the way of the enemy tanks, which were moving off in a north-westerly direction.

The 2/7 Queen's, under Lieutenant-Colonel 'Chippy' Block, had faced tough opposition throughout the day, but by the evening had reached the small village of Faiano in the foothills. After digging trenches, they settled down hopefully for a quiet night. Battalion headquarters was in the village, and an old civilian who had spent some years in Chicago bored them all stiff with tales of gangster fights and night clubs in that city.

Lieutenant Gunter Schmitz with his Panzer pioneers drove in small groups at high speed through the deserted streets of Battipaglia. They occupied the tobacco factory south of the town and spread across country to the banks of the river Sele. The Pioneers, backed by several light field guns, had a fighting strength of about two hundred men. Schmitz sent out patrols along Highway 18; in a short sharp clash with the Royal Fusiliers Second Lieutenant Klieme was wounded and several troop carriers and other vehicles brewed up near Santa Lucia farm. Orders were received to demolish the bridge over the Sele and this was done without opposition. Towards midnight, a field kitchen arrived bringing hot soup and potatoes for the men; the quartermaster's staff excitedly reported:

"Enemy in Battipaglia—we drove through the middle of them!"—
"A motorcyclist was captured."—"Several officers, en route to a
conference at divisional headquarters, were taken prisoner or
killed." Schmitz and his men spent an uncomfortable night under
almost continuous shelling.

Battipaglia was only lightly held by patrols of the Royal Fusiliers
and the battle for the town continued throughout the night.

From the German point of view the 16th Panzer Division had
acquitted itself well. By a continuous series of punches it had
caused much disorganisation and created confusion amongst the
Allies, gaining valuable time for the reinforcement divisions to reach
the area. It had been a costly battle for them, but their morale had
remained high; many were still convinced they would push the invaders back into the sea.

Several German officers have since criticised the bad handling of
tanks by the Allies. Prisoners of war kept asking "Why are you not
using tanks?" and were surprised to learn that there were some.
There is no doubt that if more tank-landing craft had been employed
to bring ashore armoured vehicles on the first day the situation could
have been exploited to better advantage. As it was, the infantry
faced massive panzers mainly armed with small anti-tank weapons,
while the few Shermans that had landed remained in penny packets,
often afraid to move.

*   *   *   *   *

In the Sanatorium at the top of the Laughing Hill, above Salerno,
Arturo Carucci with his nurses and patients had watched the ebb
and flow of battle all day, hoping the fight would prove swift and
successful for the Allies. They had found themselves in a comparatively secure area, with only a few shells landing in the nearby park.
But they were apprehensive that such a good observation post
would not be ignored for very long. At about 1900 hours a group of
anguished nuns ran to the chaplain with the news that a column of
German tanks and armoured cars was climbing the hill, with the
obvious intention of setting up a strong position. Carucci, worried
for the safety of the sick, decided to meet the commander of the
force and plead that the hospital sanctuary be recognised. Somewhat nervously, he went down the road and was directed to a
Wehrmacht major. In halting German he tried to describe the
situation of his patients and the dire peril they would be facing if a
battle was fought in and around the buildings. Receiving him
sympathetically, the major declared himself to be a staunch Catholic;

under the circumstances, however, he had no choice. The Sanatorium was an obvious vantage point for defence or attack; if he did not occupy it, the British would. Carucci in desperation renewed his pleas and offered himself as a guarantee against the English occupation of the buildings. He finally managed to evoke some reciprocal chord in the officer, who agreed to attack from another direction.

"God Bless you," shouted Carucci.

"Heil Hitler," replied the Germans.

In a few moments, the column of tanks swung round on their tracks and set off.

It is interesting to compare an entry in a German officer's diary which presumably refers to the same incident:

> I was approached by a fool of a priest, who beseeched me not to use the Sanatorium because of the patients. What a strange conception of war these Italians have. However, I was able to do him this favour, as fresh orders came over the wireless, ordering me to retire to the main road block.

As this column drove through the streets of Salerno they found the port empty of British troops. Moving northwards, they motored through several small villages, where the inhabitants crowded into the streets in the gathering dusk and, mistaking them for Allied troops, threw flowers on to the vehicles shouting: "*Viva gli Inglesi!*" The Germans were tempted, but desisted from firing at these peasants, who, only a few days before, had been shouting "*Viva i Tedeschi!*"

*   *   *   *   *

With nightfall came an increase in the hordes of giant mosquitoes. They descended in black clouds upon the troops, who soon found that nets and repellent cream were useless. The insects ate the cream with relish and settled in their millions on food, excreta and dead bodies. A diet of unaccustomed fruit was also wreaking havoc with the men's stomachs; in some units dozens of soldiers were incapacitated by violent diarrhoea and orders were issued warning troops to take care.

By the end of D-Day in the British sector the general situation was such that McCreery could report to General Clark that, although not all objectives had been taken, we had seized enough ground to make the beachhead tenable. Montecorvino airfield had not been captured and was still a no-man's-land, over which enemy and Allied tank and infantry patrols roamed.

Earlier in the day, a radio message from the 2/6th Queen's had been misinterpreted and a signal flashed to air headquarters, saying: *Montecorvino open.* Within an hour, a lone Seafire from the Fleet Air Arm had come in to make a perfect landing on the pitted runway. The pilot, looking round for the *RAF* control centre, was taxi-ing slowly along seeking his dispersal area, when the horrified troops saw it suddenly engulfed in flames, as a direct hit from an 88-mm. gun blew it to pieces. With the Germans in strong positions in the hills overlooking the whole beachhead, this airfield, from which the Allies had hoped to operate four fighter squadrons in close support, was to prove untenable even when the Army finally did get control of it. Only a few planes, which had been damaged or had run out of fuel, landed on the field and they did so under continuous fire. It finally opened on 20th September. The port of Salerno was also unusable as the enemy still overlooked it from the high ground behind. Yet on the beaches thousands of tons of war material and men were still being unloaded, and the organisation was slowly sorting itself out.

During D-Day, 1,600 vehicles and 50 tons of stores were landed on *Roger* and *Sugar* beaches. The average for the whole operation was 812 vehicles, and 1,830 tons of stores a day.

Most worrying of all from the Allied viewpoint was the existence of a ten-mile gap between the British and American Corps; this should have been closed, but owing to the intensity of the fighting neither General Walker nor General Graham had been able to spare the men to expand their fronts. In the original plan the beachhead at the end of D-Day should have covered a hundred square miles with a maximum depth of ten to twelve miles; in fact it covered a maximum of fifty square miles and in no place was deeper than six miles, with all the dominating heights still held by the enemy. Mark Clark described this as "not too serious" and confidently signalled the Supreme Commander to the effect that a beachhead had been established and he was about to start the drive to take the dominating mountain heights which covered the roads to Naples.

Chapter IX

D-DAY—PLUS ONE

10th September, 1943

AT 2100 hours men turned the knobs of their radios to get the latest news from the *BBC*. The cool, calm voice of the reader came over the speakers:

"Allied forces have successfully established their bridgehead in the Naples area in face of strong German opposition. The work of unloading ships is going ahead smoothly. . . . Operations are well abreast of the timetable."

This was too much for an *RAF* pilot who had been shot down and taken aboard *USS Ancon*. Sitting in the wardroom, he took off his shoe and threw it at the radio, voicing his feelings: "What a lot of bloody nonsense that is!"

The day, as seen by those who were there, was quite different.

* * * * *

German reinforcements arriving from the Naples area and from the south were thrown in at once; the British X Corps met severe opposition and was forced to retreat in places. The town of Salerno was finally taken over by the British, but in spite of efforts by the Royal Navy to bring the port into use, enemy artillery so dominated the area that the attempt was abandoned. Although Battipaglia was entered, fresh infantry of the 16th Panzer Division, backed by a tremendous weight of armour, captured a large number of troops, causing others to retreat in panic. The Navy, continually called upon for quick and accurate support, answered speedily, breaking up tank attacks by direct fire and silencing enemy batteries whenever they were located; there was praise from army commanders at all levels for the prompt and effective action of the ships.

* * * * *

Lieutenant Christopher Bulteel, a platoon commander of Number 3 Company 3rd Battalion Coldstream Guards, had passed an uncomfortable night in a slit trench close by a tobacco plantation. He

103

was tired after the long sea journey and a hectic day, during which most of the Guardsmen had had precious little idea of what was happening, apart from the fact that they were shelled and machine-gunned every time they moved. He had finally dossed down in his muddy trench at about midnight and tried to get some sleep. At 0200 hours he was gently awoken by his company commander, Major Mervyn Griffith-Jones, who whispered in his ear:

"There are Germans in the tobacco plants."

Shaking his head to clear the dullness of sleep, Bulteel clambered out of his trench and lay listening; to his ears came the sound of bodies breaking the stems of the plants and the rustling of leaves. Both officers loaded and cocked their pistols and moved back slightly to get a better view of the dense growth. The noise continued, but nothing emerged. Leaving his company commander and making a wide detour around the plantation Bulteel moved to the platoon positions slightly forward of the tobacco to warn Lieutenant Raymond Nares. He and his men had already been alerted and were tensely waiting.

"What do you make of it?" asked Bulteel.

"There's definitely somebody in there . . ."

"I don't think they are Germans."

"Well, I've no idea."

"I'm fed up with waiting; let's go in and see."

The platoon advanced as silently as they could, but the movement of their bodies sounded like a threshing machine. Bulteel, stepping carefully, put a foot on a soft body, tripped and fell headlong, to be then trampled on by a herd of grunting, squealing pigs which had been feeding off roots! Roundly cursing for the loss of sleep, and feeling rather foolish, they returned to their positions to await the dawn stand-to.

During the night the 201st Guards Brigade had attempted to move closer to Battipaglia and to the Montecorvino airfield. The Grenadiers, held up at a crossroads south-west of a large barracks and Battipaglia Tobacco Factory, had spent the night under intense artillery fire, with continual patrol sorties on both sides, but had been unable to get forward. The Coldstream Guards had been in reserve; the Scots Guards were on the other side of the Tobacco Factory.

Just forward of them patrols of the Royal Fusiliers had been in and out of Battipaglia, and the 9th Battalion of the Fusiliers had finally moved into the town just after midnight. The Panzer Grenadiers had withdrawn after a severe battering by naval guns and artillery, but the position was by no means secure, as the 9th Battalion was stuck well out, with nothing on its flanks and no tanks in immediate support. So fluid was the battle that a German despatch rider came calmly driving into the town in the dark and stopped near an English sentry to ask the way. He was quickly put in the bag. An armoured car following close on his tail was hit by a *PIAT*. The driver was wounded, but an officer leapt from the turret and, firing his pistol, ran off down the road, until he was captured by another sentry.

All through the night the Fusiliers, urged on by their officers, dug trenches and fortressed themselves into strong points. At dawn Spandau fire and shells from 88-mm. guns increased, until a heavy barrage was falling on all positions.

Suddenly, one sentry shouted out "Tanks!"; his cry was taken up by other watchers as, looking down the road, they saw a column of Tigers and Mark IVs advance almost leisurely into the town. The battalion's 6-pounder anti-tank guns sited in the main street commenced firing, but the shells bounced harmlessly off the thick hulls. Lieutenant-Colonel Ted Hillersden, ignoring the bullets and shells, stood just behind the guns gazing through his binoculars, although several officers warned him to take cover. Within a few minutes he had been wounded. Fusilier Albert Fitzgerald rushed out and, helped by others, dragged him under cover.

"Where have you copped it, sir?" he asked, and was told: "In the arm."

But on looking, Fitzgerald found it was a bad chest wound; after applying a shell dressing and giving a jab of morphia, he marked 'M' on the officer's forehead and stayed with him, waiting for help to come.

Major Delforce, who took over the battalion, soon found that the enemy forces were virtually all round the town in overwhelming strength. The tanks had been able to approach close to the houses by driving through the twelve-foot-high tobacco plants, the sound of their engines drowned by the guns. As the day progressed, the Fusiliers' perimeter got smaller and smaller. Delforce urged his men to hang on with the news that the Guards Brigade was on the way, and to some soldiers who were frightened of being taken prisoners he said:

"Although we are surrounded, we shall not be captured."

But privately he told the officers to destroy all maps and ciphers; the situation looked rather grim.

It is only possible to get individual glimpses of the battle as it progressed.

Lance-Corporal Harold Lampard, still carrying his wireless set, marched along roads covered in broken electric cables and telephone wires. First stop for half an hour was in a hairdresser's, where some of the troops, in a light-hearted mood, liberally sprayed themselves with sickly smelling pomades and lotions. Smelling like "pox doctors' clerks", as one Fusilier described it, they then pushed on to a house just off the main street. A platoon went into the upper rooms, taking up a fire position overlooking the Germans, whilst Lampard stayed on the stairs above a small courtyard. There they remained, unaware of what was going on, even though they had the wireless set operating. All morning they listened to the thunder of guns and automatic weapons; every now and then they would hear a rumble as a shaky house collapsed or a final shell demolished a wall. Late in the afternoon Lampard and his chum Fusilier Brown heard the sound of unmistakably Teutonic voices shouting commands and running feet. Loud shouts came through the flimsy walls of the neighbouring house; then a German broke through a door with a levelled sub-machine-gun. Lampard shouted into his microphone:

"We're about to be captured; I'm closing down now to kick in the set. Out."

His message, received at battalion headquarters, was to be re-repeated several times that day from other units. For a moment Lampard and Brown thought they would be shot out of hand, but after a long pause, as the Germans looked at them, one shouted: "*Hande Hoch!*" and they were prisoners.

The enemy troops called up the stairs to the platoon, which, cut off at the top of the house, had no choice but to surrender. They were taken out into the street, where a Wehrmacht officer warned them: "If anyone escapes, we shall shoot ten in reprisal." They were marched off under light escort for some three hours. They were aghast to see the enormous mass of tanks, armoured cars and lorries hidden in valleys in the foothills. At the end of the march, they were allowed to halt; an officer pointed to some horse troughs and suggested they should drink their fill. A German *NCO* wandered over, saying: "For you, the war is over."

Throughout Battipaglia other groups of Fusiliers were being rounded up as dusk fell on the second day; many of them were giving up the fight and surrendering in penny packets. The Commanding Officer, although weak from loss of blood, still refused to be evacuated, whilst Major Delforce kept trying to reorganise his positions, as one post after another fell. Soon all the anti-tank guns had been wrecked; there was little future in fighting Tiger tanks with rifles and bare hands. Finally, the order was given for the remnants to fight their way out as individuals. The Medical Officer and the padre elected to go into captivity, in order to remain with the wounded. The men came out of the houses firing Bren-guns and automatic weapons from the hip, aiming at the slits in the tanks' visors in an attempt to blind the drivers and commanders. Many fell as they ran; others were knocked over and run down by the armoured monsters.

Fusilier Bill Turner was on the top storey of a house, firing his Bren-gun at everything that moved; like hundreds of others, he realised that it could not go on for much longer.

From his vantage point he glanced down into the street, where a corporal, lying behind a Bren-gun, laughing and screaming, pumped magazine after magazine of bullets into the already dead body of a German. In the other direction, he saw dozens of Fusilier officers, NCOs and men walking up the street towards an enemy tank, surrounded by Germans with levelled weapons. Wondering if he would be shot, Turner clambered down the stairs, to emerge into a street full of Jerries. It was not at all like he had imagined it. No fusilade of bullets, no pushing around or hands above the head. A German just jerked his rifle in the direction he should go and soon he joined a large crowd of comrades waiting to march into captivity. Major John van Gelder and Major Sandford paraded the troops in rough lines, and a German officer in broken English told them:

"You have fought well. This was our third counter-attack; if you had beaten us this time, we could not have launched another."

Fusilier Fred Hawthorn never forgot the sight that morning in Battipaglia, when a German automobile came down a street to be met by a British car driving in the opposite direction. The officers in each car stood up simultaneously, shouted and fired; both missed; the cars reversed and screamed off. Involved in street fighting, Hawthorn soon realised the futility of throwing Mills grenades at tanks, just to have them bounce off before they exploded, often almost back at the thrower. When he saw bunches of prisoners being assembled, he went out to join them, raising his hands as he left the door. For some unknown reason he had a potato in each hand; a young German soldier, reasonably suspecting them to be grenades, was about to bash his head in with a rifle butt, when he was ordered to stop by an officer.

The Germans paid dearly for the capture of Battipaglia, and were to pay an even higher price before they finally left the area.

One platoon of Fusiliers remained behind uncaptured in the attic of a house, which was shortly taken over as a German headquarters. Lieutenant Grost ordered his men to remain motionless and kept sentries posted to prevent men sneezing and snoring. They nibbled biscuits and pieces of corned beef and sucked sweets, which were carefully rationed. They stayed there for twenty-four hours; most of them eventually escaped, apart from the officer, who was presumed to have been captured when he went in search of water.

The remnants of the Fusiliers moved out of the town as best they could. Some ran, panic-stricken, towards the sea, shouting, "Back to the beaches! We're overrun!" and "We've had it; the German tanks are right behind us!" Other groups, led by officers, moved back under control and, reaching the 201st Guards Brigade, were reorganised by Major Delforce into a compact unit.

At one point, where Panzers were threatening to break through to the beaches, a Guards *CSM* called out to some Fusiliers:

"Does anyone here know how to fire a *PIAT*?"

Receiving blank looks and negative replies, he immediately grabbed hold of a group of men and gave them an instructional lesson on the weapon and then sent two of them into action with it. Half an hour later a report came in that the men had set a Tiger on fire.

Earlier in the day the 3rd Coldstream had been ordered to advance and seize Montecorvino airfield. A carrier patrol, skirting the edge of the field meeting only light Spandau fire, managed to take up positions on the road on the far side and dig in. But the Germans in the dominating hills were still able to prevent the runways being used, by shelling them intensively every time anything moved. The 2nd Scots Guards had also received orders to attack the Battipaglia Tobacco Factory that stood halfway between the airfield and Battipaglia. It consisted of a series of buildings, surrounded by a high wire fence supported on stakes, and from the fire that had come from it during the previous night it was obvious that it was heavily defended and unlikely to be given up without a fight. To make matters worse, the Scots Guards were expected to attack in broad daylight, as orders had been received from divisional headquarters to push on at all costs. The attack did not go in till some time later.

At 0730 hours the Grenadiers were sent into a fresh attack. The Scots Guards prepared to support them with Vickers *MMGs* and 3-inch mortars.

The Grenadiers went in after a heavy barrage and reached the crossroads south-west of the Tobacco Factory with very little opposition. They quickly started to dig in, but before they had hardly scraped the surface several armoured cars and tanks supported by infantry charged down, wiping out one platoon before they realised what was happening. Panic set in; the remainder of one company began running back to the start line, where they were stopped and organised into fresh positions.

A Guards Brigade officer recorded after the battle:

> Nobody will really know what happened, and perhaps it is better to gloss over the rest of that day. The morale of the Grenadiers was not high, and it is certain that small parties considered the only plan was to return to the beaches as quickly as possible. On their right, some Fusiliers of the 167th Brigade had a similar idea. By mid-afternoon the small roads were full of frightened soldiers, many retiring pell-mell regardless of officers. Two companies of Grenadiers, however, stood firm and our brave supporters of the Royal Scots Greys in their Shermans did great feats.

Over on the left flank, Lieutenant Bulteel with the Coldstream Battalion had been having a fairly quiet and pleasant day, apart from an occasional 'short' from our own guns. At about 1800 hours, as he was supervising the loading of some wounded into a jeep, another vehicle roared past, filled with Grenadiers shouting: "They're coming! They're through! Get back to the beaches!"

Bulteel drove his jeep across the road to prevent any more passing, and then rushed off to speak to his company commander. Major Griffith-Jones was on the telephone and would not be interrupted. At last he finished.

"Mervyn," said Bulteel, "some of the Grenadiers have run away; we are to be ready for an immediate counter-attack."

Griffith-Jones cleared his throat and paused.

"Nonsense," he then said quite calmly. "Everything's quite all right. The Grenadiers have attacked again and now they are back where they started. I am going to have a sleep"—which he immediately proceeded to do.

Grenadier officers, assembled to produce a fresh plan, were horrified to see the divisional commander, General D. A. H. Graham, driving in his jeep from the crossroads they had just abandoned. By some miracle he had come across from the airfield and got through unscathed. He was in a towering rage and made some very derogatory remarks about the troops.

The German unit in the attack on Battipaglia was the 2nd Panzer Regiment commanded by Major Freiherr von Falkenhausen, which had been ordered at all costs to retake the town. Lieutenant Gunter Schmitz with his Pioneers was in the initial assault, but then received an order to report to divisional headquarters at Eboli. Puzzled as to the reason, he was sent to see General Sieckenius, who reprimanded him for retiring from his positions on the previous day. Schmitz forthrightly defended himself, explaining that he had withdrawn on orders, and ended up by getting a pat on the back He drove back to Battipaglia with a much lighter heart, and went off with his reconnaissance troop of two tanks to make contact with the neighbouring unit. He drove through the farm at Santa Lucia, which was littered with destroyed Bren-gun carriers and dead British soldiers. They came under machine-gun fire; Lieutenant Opderbeck, sitting beside him, was struck in the face. When an anti-tank shell hit the vehicle, Schmitz was wounded in the chest. Nearby soldiers hauled them out of the vehicles and, through a hail of Allied gunfire, they were taken back to a first-aid post. After a short time they were put in an ambulance with a wounded British lieutenant-colonel to be taken to the village hospital at Sant'Angelo. During the journey Schmitz tried to strike up a conversation with the English officer, but was ignored as the colonel lay on his back, swearing and cussing at his ill-fortune.

The British decided to send in the Scots Guards, who started their advance at 0930 hours. They strode along the rough lane leading to the crossroads; ahead, their path disappeared into thick bushes. Over the tops of the vegetation they could make out the high roof of the Tobacco Factory and a couple of two-storeyed houses to the left of the crossroads. The sun shone peacefully down on the bodies of many Grenadiers lying in the ditches; in the distance came the sounds of fresh battle from the direction of the airfield. As the forward companies passed the crossroads in complete silence, there was not a sign of the German armoured vehicles that had wreaked such havoc two hours before. The infantry fanned out and advanced towards the Factory. Inevitably the German reaction was swift and well-timed; 88-mms, mortars and hidden Spandaus opened up, forcing the men to go to ground.

Back at battalion headquarters a chance shell landed in the midst of a group of officers. Major Michael Crichton-Stuart was conscious of a violent but silent explosion; feeling a sharp pain in his thigh, he looked down to see a hole in his trouser leg. He also became aware that, of a group of seven men, he was the only one still upright. Looking across at his friend Hal Astley Corbett, he saw him flat on his back, his face grey and pinched. As Crichton-

Stuart fell carefully to the ground, he heard his colonel shouting out:

"It's all right, it's all right!"

Crichton-Stuart rolled on his back. "It's bloody well not all right; Hal's dead and I'm wounded."

The colonel crawled over to feel the officer's heart; then, turning to Crichton-Stuart and seeing his bloody leg, he said: "Bad luck, old cock!"

In the forward company of the Scots Guards men charged forward in face of the fire across a narrow lane, over a ditch and through the scrub surrounding the Factory fence. The six-foot-tall troops clambered over the barrier; some climbed up others' backs, some almost high-jumped it. Inside they found a maze of huts and the battle developed into one of hide and seek, grenades flying like tennis balls and gunmen snap-shooting at figures as they flitted in and out of the corridors between the buildings. But the enemy counter-attack was too strong for mere infantry to hold; orders were sent forward for the men to retire. Still in full daylight, the reluctant Guardsmen had to fall back and, once again, climb the wire fence. Small groups lay down with Bren-guns and fired magazines as fast as they could load them at the advancing Germans, trying to get their heads down and stop the deadly fire which came at them. Lieutenant D. I. Fyfe-Jamieson stayed with the support groups to urge the men on; as the last few went over the fence, he rushed with his group to a tall gate. As he clambered over the top, he slipped and found himself strung up by the trousers on a spike, with Spandau bullets whipping all round. Seeing his plight, Sergeant William Lumsden, one of the section commanders, ran back through the fire; with a knife, he cut the officer's trousers free and together they rushed into some nearby bushes for cover. For this courageous act Lumsden was awarded the Distinguished Conduct Medal.

The 201st Guards Brigade had suffered heavy casualties and had only succeeded in advancing a few hundred yards. Reviewing the situation, one senior officer remarked to a Guards colonel:

"If we don't hold these German counter-attacks, it will be just like Dunkirk again; except that there are no little ships to take us off."

To the left of the Guards, the Queen's Battalions of the 169th Brigade were ordered forward north of the airfield to occupy the foothill village of Faiano. The 2/5 Queens had become somewhat disorganised during the night and it had been reported that the

Commanding Officer and battalion headquarters were missing, presumed captured. In fact, Lieutenant-Colonel John Whitfield was at that time submerged up to his neck in muddy water in a ditch, peering through the branches of a blackberry bush, watching German tanks roll up and down the road carrying his captured troops. He had hidden there with his adjutant and several others, helpless to take any action, when they had recognised some tanks advancing towards them from the beach as Tigers; they had at first presumed them to be British, coming from that direction. The armoured vehicles were so close that they could see the men and could have called out to them. It was lucky they remained under cover, for shortly after dawn a nearby haystack disintegrated and out from its midst moved an armoured half-track. At last a troop of the 67th Anti-Tank Regiment with 17-pounders got the German tanks in their sights and gave them such a pasting that they withdrew. During the confusion a considerable number of the prisoners jumped off the vehicles and ran back into the British lines.

At 0800 hours a company of Whitfield's 2/5th battalion on its own initiative started to advance across open country, but after only a few hundred yards, as they trudged through the fields and across ditches and hedges, they were caught in a shattering barrage. Several Bren carriers and gun limbers burst into flames; only about thirty men from a company of a hundred managed to get away. The battalion had by now been so massacred that it was decided to withdraw it. A hundred and seventy-three all ranks, including four company commanders, had been killed or taken prisoner. Colonel Whitfield reorganised the remaining troops into two companies and prepared for any job that was offered to him.

The 46th Division, between the River Tusciano and Salerno town, was having a slightly quieter time, but as the day progressed it became more and more obvious that strong German forces were coming into the area and that the main attacks could be expected from the north. The 46th Reconnaissance Regiment, which on the previous day had driven all the way to the village of Cava de' Tirreni, a few miles from the Vietri defile, set out at dawn to return there. As they drove along the dusty roads, the troops picked oranges and peaches and waved to the crowds of Italians who excitedly greeted them in every village and hamlet.

The peaceful day was soon interrupted by an outbreak of enemy shelling as they rounded a corner to cross the Cava bridge. German artillery, anti-tank guns, mortars and automatic weapons had taken up a defensive position there. In the face of superior fire, they retired back to Vietri itself, where they were able to warn the Commandos of an imminent attack, which they had seen forming up.

On the flank the Commandos were already in stand-to positions. By 1000 hours, 'A' and 'X' Troops of the 41st Royal Marine Commando in the hills near Vietri defile reported the enemy infiltrating south of the pass. The Marines lay flat on their stomachs in the shallow slit trenches, facing the advancing enemy. The supporting mortars soon laid an accurate barrage, which burst among the Germans and sent some of them scattering back—but the main body crept onwards. In camouflaged uniforms, their faces painted with streaks of green, the Germans took on the appearance of characters from Dante's *Inferno* to the Marines. With instructions not to fire until given the order, the latter stayed motionless until the leading Huns were only thirty yards away.

As the officers screamed "Fire!" the Commandos let rip with every weapon they had; the enemy fell by the dozen, dead and wounded. Those continuing the advance, kept shouting a battle cry—"*Hoch! hoch!*" By sheer weight of numbers, they managed to get through. Hand-to-hand fighting with bayonets, rifle butts and knives took place, men struggling, kicking, scratching, biting and cursing.

Back at Commando headquarters, Colonel Lumsden quickly appreciated the situation and sent 'Q' Troop into an immediate counter-attack, led by Captain Martin Scott, who was soon killed. Nineteen-year-old Lieutenant Peter Haydon, only six months in the Royal Marines, took over and continued the advance up the hill. Men kept falling all round him; finally he was hit in the thigh by a piece of mortar shrapnel. By this time he had only seven men under his command, but he refused to be evacuated or to allow anyone to retreat; offered a phial of morphia, he rejected it, fearing it would fuddle his brain. With a rifle seized from the hands of a dead Marine he started firing at the enemy and directing his minute force. In the next few hours he fainted three times from pain and loss of blood, but he shot four Germans.

In the meantime, the bulk of the enemy forces carried out a wide encircling movement round the pass and almost reached Vietri itself. The lightly equipped Commandos contested every inch of ground and the Germans suffered appalling losses from artillery and mortar fire. Number 2 Commando under Lieutenant-Colonel Jack Churchill went into the attack and drove the enemy right back to the original positions occupied by the Royal Marines. There, on the top of a hill, they found young Haydon still clinging on with his tiny force, still determinedly keeping the enemy at bay. He had suffered a further wound, but had managed to conceal it from his troops. He was carried back to the beaches and evacuated.

Haydon was later awarded a Distinguished Service Order, a medal very rarely given to a lieutenant. He served throughout the war, until he was later killed on Walcheren Island in 1944.

At one stage, when the Army Commandos had dug in and were prepared for yet another attack, a forward troop saw coming towards them a man in British battle-dress, dragging along a reluctant German prisoner. As he approached, he was heard to be using Billingsgate curses:

"Keep quiet, you little bastard, or I'll cut yer throat! . . . Shut up, or I'll have yer liver for supper!"

The Commandos grinned at the sight; then both captor and captive, only twenty yards away, threw themselves to the ground firing sub-machine guns and trying to toss grenades into the British trenches. Yet another German trick had almost succeeded, and there was a short, sharp battle before both attackers were killed.

During the afternoon Brigadier Robert Laycock was visited at Commando Brigade headquarters by General Hawkesworth, who had driven up from Salerno. He congratulated the Commandos on the extremely tough fight they were carrying out and asked them to hang on, as he had no troops to spare. The Commandos, who had asked for reinforcements, were later sent a Field Company of Royal Engineers, who were meant to act as infantry. Unfortunately this was not understood by the Commandos, who, still thinking them to be specialist troops, kept them in reserve.

Gay, debonair Laycock had taken over a smart Italian villa as his headquarters, where he was keeping up a reasonable standard of living. A great advantage to this building was that, being under an overhanging cliff, it was virtually impossible to hit it with gunfire. That morning at a conference a new collective noun had been added to the British language, and it was a joke that was being passed from mouth to mouth. There were three Churchills in the Commando Brigade: Lieutenant-Colonel Tom Churchill acted as Laycock's Chief of Staff; Lieutenant-Colonel Jack Churchill commanded Number 2 Army Commando; and there was Major Randolph Churchill, the Prime Minister's son. These three, an imposing group, were christened the 'Avalanche of Churchills'.

Randolph, not a very popular character amongst some soldiers, got on well with the Commandos, and although holding no definite appointment, was helpful wherever he could be. On one occasion, when a United States mortar battery, who had come ashore to support them, seemed at first uncertain of what to do, Randolph was reported as having mounted on an imaginary soap box and harangued them in good political style about the task they had in hand, and as to where and how they should carry it out.

Lieutenant-Colonel Jack Churchill was probably the most colourful of the 'Avalanche'. He often went into action with bagpipes, although he made no claim whatever to any Scottish blood, and Laycock once saw him in battle with a bow and arrow. Asked what the hell he thought he was doing carrying a medieval weapon on a twentieth-century battle-field, he immediately demanded to be given a target. Laycock pointed to a tree about a hundred yards away. With unerring aim an arrow flew directly to the target, whilst the colonel commented:

"And think how frightened you'd be if a shower of arrows suddenly descended on you!"

Eccentric as some of his actions appeared to be, Jack Churchill was loved by his tough Commandos, who would follow him anywhere, and he was to prove his courage and determination even more in the days to come.

The 6th York and Lancaster Regiment had survived a rough night of shelling and mortaring. Early in the morning, Lieutenant-Colonel Joe Kendrew went across the rocky hillsides near Salerno to visit his forward companies. At one position, a haystack only fifty yards away was pointed out as an enemy blockhouse. Unbelieving, Kendrew decided to investigate. He walked casually towards the haystack, and the nearer he got, the more convinced he became that the troops had been imagining things in the night. As he moved to within about twenty yards, however, a Spandau opened up from within. Finally convinced that the haystack was not all it seemed, he turned and, with bullets hitting the ground at his heels, he zigzagged back at a fast gallop.

Ordering the company to stand fast, he hurried back to battalion headquarters, where he learnt that a rapid counter-attack had followed him almost immediately into the company trenches, and it looked as if they would be overrun. He hastily sent in another unit and most of the day was spent in attack and counter-attack. In the evening, as the Hun retired to regroup and lick his wounds, troops of the 138th Brigade were ordered in to relieve the Yorks and Lancs, who marched through the dusk towards the Vietri defile, where they were to take over new positions along the road leading from Vietri to Naples.

* * * * *

Atop the Laughing Hill, Arturo Carucci rose early after a restless night spent with hundreds of others in the damp, smelly tunnel in the hospital grounds and with a few nurses and colleagues went into the chapel to celebrate mass. When the service had finished, with the roar of guns and explosions in his ears, he stood outside gazing over the panorama of war which spread out all round him. A party of British troops drove into the grounds shortly afterwards, and a major of the Durham Light Infantry advanced towards him, hand outstretched, with the warning that he and all the others should return to their tunnel, as the Germans were only a few metres away. Carucci asked for an assurance that the Sanatorium would not be taken over as a strong-point, and was told that the buildings would be respected. But others were not so considerate; when fresh troops arrived, obviously looking for vantage points, an officer brandishing a pistol ordered the chaplain and his companions to go away and mind their own business. Carucci and Lieutenant Gatti, refusing to be silenced, pleaded their cause, pointing out that they had already been promised that the hospital would not be turned into a battle-ground. Finally the officer relented, offered cigarettes all round and took his men away.

Throughout the day Carucci found himself answering questions from officers of all ranks, who wanted information about the town, the health of the people and the whereabouts of the civil authorities. He did his best to supply the required details, all the time extricating promises that his beloved Sanatorium would remain untouched. Accompanied by the nuns in their long black dresses and several excited patients, he was everywhere at once, soothing and calming, encouraging and reproaching his own people and the Allied troops.

At 1300 hours a small convoy of jeeps drove into the courtyard. A bevy of senior red-tabbed officers alighted and, from the terrace, commenced surveying the battlefield with binoculars and consulting maps. The chaplain was informed that the tallest officer in a plain battledress and stars on his shoulders was the American General Mark Clark. With natural hospitality, the Italian rushed forward to greet him and to offer the party a glass of Cinzano, which was gratefully accepted; Mark Clark subsequently promised to do all he could to preserve the Sanatorium. After a while, in a flurry of vehicles, the Army Commander departed with his generals.

Fearing that Clark's endeavours would have little effect, Arturo Carucci ordered most of his staff to go back to the tunnel, as he was frightened that soon shells would start landing. As the party of nuns and patients wended its way through the park, they came upon a lone German soldier wandering amongst the trees and the flowers, looking lost and miserable. The Mother Superior, with inborn sympathy and compassion, offered him food; then from the inner folds of her gown she drew forth a Catholic medallion engraved with a picture of the Madonna. The soldier, bewildered by the fighting, afraid and lonely, took the small piece of metal, gazed at it in silence for a moment and, bursting into tears, brought out from a worn wallet pictures of his wife and children, which he passed round the group.

The chaplain remained in the hospital buildings with Gatti and Soffietti, the chief doctor.

In the tunnels and caves around Salerno, and in countless other villages, the peasants and the priests prayed for an end to the death and devastation that was sweeping their homeland.

*   *   *   *   *

General Mark Clark had gone ashore early in the morning to see for himself the exact situation, which it had been impossible to ascertain from the headquarters ship *Ancon*. He also wanted to find an area in which to put the 157th Regimental Combat Team which was still at sea as the Army floating reserve. As he stepped off his craft, he found to his astonishment Mike, his German police dog, jumping up and down, barking furiously with joy at seeing him. Strict instructions had been issued that animals would not be taken ashore, but his batman, Sergeant Chaney, had decided that the Army Commander's pet was an exception and had put a label on its collar which read: *This is General Clark's dog. He is going to Salerno.* The animal made a tremendous fuss and bother and kept getting so much in everyone's way that Clark eventually ordered the dog to be tied up on the beach, where it spent a miserable day whining for its master.

His first visit was to the American sector to see Major-General Fred Walker's 36th Division. Since the initial landings Clark had been dealing directly with General Walker and issuing orders concerning the movement and actions of that division. The excuse Clark gives for this is that Dawley's headquarters was still not ashore and, had he passed instructions through corps headquarters this would have caused even longer delays. Not unnaturally, Dawley felt he was being by-passed and not allowed to use his authority. This was probably one of the earlier of many subsequent irritating pin-pricks, which culminated in great personal dislike between the two generals. Dawley up to this time had certainly been cautious in his reaction to the enemy and in the use of the troops under his command. Whilst Clark and Walker at this stage were seeing eye to eye on the general conduct of the battle.

Despite the fact that he now knew that most of the objectives were still in enemy hands, Clark decided that the situation was favourable and the American morale was high. The Army Commander always drove his own jeep and had an escort of giant military policemen: together, they made a most imposing vehicle load, easily recognisable by all the troops, who cheered and waved as he passed by.

At McCreery's headquarters he was given the full situation, but again decided that as a whole most things were according to plan. He sent back orders that the floating reserve should be landed to back Colonel Darby's American Rangers, still fighting hard in the extreme north of the beachhead. On return to the *Ancon*, he discovered that during his absence orders had been received from Algiers that, the landing craft carrying the floating reserve being urgently needed, they must be sent to North Africa at once. Admiral Hewitt, faced with this ultimatum and unable to contact Clark, had to act immediately, with the result that he sent the troops into the American sector many miles away from where they were intended. Clark was naturally furious at the resultant delay and confusion caused by having to move a complete regiment from one end of the beachhead to the other across the lines of communication.

Despite obvious gaps and holes all along the front, with Salerno port still closed and Montecorvino airfield under fire, the Army Commander sent a highly optimistic signal to General Alexander, saying that he would soon be ready to attack northwards through the Molina Pass above Vietri and capture Naples. In his memoirs he admits this was too hopeful, but he does not explain how it was that he was misled into this viewpoint.

* * * * *

In the American sector on this day there was comparatively little opposition, the main brunt of the enemy attack having been switched to the British Corps.

Just after midnight the first men of the 45th 'Thunderbird'

Division went ashore. Under command of Major-General Troy H. Middleton, two Regimental Combat Teams had been at sea for the whole of D-Day, awaiting orders to land, with the result that they did not know until just beforehand where they would be going in. As the assault craft were swung out on the davits, a flight of Focke-Wulfs shot low over the area. Several huge parachute flares were dropped illuminating the whole zone, and then the anti-aircraft guns on all the ships opened up in a crazy multi-coloured phantasmagoria of tracer—the British Bofors, their barrels spitting and chattering, US Navy 90-mms pumping away at a slower deeper rate. The Americans huddled close to the decks, feeling helpless, as all soldiers do when bombed at sea and unable to do anything about it.

Movement of troops towards the shore continued with disembarkation planned for 0420 hours, but a thick sea mist developed, forcing its postponement until 1140 hours. Meanwhile, until dawn, German bombing attacks continued in the main anchorage. American army engineers had been busy on the southern beaches around Paestum; when the LSTs and LCIs finally drove in, many of them found pontoons sticking fifty yards out into the water, along which the troops were able to march with dry feet. For some unexplained reason, the German gunners were leaving these beaches alone and, as the doors of an LCI gaped open, a Sergeant stepped out, shouting back to his men: "It's a cinch! There ain't no enemy at all." The words were hardly out of his mouth, when a flight of Messerschmitts whined down out of the sun at fifty feet, unnoticed by the ack-ack gunners, their bullets spraying the advancing columns. Twelve men died in as many seconds, whilst the soldiers cursed their NCOs and officers, who had promised them a quiet time.

The 179th Regimental Combat Team was first ashore on Blue beach, with orders to assemble on Highway 18 near Paestum and attack up the Sele-Calore corridor. Here neither army engineers nor naval shore parties had been able to cope with the vast amount of supplies that had been continually disgorged from the vessels ever since the morning of D-Day. Right down to the water's edge, the disembarking troops found mountains of petrol cans, oil tins, boxes of rations, crates of ammunition of all types. In some cases the dumps were actually lapped by the waves and close inshore the water was littered with damaged or abandoned equipment. Bulldozers and tractors ground all over the sand, dragging material into the shelter of the dunes and winching wrecked vehicles off to clear the routes. Forcing a way through this chaos, the 179th RCT moved into the plain behind the beaches, along roads dotted with burning tanks and trucks; dead bodies of comrades and of enemy troops were scattered round erupted slit trenches and deserted gun pits. For the first time it was rammed home to these men that the invasion was not a pleasure trip and that Naples was still miles and days ahead of them.

General Dawley, on a tour of the battlefield but with his main headquarters still at sea, issued orders personally to Colonel Hutchins, Commanding Officer of the 179th *RCT*, which was divided into two columns. The 2nd Battalion was to advance south of the Calore, the 3rd Battalion to cross the river and march via Persano to take the vital Ponte Sele.

Probably owing to the delay in landing the 45th Division the attack on these two objectives was postponed almost twenty-four hours, and instead of capturing them on the 10th under what might have been more favourable conditions, the units on the 11th, after a leisurely preparation, came up against strongly reinforced enemy formations and failed to capture their objectives. The Gap remained wide open.

The two columns pushed off in the evening towards their start lines. The 2nd Battalion slowly traversed four miles of country, forded the Calore river about three miles south of the Ponte Sele and was then given a hard blow by the 29th Pioneer Battalion 16th Panzer Division. The Americans withdrew in some disorder and reorganised back on the south side of the river.

The 3rd Battalion, with the 1st Battalion in support, moved northwards toward Persano. A main bridge across the Calore, a wooden structure, had been set alight by the Germans, which meant a detour across a ford. Continuing on their route, they swung to the right towards the Ponte Sele, unwisely ignoring the high ground at Persano, which was still occupied by the enemy. The whole of this advance was across territory which Allied and enemy gunners had used as a killing ground. It was a mass of wrecked and burning vehicles, mostly German, and the enemy was not prepared to let anyone cross it unscathed. Leading elements of the 3rd Battalion reached the high bluffs overlooking the Ponte Sele, which was found to have been wrecked. Army engineers were brought forward and told to repair it as best they could. They worked throughout the night and on through the following morning under heavy gunfire to make it passable.

By the end of 10th September the 45th Division, with its two columns sticking out into enemy held ground, was savagely struck by tanks and infantry and came to an immediate full stop.

The town of Maiori showing the mountainous terrain over which the troops had to fight.

American Army DUKWs carrying ashore men of the 9th Battalion Royal Fusiliers on D-Day.

Allied invasion craft approaching Salerno at dawn on September 9th.

Pontoons being rigged up to facilitate the landing of men and stores.

German gunners in position in woods overlooking the Salerno beaches.

Montecorvino airfield after its occupation.

Major-General Hawkesworth Commander 46th Infantry Division, chats to his troops in an orchard near Salerno.

British tanks loaded with infantry advance past a road block at an exit of Salerno Town.

The 9th Battalion The Royal Fusiliers advancing inland.
From left to right: Captain Frank Rider—Lance/Corporal Lawrence Newsome—Regimental Policeman
—Fusilier Tom Richardson—Fusilier Harold Lampard—Fusilier Reg Brown—RSM George Hollings.

A German Mark IV Special in action against British troops.

The first German prisoners are hustled down the beach by British troops.

General Eisenhower tours the battlefront on 17th September with General Mark Clark (extreme left) and (centre) Admiral Kent Hewitt.

[*Imperial War Museum*

Major-General Graham, Commander of the 56th Division, talks with
Brigadier Lyne at Divisional Headquarters.

Alexander, Mark Clark and McCreery (left to right) walk along the Salerno
beach after a day spent touring the bridgehead.

[*Imperial War Museum*

Mamma Lucia at her self-appointed task in the mountains above Salerno.

Italians bombed out of their houses in Battipaglia lived in caves in the mountains.

The *RCT* of the 36th Division moved forward during the day to prepare an attack on Altavilla and Hill 424, overlooking Paestum. The 1/142nd, commanded by Lieutenant-Colonel Barron, advanced to the high ground north of Altavilla under light harassing fire and established a command post overlooking the town at about 1430 hours. One and a half hours later twenty-five Panzers attacked them, but gunners of the 132nd Field Artillery Battalion, directing accurate fire at the vehicles, drove them off with heavy losses. Other units of the 142nd *RCT* managed to reach the crest of Monte Soprano and Monte Vesole, also overlooking Paestum, meeting no resistance except from snipers, and were soon in positions ready for the next morning's battle.

By nightfall the Americans had occupied Albanella and the lower slopes of Hill 424. General Dawley was confident that his divisions were ready to strike north-eastwards on the following day.

*   *   *   *   *

At 0730 hours that morning an action of great significance occurred: the Germans brought into use for the first time a secret weapon in the shape of a radio-controlled glider bomb. There were two types of bombs, both fitted with fins and rocket boosters: one had a range of about eight miles and a speed of 570 miles an hour, the other a shorter range of three and a half miles and a speed of about 660 miles an hour. The Luftwaffe's tactics were to attack with a normal force of bombers to attract the attention of the anti-aircraft gunners and fighters, whilst the planes carrying the glider bombs stood off some miles away and released the weapons. Controlled and guided visually by the aircrew, they carried an explosive warhead of 660 pounds. The first one to come screaming into the area exploded harmlessly in the roadsteads. The Naval Command had received prior warning from British Admiralty Intelligence only a few days before; they were thus not caught completely unawares, although they had still to learn what defensive action was needed and the destructive power of the new weapon.

Aboard the British headquarters ship a radar boffin came up with the idea that the delicate guidance controls of these bombs would be affected by the tiny motors of electric razors. Clutching at any and every straw, a perfectly serious signal was despatched to all ships in the fleet, ordering every electric razor to be switched on whenever it was thought a flying-bomb attack was imminent. It was, however, never discovered if this had any effect at all.

Naval gunfire really came into its own on this day. Shore-based observers had finally got properly organised, and any unit commander who wanted support was guaranteed to get it within fifteen minutes. In the British sector at least thirty-seven calls for help were answered, most of them successfully; messages of thanks and congratulations kept rolling into the ships.

The destroyer *HMS Nubian*—was kept busy throughout the day firing three hundred and forty-one 4.7-inch rounds at a variety of targets. In her turrets sweating sailors rammed the shells as fast as they could, largely unaware of the great help they were giving the soldiers. Her log briefly records that in the early morning she broke up a tank concentration and between 1000 hours and 1145 hours she completely destroyed a German artillery battery in the distant hills and demolished an enemy strong-point.

The cruiser *HMS Mauritius* responded rapidly to seventeen calls for help and during the day fired five hundred rounds at any target within range. Her guns were largely responsible for controlling the situation south of Battipaglia and at the crossroads near the Tobacco Factory where the Guards and Fusiliers had taken such a beating.

HMS Brecon logged:

> At 2244 hours, due to a mistake, a smoke float was dropped over the stern instead of being left covered on the quarterdeck. In the light wind this drifted slowly astern. At 2247 hours an aircraft shallow-dived on the ship from over the land and straddled with five bombs. Two landed 40 yards on the port side and two 50 yards to starboard. A third delay-action bomb landed 40 yards on the starboard boom and went off with a very big shock about five seconds later. Everyone got a fright but beyond breaking most of the wardroom cups and a lavatory pan no damage was done: we were extremely lucky. . . .

The commander of 16th Panzer Division had earlier in the day sent a message to Kesselring's headquarters, reporting the situation favourable. But later in the day, when they had failed to break through to the beaches, General Herr, the Army Commander, was asking for more troops and more tanks, as he feared the Allied build-up would soon overwhelm him.

General Schmalz with the Hermann Goering Panzer Division recorded in the divisional war diary that his troops had arrived at Cava, but could not get any further forward.

> The tanks were unable to operate efficiently in the narrow valley and had a restricted field of observation. Violent fighting on both

sides of the mountain slopes, which it was important for us to occupy for artillery observation. In the deeply rifted mountain terrain the companies became dispersed. Gaps were formed in the front and through these the enemy infiltrated. Some measure of a consecutive front line was maintained by small assault parties. But it became extremely difficult to maintain control. Naval gunfire continues to cause heavy casualties.

*   *   *   *   *

The British had been forced out of Battipaglia with heavy losses. In the north, the Rangers and the Commandos faced increasing resistance from the Hermann Goering Division. And in the south, the American Corps had still not captured the dominating high ground above Paestum. The gap between the British and American sectors was still not closed and the Germans were reinforcing fast.

CHAPTER X

D-DAY PLUS TWO

11th September, 1943

"OUR forces have captured Salerno south of Naples. They have beaten off several counter-attacks and taken some hundreds of German prisoners-of-war, and are advancing steadily inland.

"It seems that in the early phases of the landing the British troops met little resistance, but later the enemy attacked strongly and often and used tanks. The Americans had hard fighting all the way. The beaches they landed on were strongly defended and taken only after a fierce struggle."

Thus the *BBC* kept the people at home informed of the way they liked to think the battle was going for the armies on the Italian mainland.

* * * * *

The German attack down the Sele-Calore corridor, which had been warming up during the night, struck with fresh vigour at dawn, hitting the 179th *RCT* from several directions. The enemy had been able to observe the unit's advance during the night; in a wide flanking movement, they now came in from the rear as well as frontally. Colonel Hutchins called his supporting tanks and tank destroyers to learn that they had fallen behind and were not available. At first the Americans doggedly tried to continue their advance onto the high ground; they were well past Persano, moving up the Tenuta di Persano road. The company that had captured the bluffs overlooking Ponte Sele was still there, although unable to go ahead. Fresh German troops well supported with artillery and tanks, pressed forward. By the late afternoon the 179th *RCT* had been pushed back from many positions and was in dire straits; ammunition was almost exhausted, with most of the artillery batteries down to their final reserve of five rounds per gun. Brigadier-General Raymond S. McLain personally ran a gauntlet of fire, bringing up a much-needed truckload of ammunition. The infantry was suffering from lack of water as, during the approach march in the heat of the night before, they had been allowed to drink from their water-bottles which it had been impossible to replenish.

Staff-Sergeant Warren Pingleton of 179th with his platoon was cornered in a gully. He ordered covering fire and most of the group escaped, leaving him and three men behind the lines. For four days he remained hidden, moving only at night; when they finally returned, he was able to give valuable information regarding enemy positions and strength. For this action he was awarded an immediate field commission.

Many of these young Americans, fresh to war, were horrified by the conditions in which many German troops lived. Nearly every position they captured was in a mess, personal hygiene being almost non-existent. In the words of one *GI*:

"There was shit all over the place and German soldiers had wallets full of pornographic photographs."

Corporal Charles F. Reynolds, of the 160th Field Battery, moved off just after midnight with Lieutenant Fourte on a jeep reconnaissance patrol, seeking fresh positions. Under constant gun-fire, having picked a new battery site not far from the Sele bridge, they returned to lead the guns forward. By mid-morning the *US* engineers had repaired the bridge with wooden beams, enabling the guns to cross to a large house, which stood battered and almost deserted. Civilians hiding in the cellars reported that the Wehrmacht still occupied some nearby woods. Only three guns having arrived, Reynolds was sent to find the remainder. As he left the house, German Spandaus opened up on him and a bullet smashed his trigger finger when he attempted to fire his carbine; disregarding the wound, he returned the fire and killed an enemy soldier at 75 yards' range. Reynolds was soon hit again in the side, yet kept urging his men on; they crawled a hundred yards and then dashed across a fire-swept road. Germans seemed to be all round them. They rushed a small house, to find it occupied by frightened civilians and equally frightened Italian soldiers, who tended Reynolds' wounds. Shortly afterwards he was evacuated to a regimental aid post, where the thirty casualties were convinced that the battle had been lost and they were on the point of being captured. Rumours flew fast and furious as men came and went, but many proved to be true.

By the end of the day one column of 179th was completely surrounded, its perimeter getting shorter and shorter. Ammunition was very low and wounded who could not be evacuated were often hit again as they lay on stretchers in the open.

Allied reports since the battle have always claimed that it was by pure chance that the Germans struck down the Sele–Calore gap at the weakest point. But most German accounts have recorded that recce patrols had easily established this gap on the 10th and that the subsequent assault was planned.

The first task of the 191st Medium Tank Battalion of the 45th Division, which had landed in the morning, had been to subdue the German garrison occupying a tobacco factory near the banks of the Sele. Named the *Tabacchificio Fiocche*, it consisted of five large buildings on three sides of a square; commanding the Grataglia, it could hold all the crossings along the rivers Sele and Calore as far as Altavilla. The factory was a vital part of the enemy defensive system and they were determined to hang on to it.

Unwisely this tank unit, completely unaware of enemy strength, went ahead of its infantry. 'B' Company under Captain Donald May advanced in massed formation, fighting its way through the front screen. The opposition, well concealed in phoney haystacks, ditches and houses, appeared to give up after initial resistance. In fact the Germans were leading them on into the clear ground near the factory; as the tanks emerged, guns of very heavy calibre opened up at short range; within seconds seven *US* tanks were blazing. The survivors withdrew some distance to await the arrival of the infantry, but found that by now they had not the strength to capture the *Tabacchificio*.

Part of the battalion under Lieutenant-Colonel Preston Murphy, avoiding the factory, swept north towards Bivio. They reached a crossroads one mile north of the village, where they set up a strongly-defended road block. But at midnight the factory was still in enemy hands and the situation on the Allied side very confused.

The 36th Division had a better day and made limited advances. The 1st Battalion 142nd *RCT* entered Altavilla at noon to the accompaniment of enthusiastic Italian cheers, and spread itself out on the high ground to include Hill 424. They were told that only a few hours before the town had been occupied by 700 Germans. All was deceptively quiet.

*   *   *   *   *

In the north, in the mountains to the west of the Vietri defile, Colonel Darby's Rangers were hitting increasing resistance, where their thrusts towards Naples had started worrying the enemy. With the capture of Monte Pendolo, the Rangers were much too thin on the ground. Darby asked for urgent reinforcements, and

Clark responded by sending several assault craft loaded with the
1st Battalion 143rd *RCT* supported by artillery and tanks. Taken
from the 36th Division, they were landed at Maiori to strengthen
the Rangers' positions overlooking the vital passes.

Captain Herbert Scheftel, *USAF*, controller in 64th Wing of the
12th Technical Air Command, was responsible for radar locating
units, which had to be placed so as to spot German aircraft taking
off from Naples airports. It was realised soon after landing that the
hills surrounding Salerno made it quite impossible for these units
to operate efficiently. As a result, during the first few days they were
unable to give to our fighters early warning of enemy air attacks.

On this morning Scheftel set off in a jeep with two other officers
to see if it was possible to establish these units in the high ground
where the Rangers were fighting.

At every bridge and river crossing the party was machine-gunned
or shelled; at one bridge in the British sector, which was defended
by a troop of Bofors guns, they were stopped by a sentry, who
warned them that the bridge was under heavy fire. A column of
vehicles formed, awaiting the opportunity to cross. Scheftel started
chatting with several British gunners, who were making bets as to
which vehicles would be hit crossing the bridge; he was horrified
to learn that the betting lay heavily against his own jeep. Nervously, they set off with engine roaring and tyres screaming, but
in spite of several near misses they arrived on the other side in one
piece.

At the Rangers' Headquarters near Venafro they enquired the
exact location of the forward units, to be told by Colonel Darby
in a pleasant manner:

"At this moment I haven't the faintest idea, you'd better go
and find out for yourselves."

They soon discovered them in a small hill town north-east of
Amalfi. The area was under command of a Ranger sergeant, who
had locked up the mayor and the Chief of Police in the local gaol.
The sergeant, delighted to have visitors from the Air Force, offered
them a variety of gifts and entertainment, ranging from a huge
Mercedes saloon car to the company of the belles of the town.
Scheftel and his brother officers decided there was not much future
in the area for themselves or for their radar sets and retired to
Amalfi on the coast.

The inhabitants of this pleasant seaside resort seemed almost
unaware of the war raging round them and the wealthy Italians
were still leading lives of luxury. The Air Force officers were advised

to stay in the best hotel, where they spent the night between clean sheets and at dinner were served by a head waiter, immaculate and attentive to all their needs. They even sent back one of the courses as not being properly prepared, and duly received the abject apologies of the chef!

Airfield construction units of both armies had started building fighter strips on D-Day, often under severe battle conditions. Owing to enemy counter-attacks, a half-finished strip in the American sector near the Sele had to be abandoned, but on the 11th they were able to return and finish it. British Royal Engineers built two other strips, one near the Tusciano and another close by the River Asa. As they were all, however, under enemy observation and direct line of fire from the guns in the hills, they were of little use to the air forces for the first few days, except for emergency landings. This was a particularly hazardous operation for pilots. Anti-aircraft units of the 36th Division, who had been warned by Major-General Fred Walker to be particularly alert for German para-trooper and Luftwaffe attacks, took his warning so seriously that at least one British fighter plane out of fuel was shot down by the gunners, as he tried to come in to land.

In operation it was found that the Sicily-based Spitfires, with long-range tanks, were capable of remaining over the bridgehead for at least thirty minutes. This led to some speculation by the Air Force that it would have been possible for the assault to have been launched in the Gulf of Gaeta, north of the narrow passes and closer to Naples.

*   *   *   *   *

General Dawley, who had finally moved his headquarters ashore, was by this time getting a truer picture of the position. His reports caused the Army Commander to order the move of a reserve of the 2nd Battalion 143rd Infantry to provide a defence between the Sele and Calore. General McCreery was also told to reduce the area assigned to the British and concentrate his forces.

General Dawley called his two divisional commanders to a conference at Corps *HQ.* In view of subsequent events, including the near-annihilation of American forces in the Gap, it is interesting to read Major-General Fred Walker's account of this meeting:

> Major-General Troy Middleton, *CG,* 45th Division, was present. He arrived before I did. He heard the instructions. When General Dawley indicated the front line of the area the battalion (2nd Battalion 143rd Infantry) was to occupy and stated that the right flank of

the 45th Division would be on the left of this battalion, across the Sele. General Middleton made no comment. I presumed that he and Dawley had discussed the instructions prior to my arrival. I had served previously with Middleton when we were both instructors in the tactical section at the Infantry School. I had also served with him on other occasions and I had a very high regard for his ability as a soldier. I had met Dawley in the Philippines in 1913, where we were associated together on field manœuvres; he in the artillery, I in the infantry. I had been associated with him since on several occasions. I also had a very high regard for his ability. When Dawley finished his instructions and Middleton did not make any comment, I assumed that the information I had been given regarding the 45th Division was authentic and reliable, and passed it on to the battalion commander.

The right flank of the 45th Division was two and a half miles to the south-east of the point indicated to me. The result of all this was the disaster the next day. I know now and I knew then that the best of generals are sometimes misinformed. I should have been more cautious and should have had my staff ascertain the location of the 45th Division. All three of us were equally to blame for this unfortunate misunderstanding of the facts; Middleton and Dawley for passing on unverified information; and I, for not having it checked.

*　　*　　*　　*　　*

In the British sector, a few minutes after midnight, a platoon of the 9th Royal Fusiliers, hearing the sound of wheels coming up a small lane, stood to anticipating a night attack. The men crouched low in their trenches and waited their fire orders. It was a bright moonlit night and observation was good, when round the bend in the lane, just as trigger fingers were taking up the pressure, they saw two men between the shafts of a donkey cart struggling along with others pushing from behind. The regimental quartermaster sergeant and his cooks had brought them a hot meal; without transport, they had requisitioned the cart from an abandoned farm stable. In vain they had searched for a donkey or even a cow to pull it along, and eventually two 'volunteers' were ordered into harness. They were not amused when they learned that their efforts had almost been greeted with machine-gun bullets.

*　　*　　*　　*　　*

Luftwaffe activity during the night 10th/11th September and during the day was the heaviest yet. Over a hundred and twenty planes put in a determined effort on the assembled shipping, and six hundred Allied fighters fought them off through daylight. Many troops, strafed by marauding German planes, were complaining bitterly about the lack of Allied fighter cover. Yet in fact the Air Force was doing a magnificent job further north, intercepting aircraft before they ever reached the bridgehead. But some planes did get through and the enemy were able to score the first victory with their new flying bomb.

General Mark Clark, who still had his headquarters aboard the *Ancon*, owing to the lack of space ashore for an Army headquarters, was standing on the bridge with Admiral Hewitt prior to going ashore, when they heard a tremendous screaming roar indicating the approach of one of these weapons. Absolutely convinced that their ship was the target, they waited resignedly for the explosion. The bomb, however, shot very low overhead and hit *USS Savannah*, a cruiser which had just passed them two hundred yards to the port side. The bomb struck forward of her bridge with a fantastic crash, went through the deck and exploded below, sending roaring flames fifty feet into the air and causing hundreds of deaths in the packed decks. Tugs rushed to her aid and she had to be eventually towed to Malta. Four sailors were trapped in the auxiliary radio room, completely surrounded by water which was only kept out by the water-tight doors. One small pipe led to fresh air, down which food and liquid were passed to them, together with encouraging words. Only their ingenuity kept them alive for four days, until the water was pumped away and they were released.

At 0800 hours *HMS Barndale*, a boom defence vessel, accompanied by the tug *Favourite* and a small coaster, under command of Lieutenant R. L. Jones, *RNR*, steamed into Salerno port in the hope of opening it to get supplies moving more rapidly ashore. A German reconnaissance lieutenant in the hills above the harbour was warned of the approach of these vessels by a lookout. He instantly alerted an artillery regiment to stand by, and allowed *HMS Barndale* to steam right into the port before giving the fire order. The barrage was so effective that Lieutenant Jones, quite rightly, decided it was useless to try and operate the port under these conditions and, having reported to his superiors, was ordered to retire.

Out in the bay lookouts gazing seawards were astonished to see the conning-tower of a submarine emerge dripping from the waves. It proved to be the Italian *Nichel* on her way to Malta in compliance with the armistice terms. Its Commanding Officer, taken aboard the *Ancon*, revealed that he had not fired a torpedo for five weeks; yet, shortly after receiving the armistice instructions, he had seen through his periscope the fantastic sight of the Allied convoy approaching Salerno.

"*Mamma mia*," he exclaimed. "What a temptation it was!"

He asked permission to proceed on his way, but was refused by the Navy, who thought his chances of getting through to Malta unescorted pretty slight. The generous American sailors presented the captain with a large tinned ham; in return, a negro steward was given a small fluffy puppy, one of a litter born aboard the submarine. *Nichel* was tied up alongside a battleship for several days and eventually escorted to Malta.

The Navy were getting slightly worried after a small attack by E-Boats in the early hours of the morning. The American destroyer *Rowan* had sighted a torpedo track about a hundred feet off her starboard beam, and running down the trail with her radar beam, contacted a surface target about 6,000 yards in a north-westerly direction. Commander Ford, the captain, immediately increased speed to twenty-seven knots and gave chase. At 4,800 yards he opened up with the forward 5-inch guns, but the target, which proved to be two E-Boats, rapidly outdistanced them. *Rowan* turned back to rejoin the convoy, but at once sighted another torpedo wake and made a fresh contact at 200 yards. Rapidly changing course, she shot off in another direction, coming into torpedo range at about 2,000 yards. Expecting an attack, the captain ordered the helmsman full right rudder; the vessel was slow in responding and she was struck amidships in the middle of her turn. A tremendous explosion shook the ship from stem to stern; she sank within forty seconds. Rescue ships only managed to save 71 members of the crew out of a complement of 202.

This action was carried out on the personal initiative of three E-Boats who had been sweeping the area. The commander later reported to German headquarters that he had sunk a 10,000-ton cargo ship, evidently mistaking the destroyer for a merchant vessel.

At 1000 hours Admiral Sir Philip Vian from his flagship sent a signal to Admiral Hewitt couched in the following terms: *My bolt will be shot this evening, probably earlier.* He requested permission to retire to Augusta for refuelling. Hewitt was at this time in conference with General House of the *USAF*, preparing a protest to the North-West African Air Force over the reduction of fighter coverage. The North African Tactical Air Force had somehow gained the impression that Luftwaffe activity in the area was slighter than had been anticipated and were anxious to switch planes to more profitable targets inland. They did not know about *Savannah* having been hit, about the increasing danger from the guided bombs, or of the impending departure of the Fleet Air Arm. Hewitt sent a strongly-worded urgent radio message of protest; he was promised the return of one P-38 Squadron, with a request for evidence that the planes were really needed. After this Hewitt contacted Vian:

Air situation here critical. Status of the airfields ashore uncertain. Can your carrier force remain on station and furnish early morning coverage tomorrow?

Vian typically replied at once: *Yes, certainly. Shall just be able to make Palermo.*

Already in some senior circles, particularly amongst Army officers, there were pessimistic thoughts about the outcome of the battle. Yet worse was still to come. Quentin Reynolds, the American correspondent, recorded at the time that some senior officers and correspondents were talking in terms of another Gallipoli!

* * * * *

On land in the X Corps sector the troops were manfully trying to push ahead, but were successful only in a few places.

Lieutenant-Colonel John Whitfield, with the 2/5th Queen's, was in position on the railway to the left of Montecorvino airfield, but they were blocked in every move they made by enemy artillery barrages. Whitfield, with a badly battered battalion, appreciated the seriousness of the situation and saw in the wondering eyes of his troops doubts beginning to form about the whole operation. During the day, doubling from platoon to platoon in the thick of shell-fire, he made thirty-six speeches to all the men in the unit. He told them the truth, but demanded them to give of their utmost:

"I have come along to speak to you all in order that there may be no doubt in your minds as to the gravity of the situation. We hold the airfield, which the enemy badly needs. I am certain he will attack tonight, tomorrow, or the next day. It is a position which I would much rather defend than attack. If the enemy does attack, it is our duty to ensure that he only gains a foothold over your dead bodies and mine. I have complete confidence in every one of you."

In some places he received cheers; in others, a bewildered silence as men thought: It must be bloody serious for the old man to come round like this. His words were to produce a dividend, however, because although they were attacked and shelled consistently during the next ten days, this battered battalion stayed put and never gave an inch. Together with the 2/6th and 2/7th Queen's, the Brigade stuck it out, and this sector was to remain one of the few stable areas in the coming ebb and flow of battle. The troops dug deeper trenches, improved their communications and every night in the maze of lanes, fields, vineyards and orchards played hide-and-seek with enemy patrols.

The 2/6th Battalion advanced during this day about 3,000 yards to Hill 210 in the centre of the brigade front. They moved across the open green fields, expecting at any moment to be shelled, but strangely the German gunners must have been paying attention to other zones, for the Queen's remained untouched and arrived on the hill without opposition. They ambled along in the sun, sweating under their loads, picking black grapes as they passed the vines. Sergeant Fred Peart, a section commander, enjoyed his fill of fruit to discover within a few hours that he and many others had what was popularly known as "the back-door trot"; for the next few days they found themselves digging plenty of little holes all over the place and having to face shell fire with their trousers down.

The main action that day for them was when the American pilot of a Lightning zoomed down out of the sky and calmly machine-gunned them as they were digging trenches to the accompaniment of shouted oaths: "Trigger-happy bloody Yanks!"

The Guards Brigade, the Fusiliers and the Ox and Bucks were to have another day of heavy combat with an eventual retreat and consolidation of the line.

The Grenadiers again went into the attack at Battipaglia, which had been lost the day before, edging their way step by step, inch by inch, along the littered roads and through the smashed houses and alleyways. They fought magnificently, determined to succeed, but once again the overwhelming weight of armour and infantry crushed them. It looked as if the line would be broken by sheer weight of numbers. The defending Germans consisted of a parachute regiment, supported by tanks of the 16th Panzer Division. These were the men who had captured Battipaglia on the previous day and on this morning at 1100 hours they launched the attacks which forced the Grenadier Guards back towards Belvedere. The Cold-stream Guards were ready to rush in; but after giving some ground, the Grenadiers stood firm south of Battipaglia.

To the Grenadiers' left were the Scots Guards. During the evening a returning patrol reported that the Battipaglia Tobacco Factory appeared deserted. Plans were made for an immediate occupation, with the added insurance of an artillery barrage in case the information was wrong. They went forward in bright moon-light at 2130 hours; the leading platoons had climbed the wire and were inside the Factory before German tanks appeared. 'C'

Company found itself in the middle of enemy positions, fighting in and out of the buildings, whilst the Germans confused the situation even more by broadcasting misleading instructions in English. Voices were shouting out: "All right over here!" and "This way, men!" Those Scots Guardsmen who unwarily obeyed the instructions were either killed or captured. The Panzers finally overran them and most of the company was taken prisoner.

On the right flank of the British sector south of Battipaglia, the two battalions of the Royal Fusiliers and the 6th Ox and Bucks lining a railway, had initially a moderately quiet day, but in the early evening they were confronted with a heavy tank-infantry assault. The 8th Royal Fusiliers, which took the brunt, had been cut up into small packets by 2000 hours. Stragglers were streaming back in the direction of the sea. Lance-Corporal Tom Whittaker was in an observation post at the top of a farmhouse tower, reporting enemy movements on his front, and not too happy about all the shells coming his way. He saw the forward units break and run towards him in a panic; no one could get control. A motorcycle went past the farm laden with eight men, all shouting: "Tanks are coming."

Whittaker could see this for himself and hastily climbed down to get a lift on another motorcycle. Many of these troops got back almost to the beach, but were stopped at brigade headquarters by officers and by *RSM* George Hollings and Provost Sergeant Jack Ward, who drew their pistols and made it quite plain that this was as far as anyone was going. A Guards' officer, horrified by the event, was actually crying in frustration that such things could happen.

Hollings was not in the best of tempers. He had just returned from an ammunition dump, where he had been sent to obtain supplies of 3-inch mortar bombs. On arrival at the depot not far from the beaches he was told by an *NCO* that, as the organisation was not yet complete, no issues of ammunition could be made.

Hollings demanded to see the depot commander, who greeted him brusquely: "Who are you and what do you want?"

Again Hollings explained and received the same reply, with the added instruction that ammunition indents were to be made through divisional headquarters.

The *RSM* was indignant: "If you don't give me the bloody ammunition, we'll all be back in the sea very shortly, and your precious shells and bullets will be in German hands."

He got his supplies, but drove back to battalion to be faced by a new and difficult situation.

Fusilier D. Needham was with a forward company during the evening when the attack developed.

The Germans broke through; half-tracks and tanks appeared just before Battalion *HQ*. Captain Clarke ordered a withdrawal across a field towards the wood to the beach—I thought at this time how bad things were going. I noticed several wounded left where they fell. We heard tanks on one side and in front of us and heavy firing, and it seemed that the Americans had withdrawn before us.

Under Lieutenant Goldstone we occupied a ditch two feet deep in water and opened fire with rifles and machine-guns on German infantry in some woods. At this stage Sergeant Brown of the Signals pointed out that the ditch farther along was dry, but we were ordered to stay where we were. It was now getting very dark and completely disorganised fighting was taking place.

At this stage, Lieutenant Goldstone decided to withdraw towards the beach and we moved off. As we started, the shelling increased and a tank crossed our front, firing at us. Quickly we began to run towards the rear, with shells and bullets coming around—I remember thinking of the strange whisper the bullets made as they went by. Suddenly, I heard a loud crack and something hit me. I was flung on my face; Colour Sergeant Rye shouted to me to get up and helped me. We eventually reached some high ground, where we were re-formed. Slowly, things began to be sorted out and contact was made with other companies . . .

In every unit officers lectured their troops and gave pep talks to try to raise the morale.

Orders were issued from divisional and brigade headquarters that every possible man was to be put into the line to stop the enemy reaching the beaches. Cooks, clerks and storemen got their rarely used weapons out of their trucks and hastily dug in, commanded by Administrative *NCO*s. A group of American Airfield engineers in the same area refused when ordered to join the battle, saying they were there to build an airstrip. Told that the ground they wanted was still in enemy hands, they again declined to move. A Royal Fusilier *NCO* then drew a pistol and, walking up to the senior sergeant, offered them the choice of taking a chance in the fighting or being shot where they were. Choosing the former, the Americans went into action.

Another American, who had been sent over from VI Corps on liaison duties, was near battalion headquarters trying to operate a vast radio set that stubbornly refused to emit a sound. Hollings chatted with him.

"Are your chaps good fighters?" he asked.

The American frankly admitted: "They might fight, they might run away—I sure don't know."

Offered some thick sugary tea, the American took one sip of the sergeant-major's brew and commented: "Gee, hot ice cream!"

Morale was certainly very low at this period. During the night troops in a section position saw armed figures coming towards them through the trees of an orchard. Before a shot was fired, several men had risen from their trenches and gone forward with their hands up to be greeted by an unmistakable Transatlantic voice: "O.K., bud, we've come over to find what it's all about."

*   *   *   *   *

North of Salerno and Vietri, German attacks with fresh units from the Naples area were gradually increasing momentum and the 46th Division and the Commandos were hard at it all day resisting under very difficult conditions.

The Commando Brigade, with its light equipment, had been very badly mauled; General Hawkesworth decided to relieve them to give them the chance of a rest. The 6th Lincolns, the 2/4th King's Own Yorkshire Light Infantry and the 6th York and Lancs were sent up to take over.

Colonel Kendrew took his battalion to the top of Commando Hill, where he had been told to relieve some Army Commandos. When they arrived they found only dead troops. It was a grim sight that met these men's eyes. The stark brown rocky hill was covered with British and German dead and mounds of abandoned and wrecked equipment. Many of the bodies were burning from a barrage of phosphorus bombs that had been poured on to the slopes and the smell of baking flesh and acrid phosphorus clung to the ground and to their clothing. Kendrew decided to defend the hill from the slopes and the flanks and not from the peak, which he wisely recognised might be heroic but would be too costly in lives.

The 5th Battalion Foresters, who on the previous evening had captured Taborre on the left side of the Sanseverino road, due north of Salerno, were pushed off in the early morning and fell back towards Ponte Fratte, where they took up fresh positions on either side of the main road. In the afternoon, as they prepared to move out for a new attack on Taborre, the Germans reacted with another assault which drove them off the Fratte bridge. Two companies of the Leicesters went in to help, but, having lost their way, were cut off by an enemy thrust. They held out for three days behind the lines, until they were eventually able to break through. As they approached the Allied lines they were aghast as they realised that the shells landing amongst them, killing and wounding, were coming from a field regiment of the Royal Artillery, which had mistaken them for the enemy.

The Commandos, who pulled out, had hardly got back into Vietri, when they were told that the Lincolns and *KOYLI*s had been overrun. They wearily turned about and went back to the hills. It was only in places that the Germans had broken through, but the situation was extremely dangerous, with small pockets of men cut off and well-armed hostile groups shooting up the rear areas.

The Commandos rushed in. Major John Edwards, having taken over the Royal Marine Commando, led one attack towards the left flank, where the Molina Pass itself was being threatened. In a few hours the situation was clarified and the Germans were sent scuttling away, leaving many dead behind. A Number 2 Army Commando force, led by Captain the Duke of Wellington on the right flank, slowly pushed the Germans back, with the help of a field regiment of 25-pounders firing shells just ahead of the advancing men. The counter-attack succeeded, the Commandos recaptured all their original positions, but in the action the Duke of Wellington was killed and the troops were unable to find his body.

A German account of this action by the 2nd Parachute Battalion of the Hermann Goering Division, written by Paul Löw, records: *What they accomplished will rank with the best performances of the war.*

The German attack was led by Captain Fitz, who wore the Knight's Cross of the Iron Cross and the Gold Wound Badge. He had already been wounded seven times on almost every European battlefield and was a legend amongst his men.

They attacked from the area of Cava de' Tirreni with the object of capturing the village of Dragonea, just north of Vietri, which it overlooked. After four days without sleep under an uninterrupted bombardment from land, sea and air, the Germans were fatigued and shaken. Yet, given the order for a counter-attack and rallied by Fitz, they bravely shook the lethargy from their limbs and, screaming war cries, swept down through a fury of mortar and machine-gun fire into the positions held by the *KOYLI*s and the Lincolns.

Fitz was wounded in the thigh from a mortar fragment as he ran at the head of a company. Cursing, he ordered a medical orderly to wrap a shell dressing around his leg and then, despite the intense pain, continued to run ahead. His example inspired all. The enthusiasm spread to an *NCO*, who increased his pace and, firing a sub-machine-gun from the hip, reloaded fresh magazines of ammunition as he ran. Many of the British County troops staggered from their trenches hands in the air and the Germans occupied the village, shooting at the retreating Englishmen as they retired down the hillside.

The German report claims that Dragonea was taken and held, preventing the Allied advance up through the La Molina Pass. No mention is made of its subsequent recapture by the Commandos.

That morning a group of war correspondents decided to visit Commando Brigade headquarters. On arrival in the middle of a mortar 'stonk', they were greeted with the astonishing statement that the brigadier was having his morning bath. Laycock, not a bit put out, cheerfully called them into his bathroom and answered their questions as he continued with his ablutions.

There was some criticism of the apparently casual manner in which the staff of the Commando Brigade went about their duties. People were envious of their villa quarters, their food, their wines, and the general standard of living. There was even in the mess a resident barber, who liberally sprayed a particularly violent-smelling hair lotion on his customers! But the criticism was ill founded. "Why be uncomfortable when you need not be?" was their reply. "Any *BF* can live rough."

The troops worshipped their commander and knew they could rely on him whatever happened.

* * * * *

Salerno town, which had been a hunting ground for parties of both sides since the landing, was officially occupied on the 11th. The Port of Salerno gave its name to the battle, but owing to the inability of the Navy to use the port, the town itself played very little part in subsequent operations. Only a few civilians remained in the shell-torn houses; as a convoy of vehicles drove into the main square, some of them gathered to see what the *Inglesi* and *Americani* were like. The Italians were haggard and unshaven, and their women had given up bothering about appearances. Tired and hungry, all they hoped for was food, drink and peace.

The convoy drove along the Via Roma past the deserted shops and shuttered windows, bumping over rubble and avoiding shell pits. In command as Allied Military Governor was Colonel Thomas

Aloysius Lane, a tall strong Irish-American born in Washington, with a Catholic background. His *ADC*, Captain Riola, was an Italo-American whose forebears had emigrated from Southern Italy.

The vehicles stopped and the Americans started questioning the inhabitants.

"Where is the Mayor?" asked Colonel Lane.

With shrugs of shoulders and outspread hands, he was told: "Who knows!"

To questions about the police chief and the town clerk he received the same uninformative reply.

"There is no one in authority left in Salerno," said a short, unshaven man.

"Surely," suggested Captain Riola, "there must be some priests?"

"Oh yes!" came a chorus. "All the priests are still here."

"Then fetch one to me."

At the church of the Annunziata a group of self-appointed messengers found Don Aniello Vicinanza and hustled him to the Military Governor. Colonel Lane, on greeting him, went down on his knees to receive the blessing and then gave the priest a warm handshake. This act impressed the Italians, who immediately dropped their reserve and gathered closer.

Colonel Lane and his staff took over the Town Hall, whilst the rest of the governmental party of clerks, medical officers, public health officials, security police and traffic controllers were soon installed in offices all over Salerno.

A few hours later the Governor paid a formal call upon Monsignor Monterisi, the Archbishop of Salerno, who requested that Allied troops should be kept under control and prevented from looting and raping. Colonel Lane assured him that this would be done. The archbishop, impressed by the sincerity of the party, took them to visit the tomb of Pope San Gregorio VII in the cathedral, where the colonel and some of the soldiers knelt in prayer. As he said goodbye to the Archbishop, Lane told him:

"Hildebrand defeated the German Emperor. He will help us too to chase the Germans from Salerno and Italy."

At the Sanatorium, Arturo Carucci found his hospital surrounded by the British and the parklands dotted with narrow slit trenches and mortar pits. In small stone out-buildings, petrol cookers roared as the cooks in khaki prepared hot meals for the troops; telephone wires festooned the lower branches of trees and drooped from wall to wall. A British Major had asked permission of Carucci for his soldiers to draw water from a tap near the gatekeeper's office; reiterating once more his appeal for the sanctuary of the hospital to be recognised, the chaplain had agreed.

The Sanatorium was now placed in a temporary no-man's-land, with German troops to the north and the British west and south. Occasional shells, falling short from both sides, spattered the old stone walls and the inmates were kept busy boarding up windows and replacing red pottery tiles that slid in time to the vibrations. Some of the staff, unknown to Carucci, were trading fresh eggs and bottles of local red wine with the troops in return for cigarettes and tins of bully beef.

Remaining in the buildings were only about fifty patients, who were too ill to go to the damp and musty tunnel. But the journeys from the kitchens to the refuge were becoming more hazardous hour by hour. The nuns, who had started cooking huge coppers full of vegetable and meat stews, preparing sufficient food for several days, scurried in between the artillery barrages to and fro, placing the stores in the underground cavern. It was the last day of comparative peace for these people; they did not know that within twenty-four hours the area would become a holocaust of fire and the scene of violent hand-to-hand bayonet fighting between the opposing armies.

* * * * *

By the evening the 46th Division had carved out a more orderly perimeter and the situation seemed easier. North of Vietri, blocking the Molina Pass at the head of the Vietri defile, were the Commandos; then came the 138th Brigade, followed by the 139th Brigade and the 128th Brigade. General Hawkesworth reported that the situation was in hand and the troops capable of preventing a break-through.

Aboard the *Ancon* a message from General Alexander had been received, informing Clark for the first time that the American 82nd Airborne Division had not been dropped on Rome and was therefore available for use at Salerno. Alexander's cable read: *Use the 82nd in any manner you deem advisable. All combatant elements of 82nd are now concentrated on Sicilian airfields.*

Clark's first decision was to drop the whole division near Avellino on the 13th, in order to strike and hamper the enemy in his rear areas. Subsequent events were to change his plan, but these airborne troops were to supply invaluable help in the days to come.

Worrying reports were received during the day by Admiral Hewitt's staff that air interceptions of Luftwaffe messages indicated that a particular ship had been chosen for a heavy air attack that night. They decided that the ship in question was undoubtedly the *Ancon* and consequently at 1930 hours she upped anchor and at twelve knots, escorted by two destroyers, set sail on a zigzag course, remaining at sea all night. This necessitated the transfer of fighter direction units to other ships; control from the *Ancon* was virtually impossible, as she was too far out to sea. At 0235 hours the Luftwaffe attack came in; monitor operators listened to puzzled German pilots asking each other the whereabouts of the headquarters vessel. A store ship was, however, hit by several bombs.

British officers expressed themselves volubly on this 'bug-out' and were horrified by the decision to remove such an important *HQ* from the scene of operations.

The optimistic planners had forecast that by the end of this day Naples would have been captured; as it was, the 5th Army was still in a small and comparatively tightly packed beachhead with no immediate prospect of advancing. There was still a gap between the two sectors.

By the end of the third day of the battle, Allied maps showed that the 5th Army's beachhead at its deepest point was ten miles inland whilst in the north it thinned down to about one mile. Still optimistic, General Clark reported to Alexander that he would soon be in a position to advance through the passes to Naples.

CHAPTER XI

D-DAY PLUS THREE

12th September, 1943

EVEN the *BBC* on 12th September were a bit uncertain how the fighting was going and limited their references in the war communiqué to the following:

"The heaviest fighting in Italy is going on at Salerno, but the 5th Army is advancing steadily.

"Twelve Lightnings met 25 Me-109's and shot down five without loss."

That was about the only success of the day that could be reported and the mention of a "steady advance" was hardly in accordance with the facts.

*   *   *   *   *

In reality, 12th September saw the start of very strong German attacks at all points and was a day of decision, particularly for General Mark Clark. Having moved his headquarters ashore that morning into the American sector, he immediately altered a staff plan for the use of a large mansion in fairly habitable condition but which, in his own words, "stuck up like a sore thumb" inviting shells, and decided to remain in his operational caravan in a small wood not far from Paestum. He spent the day roaming the dusty roads in his jeep, seeing for himself and consulting with commanders at all levels. He learned only of setbacks and weaknesses all along the line.

Field-Marshal Albert Kesselring was feeling very content; he was confident that with the reinforcements reaching the Salerno area he would be able to push the 5th Army back into the sea before he was outflanked by Montgomery's 8th Army, which was making only very slow progress up from the south.

Elements of the Hermann Goering Division were in the line facing the British; units of the 15th Panzer Grenadier Division were also arriving. Having broken contact in the south, the 26th Panzer and 29th Panzer Grenadier Division moved into opposition against the American VI Corps.

At this time Montgomery was issuing communiqués reporting his troops in hot pursuit of the Germans. General Alexander was not convinced and, having sent one "Hurry up" message to Monty on the 10th without result, he despatched General A. A. Richardson, his Chief of Staff, to 8th Army headquarters on the 12th to explain the full urgency of the situation. By now Kesselring had a total of six hundred tanks and many mobile guns at his disposal, whilst the Allies were powerless to get reinforcements from North Africa at the same speed.

As far as the 46th Division was concerned in the north the battle concentrated in three main areas: the Vietri defile, which was the main route to Naples; the Sanseverino road; and round the Laughing Hill (nicknamed by the troops Hospital Hill) and White Cross Hill—both of which covered the likely starting points of a German counter-offensive.

At Laughing Hill the Durham Light Infantry were spread all round the zone and on some of the adjacent hills, but there is no doubt that their punctiliousness in observing the neutrality of the hospital was to their disadvantage. The stone building was an admirable observation point. Although decorated with huge red crosses on the walls and the roof, it could not be ignored for very much longer. Baker Company during the night had pushed forward into the vineyards to the north of the Sanatorium, but a dawn counter-attack drove them back a few hundred yards; they fought a good withdrawal through the houses that lined the narrow road, causing numerous casualties amongst the Germans. The close country of orchards and vineyards was of great help to the numerous snipers of both sides, who could frequently change positions in the confused fighting that followed throughout the hours of daylight. In the afternoon two companies of the 2/4th Battalion *KOYLI* moved through the *DLI* to take some high ground ahead, from which enemy fire dominated the area. Backed by heavy artillery, the *KOYLI* managed to get to the objectives, but were pinned down and unable to exploit any further. To add to the discomfort of these North Countrymen, an enemy machine-gun post was slipped between their lines to be mounted on top of one of the hospital buildings, from where it covered all approaches.

Carucci and his staff, still trusting that God would deliver them from the battle, started the day—a Sunday—with the customary celebration of Mass in the battered chapel. On emerging from the building, the first sight to meet the chaplain's eyes was a heavily armed German sentry standing by the kitchen door. They looked at each other, but the German turned away, ignoring the padre's presence. Then, from the other side of the building, a message reached him that British troops were demanding water, whilst a group of Germans had raided the kitchen, locked the cook in a larder and were asking to see the Hospital Director. As Soffietti was absent, Lieutenant Gatti, by now in civilian clothes, decided to dress himself in a white gown and pretend to be the chief doctor. He was interviewed by an officer, who demanded to know if there were any Allied soldiers in the buildings. Gatti hotly denied that any troops were there, but the words died on his lips as a door opened and a nurse and two British Tommies emerged carrying water. The Germans raised their weapons and were about to fire, when the German officer ordered them to stop to avoid the possibility of wounding the nurse.

In the park two patients were approached by a group of Germans, who warned them it was unwise to remain there as a bombing attack was due. The patients rushed to the padre with the news, which was later confirmed by a message from the German commander to say that the bombing had been planned.

The battle for the no-man's-land continued in scattered skirmishes and furious barrages. Wounded of both armies were being brought in for treatment and it was with the utmost difficulty that the Italian doctors and nurses managed to keep each side unaware of the presence of the other. At 1800 hours a German battery commenced shelling the buildings. In a small room the Mother Superior and two nurses were tending a British soldier suffering from shell shock, screaming and crying in an effort to get up from his bed and rush aimlessly into the open. As the noise and the dust sent him nearly mad, the women had to use force to restrain him.

Carucci ordered everyone to the boiler-room in the basement, where the frightened people, thinking the end had come, begged for the absolution. In the gloom of the boiler-house, full of dust and fumes from the falling shells, they fell on their knees, resignedly waiting for the end. After some time the shelling lifted and moved away; it was decided to evacuate in small groups from the buildings to the tunnel. Fired on by Allied and German patrols, they had to crawl most of the way on hands and knees along terraces and ditches; by the time they reached the tunnel it was dark. Thousands of people had crammed themselves and their possessions into this underground shelter. The smell of humans mixed with animals was overpowering. An air of helpless hopelessness had overcome them, as few had any hopes of ever emerging alive. Men, women and children sat cheek by jowl or lay touching each other on the damp filthy soil. Adults and children relieved themselves, too frightened to go into the fresh air. Nuns, dishevelled and tired, tended to the needs of their tubercular patients with rapidly diminishing supplies of food and drink, whilst the screams and cries of the wounded and of hysterical women turned the place into a bedlam, which it was impossible to control.

North and east of Salerno small isolated British units fought independently against increasing Wehrmacht counter-attacks. At divisional headquarters confusion reigned.

A company of the Leicesters still being cut off and surrounded, a patrol from the 5th Foresters was sent out to relieve them. They ran into another patrol in British uniforms, but, having been led off their route, this turned out to be German; after the ensuing fight, only two Foresters returned to their lines.

*   *   *   *   *

Facing the Commandos, a Panzer Grenadier regiment was battered on a rocky hillside by the massive fire coming from several destroyers and a cruiser. Two brothers, Hans and Josef, the latter only sixteen years old, crouched in a trench surrounded with boulders they had piled around to increase protection. Josef was crying for their mother and sobbing uncontrollably as his elder brother tried to calm him. He knew sympathy was useless under the circumstances; finally, his tone hard and rough, he ordered the youth to be quiet:

"You are a man, no longer a child. Keep quiet! Soldiers are not frightened." He slapped him hard.

The young boy, his eyes full of hatred, grabbed his rifle and started firing furiously in the direction of the enemy. A minute later a shell landed in the trench, killing him outright; his brother, who to this day cannot forgive himself for his roughness, had both legs amputated.

The 56th Division, farther south, was strongly engaged all day. Atop Hill 210, south of the Tusciano, men of the 2/6th Queen's, who, still without opposition, had started the morning in bright sunshine, were consolidating their positions. Sergeant Peart and a companion had removed their gear and were washing and shaving in half a pint of precious water placed in a mess tin. In the middle of their toilet a mortar barrage descended on the trenches; with shaving soap still on their cheeks, they struggled into their equipment and peered from the trench, awaiting the expected attack. For half an hour bombs rained on them, preventing any communication with the rest of the platoon.

When the bombs stopped, Sergeant Peart climbed from the dug-out to see how his men had fared. The trenches were deserted except for dead bodies; most of the troops had run away in the initial stages, many being killed by the barrage as they descended the slope. Shocked by what he found, Peart went down the hillside and came across a group of frightened men taking cover amongst the rocks and boulders. A wounded officer, Captain Rees, was loudly urging them to go into a counter-attack. Ordering two soldiers to support him on their shoulders, Rees gathered twenty men around him and encouraged them back to their posts. Impressed by the sight of their officer courageously pushing on, the men rallied, and, running from rock to rock and bush to bush, fought back to their original trenches, where they had the gladdening sound and sight of a naval bombardment landing in the middle of a German infantry attack. But their pleasure soon turned to dismay, when the naval guns shortened range and started landing shells all round them. News of the retreat had reached the Navy, who had switched targets to deal with the situation, but the reoccupation had gone unnoticed. Luckily in the short time they had been there they had built rocky sangars around the dug-outs, and although the hill shook under the enormous concussion, only one man was wounded: yet the trees were stripped of every twig and the leafless vines stood like bare crooked fingers pointing into the sky.

Fusilier D. Needham with the 8th Royal Fusiliers spent the night in a wet trench with nothing to eat and awoke with a completely numb foot, fed up and wishing he were out of it.

I remember coming off sentry at 3 a.m. and falling asleep in the wet and filthy ditch.

At 5 a.m. I awoke trembling violently and feeling sick—I saw the padre, who suggested I report to the *RAP*, which I did. I was given hot tea and a sandwich and told by the medical officer to lay down—at ten o'clock he looked me over and on taking off my left boot showed me a one inch tear through its sole, pointing to congealed blood on my toes. He ordered me to be sent back to 167 Field Ambulance on a Bren carrier. I got there at about twelve o'clock and found it under long-range fire, as shells meant for the shipping were dropping in its area. I was put in a small shed with other lightly wounded soldiers and given drugs and attention.

D-Day Plus Three

At about four o'clock in the afternoon I awoke to notice that the shelling was much heavier and rifle fire very close. Half an hour later, an officer came in and said that anyone who had arms and ammunition must give them up. We all looked at each other: it seemed certain that we would be prisoners soon and that the battle was lost.

A Major came in one hour later and informed us that things were going very badly and every available man was required. As we were lightly injured, he asked us to go back to our units, adding that, as we were wounded, he could only ask, not order us to go.

We formed up outside—seven men of different regiments. None of us shaved or washed, very hungry and with dirty bandages on wounds. We moved off under a wounded officer, Lieutenant Fish, on a Bren carrier towards Battipaglia and very soon came across heavy fighting.

At approximately 2200 hours we were mixed up in a battle in a village street—all around lay dead, smashed guns, and the terrible smell of burning flesh. It did not take long to realise that the screams I heard came from a blazing German tank, in which an officer was half jammed in the turret.

*   *   *   *   *

Officials of the Allied Military Government in Salerno were endeavouring to get the city alive once more. Engineers under fire tried to repair the electricity services and to block the gaps in the drainage system that were polluting the water supply. At the town hall a British Pioneer officer recruited sixteen scared and hungry men and set them to work clearing the roads. By the day's end all had deserted, failing to return for wages or food.

A serious problem was the number of convicts escaped from the town gaol, who were breaking into the houses and shops looting, raping and attacking defenceless civilians. They were joined by some Allied service troops, who, with too much local liquor inside them, were preying on women and making life unnecessarily difficult for the population. The wine sold by the Italians at about three-pence for a five-gallon Jerrican had the most disastrous effect on the troops.

Plans to bring immediate supplies of food ashore had been delayed owing to the failure to open the harbour. The Italians left in the town found it hard to get food from any source. Every army cook-house that operated in the area was constantly surrounded by a crowd of civilians, adults and children, begging for scraps. The troops, as always, were generous, but their contributions were not sufficient to solve the problem.

By the evening the situation north of Salerno, from which the strongest opposition could be expected, was uncomfortable, insecure and unpleasant for the Allies. A series of strong attacks accompanied by shelling had come in all day long around the Laughing Hill, and the presence of German troops in parts of the hospital block could no longer be tolerated. It was decided to launch the 2/4th Battalion *KOYLI* to capture the entire zone, eject the Hun and turn the buildings into a strong-point. Lieutenant-Colonel N. A. W. Joynson, the Commanding Officer, crossed the start line in the north-eastern outskirts of Salerno at 1600 hours; yet the assault did not go in until 2000 hours. It was typical of operations at that time that they seldom did go according to plan.

Nobody had taken into account the appalling mountainous country over which the troops had to advance. The hills were terraced with walls often seven feet high, up which heavily laden soldiers had to climb. When they were not crawling along like mountaineers, they were dragging themselves through thick woods of firs and olives, and could only proceed at a snail's pace. To make matters worse, 'D' Company was caught in the midst of a barrage while marching through the streets of Salerno and suffered severe casualties. When the assault started, a fresh German counter-attack, strongly backed by tanks, came down the Avellino road; the Yorkshiremen were caught in the open. Some troops on the right flank were driven back; it was not until the outskirts of Salerno were reached that the attack was held.

Yet the *KOYLI* did manage to chase the Germans out of the Sanatorium. Colonel Joynson decided to shorten his perimeter and turn the hospital into a strong-point; strict instructions were issued that all possible help was to be given to the medical staff, and the patients evacuated into the already overcrowded tunnel on the other side of the park. The voluble Italians, protesting all the time, were finally persuaded that it was safer to leave the buildings.

Soon small groups of soldiers were carrying patients, piles of blankets, medical stores and pots of prepared food from the wards into the underground cavern. Others removed the Red Cross flags and erased with mud the large red crosses painted on the walls. Windows and doors were barricaded; Bren-guns were set up at every vantage point; patrols constantly ranged the grounds, fighting isolated skirmishes with enemy groups. Inside the buildings, which were paved with marble, troops were ordered to cover their feet with strips of blankets to deaden the noise of their hob-nailed boots. This was a wise precaution because, although the men slipped as if on ice, when the enemy later broke into the hospital the British were able to move silently and the Germans were unable to locate them.

At one stage, after a patrol clash in the grounds, a lone wounded Yorkshireman, cut off from his group, wandered into the tunnel when it was under enemy control. He was quickly hidden by the nuns, who dressed his wound, covering him with blankets just as two Germans arrived. They stopped at the side of the Englishman and the Italians were terrified that he would be discovered and reprisals taken. But they were only looking for a doctor. After having a broken arm set, they departed with profuse thanks to the staff.

Major Richard Bell, who had led an unsuccessful company attack on to a hillock dominating the sanatorium, failed to return with his men; it was presumed that he had been captured. Twenty-four hours later he was back in the lines, unshaven and highly indignant at the unchivalrous treatment accorded to him by the crew of a German machine-gun nest. He described how, having taken refuge in a ditch very close to the strong-point, every time he moved he was shot at; yet the enemy, probably assuming that he was not alone, seemed unprepared to chase him out. As the hours went by and the heat of the sun increased, his thirst became almost unbearable. Hanging overhead was a huge bunch of blue grapes, ripe and fresh and juicy. As he raised a hand to pick the fruit, a burst of bullets tore into the vine all round his outstretched hand. Hastily withdrawing it, he allowed a lapse of time and then tried again. But the eagle-eyed watcher was ready; the bullets, buzzing dangerously close to his hand, forced him once more to give up the attempt. Time and again he struggled to pluck the fruit, with the same result. When night fell at last, enabling him to creep away, he was most upset over what he described as such "uncharitable behaviour".

*   *   *   *   *

In the central sector the battered 56th Division had withdrawn after their desperate battles in Battipaglia. By this time most of the officers had realised that, without reinforcements, they could not hope to push forward. General Graham, commander of the 56th Division, decided to shorten and thicken his line. A new defensive front was formed 3,000 yards south-west of Battipaglia, and by dawn 12th September the line stretched from the small hamlet of Santa Lucia north-west across the Tusciano to Montecorvino station, then, curving slightly outwards, to the area of Faiano and Hill 210, which had been taken by the 169th Brigade. On the right flank were the Fusiliers and the Ox & Bucks. In the centre the Guards; the wide-open gap between the 56th Division and the Americans was patrolled by armoured vehicles of the 44th Reconnaissance Regiment, which was trying to make contact with the Americans. Supplies of barbed wire and anti-tank mines were hastily brought up from beach dumps and all day long the troops toiled to strengthen their positions.

A German lieutenant recorded in his battle diary:

> A counter-attack was planned by one regiment with two additional battalions to capture the hills dominating Salerno during the night. Following this, my battalion was to remain in fire positions in the hills, and another unit would go through us to capture Salerno and 'Faiano. The Hermann Goering Division then planned to capture Vietri from the north and, moving eastwards, cause the collapse of the entire British front in this sector.

The attack failed and the German officer added what, in his view, was the reason:

> The Commanding Officer was over-confident and underestimated the British strength.

*   *   *   *   *

Far to the north of Italy German Parachute Commander Colonel Skorzeny swooped on the Gran Sasso to rescue the imprisoned Italian Dictator. The German radio later announced that a new National Fascist Government had been formed under the leadership of Mussolini.

During this Sunday, the whole weight of the Middle East Strategic Air Forces was thrown into the beachhead and the surrounding countryside. The first air strip, carved out of the wet soggy ground by American engineers, two miles north of Paestum, was opened. Before Admiral Vian's carriers departed for Sicily, twenty-six Sea-fires were flown in to act as close-support fighters and operated until relieved by planes of *NWAAF*.

The Navy, as on previous days, was responding to calls for help with an impressive weight of shell, harrying every move the Germans made. Yet although these guns could in places batter the enemy, they could not occupy the ground—this was the infantry's task and only they could do it.

*   *   *   *   *

British hospital ships, which had sailed in with the original convoys, were, as always, painted white, decorated with huge red crosses and brilliantly lit during the hours of darkness. This, however, gave them no immunity from the Luftwaffe pilots, many of whom preferred an innocent target to others which could defend themselves. At 1327 hours, just after a padre had finished a round of the wards holding church services, the *Leinster* was attacked by several bombers; yet, despite numerous near hits, the ship was undamaged. Other attacks, in defiance of the Geneva Convention, were to be made in the following days.

Robert Scheftel and his companions had awakened in their bedrooms in Amalfi in bright sunlight. After enjoying a luxurious breakfast, they tore themselves away from civilisation to return to the war. At Darby's headquarters they asked if they could be shipped back to the bridgehead by *LST* to avoid running the gauntlet of fire across all the bridges. Darby, with a disarming smile, informed them that the *LST* was being kept handy in case he had to evacuate his troops, and suggested they make the best of it by jeep. They returned unharmed to report that there were no suitable positions in Allied hands for the radar installation; subsequently most of them were transferred to the Isle of Capri, from where they were able to cover the Luftwaffe airfields.

*   *   *   *   *

Most of the fighting for the 45th Division on 12th September was centred around Persano. The American Regimental Combat Teams struggled all day against ever-increasing resistance from the enemy, who received fresh reinforcements in the shape of elements of the 26th Panzer and 29th Panzer Grenadier Divisions.

The situation in the American sector was extremely confusing, and it is difficult to pin-point every action. There is little doubt that Commanding Officers lost control in many areas and it was often only the doggedness and bravery of individual soldiers which managed to save the day.

The 1st Battalion 142nd Infantry under Colonel Barron was in occupation of the hill mass around Altavilla, but the line was thin and his men spread out over too great a distance. The 2nd Battalion

15th **Panzer Grenadier Regiment**, which had infiltrated round Hill 424, was firing on the Americans from all directions. Allied shore and naval guns were called in to help and fired into the valleys, where German troops were forming up. The enemy artillery replied with renewed vigour: for two and a half hours it pounded Hill 424 mercilessly, blocking the roads, breaking all field telephone cables and wrecking communications.

Lieutenant Royal H. Seward, of 'B' Battery 132nd Field Artillery, had been forward looking for a suitable observation post, when during the night the platoon he was with became surrounded. The vital radio linking the infantry with the guns was destroyed in order to save it from capture. As the day progressed, conflicting reports came back from the front; the situation became rather cloudy. So heavy was the enemy shelling over this ground that it became almost impossible for reconnaissance parties to get to and fro; with nearly all the telephone lines destroyed and radio batteries fading out, it was impossible to form a clear picture. The Infantry were forced out of Altavilla late in the afternoon, and signallers and artillery observers going forward to link up found the streets full of German troops and vehicles. The 1st Battalion 142nd Infantry retreated in disorder, some of the troops in a panic, and were not stopped until they reached the gun lines. The 3rd Battalion 143rd Infantry was brought to this position; military policemen went out on the tracks and roads, stopping every vehicle that came along to order the truck drivers, signallers, clerks, storemen and even bandsmen to get straight into the front-line trenches. The German artillery never ceased from bombarding the front, and the ground immediately to the rear; the Americans began to wonder if they would be able to stay put. In no-man's-land isolated troops still fought on, trying to break out.

The sound of heavy guns from the west could be heard. From time to time messengers brought in stories of a big tank battle in that direction, and everyone was thinking that a further retirement would be necessary.

Sergeant Billy Skidmore, from Paris, Texas, and his command post group settled in an old deserted house. It was nearly midnight, so the men unpacked their bedrolls and went to sleep.

Sergeant Skidmore's men had never seen the position in the light of day, so they all slept in a small room on the ground floor. They were very much aware of the fact that they were close to the German line. Shortly after they fell asleep they were awakened by a continued hammering on the upper floor. The men grabbed their rifles and crept up the stairway to capture the German they felt sure was hiding there.

They dashed into a huge room and turned on a flashlight. There in the centre, sitting before a pile of nuts, was Sergeant John Hawkins, from Richardson Park. When the laughter died down, Sergeant Hawkins was asked what he was doing up there.

"I was hungry and so I got up to see what I could find," answered Hawkins. "I found the nuts and the hammer and was having a good time until you guys barged in."

The men went back to sleep, but Hawkins continued to eat nuts.

Lieutenant-Colonel Forsythe, commander of 143rd Infantry, called for urgent reinforcements, but was informed that, as no transport was available, fresh troops could not be sent to him. It never seemed to occur to anyone to order the soldiers to march into battle.

In the Sele-Calore Gap 179 RCT had been forced back from the bluffs overlooking Ponte Sele, and the enemy holding Persano found himself with a strong spearhead thrust into the beachhead through the American lines. Colonel Charles Ankorn, commander of 157 RCT, expecting an attack from the tobacco factory near Persano, called upon tanks and artillery to blanket the buildings with fire. By 1100 hours, as the last shells were still falling, a company of the 157th rushed the factory, forced out the few remaining dazed Germans and prepared to fight it out. They had hardly been allotted their positions, when a counter-attack solidly backed with Panzers came rolling down the Eboli road. By pure chance a battalion of Howitzers of the 158th Field Artillery Battalion was there; using their guns at point-blank range and firing as fast as the gun numbers could load, they managed temporarily to halt the attack; yet by 1400 hours the 1st Battalion 157 Regimental Combat Team had been ejected from the factory. Once more naval guns and field artillery were called in and loosed a tremendous barrage on the buildings. The Germans, unable immediately to reinforce themselves, moved out under cover of a smoke-screen at 1500 hours.

Plans were speedily put into operation for an advance; by the evening tanks and infantry were in strong positions in the factory area and in a line west and south of Torre Palladino. The 2nd Battalion 179th RCT had commenced an advance from La Cosa Creek, when to everybody's surprise General Dawley intervened and, stopping the advance, organised extensive shifts of units to strengthen his left flank. The 179th *RCT* was ordered to move out of the Persano area and take up a fresh position covering the wide-open hole between the American and British corps. Even so there remained a gap of about five miles, which was only held by patrols of the British 23rd Armoured Brigade.

$$* \qquad * \qquad * \qquad * \qquad *$$

The account for this day showed considerable losses: Altavilla, which covered Paestum, in the *US* sector; and Battipaglia, the centre of communications for the whole area, in the British sector. Plans had to be made to recapture these vital points. General Fred Walker of the 36th Division, who was up front, realising the danger of allowing the Germans to overlook them, immediately ordered an attack to be planned by the 3rd Battalion 143rd Infantry for execution the following day.

General Mark Clark was aware of these losses. He was reported as standing by the side of the road watching the *US* troops march from Persano with an "expression of concern" on his face. In fact, he soon realised that the situation was even worse than he had originally thought. In the centre of the bridgehead the Germans were pushing down the Sele-Calore Gap and there was little to hold them. Clark in his memoirs is critical of General Dawley:

> General Dawley had not been fully aware of the strength of the enemy on his left flank, and had not taken steps, or been able to take steps, to protect himself from counter-attack in that sector after the failure of our thrusts towards Ponte Sele and Battipaglia. Furthermore, as the attacks developed, it was disclosed that all the troops had been committed in a cordon defence, leaving none in reserve to meet an enemy breakthrough. We were getting into a very tight place.

By the evening General Mark Clark was thoroughly depressed, and although at this stage he kept his dismal thoughts to himself, he was seriously contemplating the necessity for a withdrawal from the entire beachhead. In his memoirs he wrote:

> I recall that about this time I had to consider the possibility that we would be driven back into the sea. A commander is always supposed to have an alternative plan, and I felt that if it came to a point where we had to abandon part of the beachhead, we should be able to evacuate some troops by sea to the British sector and continue to fight from there. It was routine in such circumstances as we then faced to issue orders for the destruction, if necessary, of all supplies

and equipment on the beaches. I went down to look over the vast piles of supplies on the beach and to recall the stern admonitions that had been drilled into us at school about taking precautions to prevent stores from falling into the hands of the enemy. I knew that if I were involved in a theoretical problem at the War College, I would at this point get hell from some instructor if I failed to issue orders to be prepared for the possible destruction of those supplies; but this wasn't a theoretical problem, and I couldn't see how I'd do anything but damage morale if I issued such orders at Salerno. I thought it over carefully as I walked along the beach. I was dirty and tired and worried, and finally I said "To hell with the theory. I am not going to issue any such orders." Furthermore, I decided, the only way they're going to get us off this beach is to push us, step by step, into the water.[1]

In fact his memoirs are at variance with the facts. At a later date he did consult with other Army commanders and the Navy and orders were issued for the preparation of re-embarkation plans. They were hotly contested, especially by Lieutenant-General Sir Richard McCreery and Commodore Oliver, and received with ill grace by the American Navy. But for the present Clark kept his thoughts to himself.

However, he did signal to General Alexander that the situation was unfavourable and that the 56th Division was exhausted. At Allied headquarters the planning staffs worked through the night organising more men, more ships and additional aircraft, but as these all had to come from North Africa, transport was badly needed. Three ships, HMS *Euryalus, Scylla* and *Charybdis* were sent off to Tripoli at full speed with orders to return crammed with reinforcements.

The total casualties in the British Corps by the end of this sunny Sunday evening were 3,000 killed, missing and wounded, about five to seven per cent of its total strength.

It was obvious to all concerned that the Germans were rapidly and dangerously building up their strength on the Salerno beachhead and that worse would be happening in the coming days.

[1] *Calculated Risk*, by General Mark Clark, Harrap, 1951. The extracts have been reproduced by kind permission of the publishers.

Chapter XII

D-DAY PLUS FOUR

13th September, 1943

FROM Broadcasting House, London, the news reader announced the following communiqué issued from Middle East Headquarters:

"In Italy the Fifth Army is fighting in one of the fiercest actions of the war in the Salerno Bridgehead, and the battle is at its height. The Germans are desperately resisting our determined thrusts to break through their positions. Tanks and lorried infantry of the 16th Panzer Division are counter-attacking repeatedly. German field artillery and mortars are plastering the Allied positions, while overhead the Luftwaffe is making a vigorous attempt to reassert itself. But the British and *US* formations of the Fifth Army are maintaining their forward pressure, and reinforcements, including Sherman tanks, have arrived. Almost the whole strength of the North West African Air Force has struck the enemy in a wide arc round Salerno."

It was indeed a change from the previous day's communiqué, which spoke of "steady advances".

*   *   *   *   *

Encouraged by Wehrmacht successes, the Luftwaffe plucked up its courage and launched a series of attacks throughout the night on the concentration of shipping in the bay. In the morning twilight a group of planes swooped on the brightly lit hospital ships *Leinster*, *Somersetshire* and *Newfoundland*. *Leinster* and *Somersetshire* suffered only slight damage from near misses, but *Newfoundland* received a direct hit amidships, causing numerous casualties among the medical staff and the patients. She was soon blazing from stem to stern.

Wireless interceptors were horrified to hear from a German plane a pilot shouting exultantly into his microphone:

"I have hit a hospital ship! She's on fire and will certainly sink."

Eighteen-year-old Cadet Michael Aston was asleep in his cabin. He recalls:

At 0520 hours there was a terrific explosion; I could hear the glass in the electrically lit red cross, which shone skywards from the top of the cabin, shattering as debris fell on it. We had not undressed; as I came out of my bunk Harry Bass rushed in saying: "She's got it just abaft the bridge and is on fire amidships." There was no panic, but the flames prevented us from getting to proper boat stations. The engine room was functioning, but the main water fire line had been fractured and it was not possible to get water to the fire. Many people had been sleeping on deck and quite a few American nurses had been wounded. We carried these girls aft. In the starboard alleyway a number of *RAMC* Orderlies had been killed and, owing to the heat, we could not get to them. We could hear someone screaming in the fire; it was probably the Assistant Purser. Our staff nurses, who were all *QAIMNS*, were in cabins on the port side; Sister Lee was at a porthole and we tried to pull her through, but were unable to and she was lost in the fire. Captain Wilson ordered boats away; an emergency hose was being played on the falls so that they would not burn. The boats were dangerously overloaded. As two destroyers, *USS Plunkett* and *USS Mayo*, came alongside, the Captain asked for volunteers to return aboard to try to save the ship. With American seamen and ourselves, we poured water on to the fires; then *Newfoundland* listed heavily and an urgent order was given to abandon ship. Shortly afterwards we returned again and Captain Wilson was convinced he could save the ship, but then a signal was received from Naval *HQ* that she was to be sunk. We were forced to watch, while the destroyers at point-blank range poured forty shells into her, setting her on fire again before she sank—a sight that none of us will ever forget.

* * * * *

Throughout the night the troop formations on both sides had been hastily reorganised; in many places, where Allied units stuck out in dangerous salients, they were pulled back to tighten the defences. Early in the day, Clark sent an urgent message to Ridgway and Alexander asking for the 82nd Airborne Division. To Ridgway he opened his heart far more than he had to either of his corps commanders, admitting that the fight for Salerno had taken a turn for the worse and that it was very much touch and go.

> I want you to accept this letter as an order. I realise the time normally needed to prepare for a drop, but this is an exception. I want you to drop within our lines on the beachhead and I want you to make it tonight. This is a must.

Captain Hamilton, a *USAF* pilot, flew from the Paestum airstrip to Sicily, but on arrival at Licata was told that the divisional commander had just left in a transport plane. The pilot dashed to the control tower and somehow or other managed to convince the airfield controller that General Ridgway must be brought back immediately. It was a pretty tall order for a mere captain to issue to a general, but Ridgway instantly agreed and returned. After reading Clark's letter, he sent back a simple message: *Can do*. Then he hastily prepared his soldiers for a brand-new operation to be launched in a matter of hours. Orders for Operation *Giant* were issued to pilots of Transport Squadrons at 1330 hours; troops received their instructions at 1800 hours and the planes took off at 1930 hours. It was a remarkable achievement.

General Alexander at his headquarters was still not entirely aware of the extremely dangerous situation. Reports from the battlefield were often highly confused and contradictory. But he did realise the obvious danger arising from the fact that the German build-up was proceeding at a greater pace than our own and there was a possibility that Kesselring would be able to grab a quick success against the 5th Army. The Allies were hampered through not having a port available in the area, nor a serviceable airfield. On the credit side was the fact that the first units of the 7th Armoured Division were scheduled to land on this day; in addition, on 11th September, Alexander had been able to persuade London to let him take over eighteen tank-landing ships, which had been in harbour at Oran en route to India, and these started ferrying infantry reinforcements immediately.

*   *   *   *   *

Colonel John Whitfield, with the tattered remnants of his Queen's Battalion, was still in defensive positions not far from Montecorvino airfield. During the morning a small convoy of lorries, having come into their lines from the rear, drove without stopping into no-man's-land in full view of the enemy. Inevitably the German spotters responded with a shower of shells; two lorries were wrecked and caught fire, whilst the occupants ran back to the Queen's trenches. They were men of the Pioneer Corps, responsible for preparing the runways. They had taken a wrong turning and reaped the benefit of their carelessness. The remaining few lorries attracted continual shellfire; Whitfield suggested to the Pioneer officer in charge that he should get them moved, but with no concrete result. During the hours of darkness Whitfield sent out a section of men, who drove the good vehicles back behind the lines, a welcome addition to their very limited transport pool.

News of their recapture leaked back to corps headquarters. The following morning a Pioneer major from *GHQ* arrived with written instructions demanding that the six vehicles be handed over forthwith. Somewhat tired and weary, Whitfield had taken advantage of a lull in firing to freshen himself up; when the staff officer arrived, he was sitting by his trench washing his feet in a bowl of water. He was not in the mood for officious red-tape: to all the officer's arguments he replied that, as the Pioneers had refused to remove the vehicles themselves, they had automatically lost any right to them.

"They are the only tipper lorries in Italy!" stormed the major.

"Yes," replied Whitfield, "and if it hadn't been for my men, they would have all been blown up."

The officer, threatening action from corps headquarters, strode off. Bending to wipe his feet on a towel, Whitfield called out:

"You'd better let me have your name for the records."

The major shouted back: "It's Yeldham and you'll be hearing more of me."

This was a family name of Whitfield, who asked the officer to return. They discovered that they were first cousins. A more reasonable discussion ensued, ending with Whitfield agreeing to return the vehicles in three days, by which time his own heavy lorries would have arrived and he would have no further use for the others.

* * * * *

The main German tank and infantry drive went down the gap between the rivers Sele and Calore, battering away at everything in its path in the wide-open corridor between the two corps. In order to accomplish this, the majority of the combat groups of the 16th Panzer Division had moved out of their positions during the night, and had occupied new positions on the line Giffoni–Montecorvino–Rovella–Olevano, ready for the attack. The Allies seemed unaware of this move and failed to follow it up. The German Division, having joined forces with the 26th Panzer and the 29th Panzer Grenadier Divisions, launched into the assault encouraged by reports that some Americans had already returned to their ships.

The History of the 16th Panzer Division records:

> The engines were started up again, once more the dust rose in clouds above the hot, narrow roads. Back again into the hell gulf! At 1500 hours the 2/64th Battalion assembled for an attack on Bellizzi. The 1/64th were to follow. But already at San Martino opposition was encountered; shells began to fall; stones, shell splinters, dust rained down on armoured vehicles—they became veritable mobile coffins. The fire increased in frenzy at Bellizzi. Watch out for fighter-bombers

ahead! A cone of fire from 2-cm. guns cuts through the columns. Let's get out of this! Red-hot shell splinters tear up the road.

The western outskirts of Battipaglia were at last reached at about 1700 hours. The 1st Parachute Regiment Number 3 advanced through the ruins. The Bellizzi–Belvedere–Battipaglia road was clear of the enemy.

Scouts who advanced beyond the road reported only weak enemy forces. The artillery fire had decreased in violence.

Since communications with the division had been cut, Colonel Stempel decided at 1730 hours, on his own initiative, but in line with the general plan, to attack towards the coast in the direction of *Lilienthal*. The 3rd Artillery Regiment Number 16 moved its positions forward and gave support from gun positions at Macchia. To protect the left flank, parachute troops advanced towards San Mattia with their right wing on the Tusciano and reached the line San Mattia–Santa Lucia. At 2000 hours the Spetzler Battalion reached Fosso, reformed for a further attack, and established communication with the 1/64th Battalion. They made a spirited advance on a broad front; by midnight the head of the column was close to the coast.

This part of the attack by the 16th Panzer was against units of the 56th Division, whose line extended roughly from the airfield in a semicircle round the Battipaglia Tobacco Factory, southwards to the Fosso bridge and towards the American sector. There were around Santa Lucia some limited withdrawals, but a tank assault by the Royal Scots Greys restored the situation. The troops, dog-tired and battle-weary, had been relieved by an earlier announcement that it was not intended to advance again until sufficient reinforcements had been landed, but they were also told not to give up another inch of ground. This was as far as they were going. Yet the general feeling amongst the men was one of desperation, and the Scots Guards' official History records: *There was a general feeling in the air of another Dunkirk.*

During the morning sporadic attacks were launched against the Guards and the Royal Fusiliers mainly in the nature of probes to find the weakest spots.

Fusilier Needham in his improvised unit of wounded soldiers found himself that morning near the 9th Royal Fusiliers. They had breakfasted on water and biscuits, with tubes of cheese taken from dead Germans just in front.

Lieutenant Fish contacted a wireless operator from the Ox & Bucks and asked for air support to destroy two Mark IV tanks that were firing at them; it came one hour later, but its effect was not as intended: the bombs fell amongst the buildings they were themselves using as a strong-point, with the loss of several men and guns. The blast and destruction were terrible and for some time the surviving soldiers could not hear or speak properly.

At this stage German infantry started advancing.

Needham and his companions crawled through the rubble to where they could watch an attack on a corner house. A Vickers machine-gun was nearby: they crawled to it and, moving the dead gunner, took over the gun and opened fire. A few minutes later German shelling was concentrated on them; the wall behind was hit, covering them with debris and killing Corporal Edward Leigh. Needham, lying dazed, watched a tank lumber up to the house and slowly smash it by destroying a corner at a time, until it fell in on the men inside.

The tank then withdrew from the rubble and started to rumble up the street towards a small series of strong-points; but it had only gone about twenty feet when it blew up with a tremendous explosion.

Taffy Evans crawled out of the section and then came back to tell Needham that there was a strong enemy patrol resting just outside. About two hours later the Germans moved off and an ambulance station was set up, in which wounded from both sides were attended to.

The men crawled out of the rear of the house, through a hole in the wall and over the body of a German officer, the top of whose head had been removed by a shell. Slowly they made their way in what they thought was the direction of the British lines. Climbing through a house, they met a sergeant and a lance corporal of the 9th Battalion Royal Fusiliers. Together they crept into a house to await darkness—they had no food, no water or cigarettes. Sleep was impossible, as German patrols could be heard moving about and tanks were rumbling around.

The group left the ruins at midnight and crawled to the outskirts of the village into a small battered and scarred wood, where they found the ground covered with dead from an earlier naval bombardment: whole trees had been ripped out and the earth dotted with huge craters.

In the afternoon a patrol from the Coldstream wormed its way forward along the ditches with short rushes across green cultivated fields towards the railway line. Near the objective it was set upon by an enemy patrol, armed with automatic weapons and several vicious guard dogs, and it withdrew with slight casualties. As dusk fell, Numbers 1 and 3 Companies of the Coldstream, lined up along the bank of the Fosso Canal, heard the sound of German tanks and half-tracks taking up position not far from the Fosso bridge. The Guards had not been idle; they had planted innumerable mines, laid belts of wire, synchronised machine-gun lines and arranged defensive fire tasks for the field regiments. Every conceivable situation was envisaged and plans made accordingly.

Major Ken Sweeting, in command of Number 1 Company Coldstream Guards, was at dusk waiting for an armoured patrol to come back into the lines. As tracks were heard approaching, the men stood aside to let them roll home. But they were not their carriers: they were three German half-tracks packed with Panzer Grenadiers. The leading vehicle was over the bridge before the startled troops could take action. The first man to realise the situation was Sergeant Jackson, who fired a *PIAT* at five yards range and missed, but succeeded with his next round in setting the rear one on fire.

Way out in front in the middle of a thick wood was a listening post manned by Corporal Mountford with a field telephone. He continued to report enemy movements in spite of the fact that the vehicles often drove within yards of his hideout and troops very nearly trod on him. He remained there until the last moment, when he was ordered back to friendly lines before a defensive barrage was put down. He had hardly returned before he was volunteering to go forward again, and throughout the night kept the battalion informed of every enemy move.

Lieutenant-Colonel Sir Terence Falkiner, Commanding Officer of the Coldstream, gave strict instructions that not a shot was to be fired until he gave the order; he told the men that every bullet must count and there should be no indiscriminate shooting. The barrage plastered the opposite bank of the canal and the woods beyond them. Just after 2000 hours several tanks emerged from the trees, followed by a number of half-tracks. The Royal Artillery started firing and managed to catch the Panzer Grenadiers moving in mass towards the canal. The Coldstream and the Grenadiers received the order to fire and a holocaust fell on the advancing enemy. Very few of the German infantry ever emerged from the wood: the Guards could hear terrifying screams coming from the undergrowth, as the shells tore into flesh or blew bodies sky high. Enemy vehicles twisted and turned in the mud trying to find safe positions. Many were hit or limped away from the battle. Some tanks, managing to get hull down behind the dykes, plastered the positions with shell fire, but they did little damage to the dug-in Guardsmen.

Every single weapon in the two battalions was used to deadly effect; by the time the Germans were routed 54,000 rounds of small arms ammunition had been fired from Vickers, Brens, tommy-guns and rifles. Luckily the attack had come in on the strongest part of the line and the Grenadiers and Coldstream certainly made up for any shortcoming on previous occasions. Only one half-track broke through the lines and continued in a mad rush right to the beaches. As the sun rose the following morning, some startled administrative troops to their utter amazement saw the half-track and a dozen Panzer Grenadiers sowing mines along the sand, blissfully ignorant that the attack had failed! They were quickly rounded up.

Lieutenant Lloyd on the next day took out a patrol and on return reported the wood an utter shambles, with dead all over the place, the ground strewn with abandoned weapons, vehicles and half-tracks.

The Navy also had backed them well: the monitor *HMS Roberts*, three carriers and six destroyers responded to every call from the naval *FOO*s.

Commodore Oliver's despatches for the day are written in terse naval language, but they do reveal the amount of support the Navy was giving to the men in the trenches:

13th *September*.

102. Naval bombardment continued during the day.

103. At 1440, *HMS Uganda* was hit aft by a rocket bomb. There was no alert in force at the time, and the aircraft was not seen. *HMS Uganda* subsequently got one engine working, and moved inshore to anchor.

104. At 1500, it was reported that an enemy attack on Salerno might develop from the northward during the night. As no guards could be provided for the port and the port party were performing no useful function whilst the harbour was under heavy fire, it was decided to withdraw them temporarily, leaving a nucleus party with communications.

105. At 1530, *HM* ships *Nubian* and *Loyal* were near-missed by rocket bombs.

106. At 1730, a signal was received from Commander-in-Chief, Mediterranean, ordering 16 *LST* to be detached to proceed to Palermo to lift the 3rd United States Division to the *Avalanche* area.

107. Shelling of the beaches continued intermittently throughout the day.

108. In addition to the rocket-bomb attack, there was one alarm at 1800. There was an air attack on the beaches at 2100, during which a petrol dump ashore was hit. Otherwise, no air attacks developed during the night.

The 56th Division were to stay in these positions, harried night and day by shells, mortars and infantry. They could not advance and they did not retreat; not until reconnaissance patrols reported the Battipaglia Tobacco Factory and the town itself free of the enemy were they able to make a move. Their stand on the night of the 13th, however, was decisive, as never again were the Germans able to attack in the same strength on this front.

In the hill village of Olevano, Carlo Carucci from his vantage point had been watching the battle day by day and wondering if it would ever end. The village street was a main supply route for the German forces; trucks and motor cycles roared through at all hours, brushing aside the Italians and more or less ignoring them. In the piazza that morning there had been a violent argument between several villagers and a man named Errico di Gaeta.

A German soldier, jumping from a truck, had asked for food and wine; di Gaeta had taken him into his shop, saying: "Help yourself."

His fellow citizens were berating him for such generosity whilst he, shaking his arms in anger and shrugging his shoulders, shouted back: "And do you think, if I had refused him, that he would have saluted and gone on his way? No, no! He would have kicked me or even shot me, and helped himself—and what good would that do me?"

The logic of his argument was not entirely lost on his listeners.

To the watching Italians it seemed as if the Allies would lose their fingertip grip on the narrow bridgehead. They could see the vast fleet of warships and cargo vessels, and they knew there was no lack of fire support, but they were at a loss to explain why the British and American infantry were not advancing. They could see for themselves the German strength, which was increasing daily. On this day fresh troops of the 3rd Panzer Grenadier Division had marched singing through the villages, and the pathetic strains of *Lili Marlene* had alternated with the mockery of Germans chanting martial bars of *Giovinezza*, the popular Fascist song. The morale of these Huns was high; they took every opportunity of reminding the people that now Mussolini had been liberated he would once more bring Italy into the war on the Axis side. Bewildered, the Italians could only hope and pray, as they felt their destiny was beyond their control.

After a sleepless night spent tending the patients and calming the frightened women and children, Chaplain Carucci decided at dawn to return to the Sanatorium. Luckily for him there was a lull in the battle and he managed to cross the park without incident. He found that Soffietti, the Mother Superior, and some nuns had spent the night gathering food; with the help of some British Tommies they had cooked large quantities of soup and acorn bread. The small group, shouldering pots and pans, recrossed the gardens to the tunnel, where they were greeted with cheers by the refugees. There was some scuffling as mothers fought to get at the bread and soup, but soon a small quantity had been shared amongst them all. Yet how long could they go on feeding over a thousand hungry people, with their stores almost gutted? This was the main problem facing Carucci and the doctors. The chaplain suggested that he should try to make his way to German headquarters to ask for a truce so that the sick, the women and children could be evacuated to a safer place. It was agreed that he should leave at 1300 hours with Gatti and Soffietti, who asked to accompany him.

The trio set off promptly at the appointed hour, but had hardly left the tunnel when they were caught in an artillery duel that forced them to return. Two hours later they made another attempt, but again had to give up after a few hundred yards. Having realised the hopelessness of trying to get through to the Germans, they changed their plans and decided instead to go to Allied Head-quarters. At 1700 hours the three of them, on hands and knees, crawled across the park following a rocky path, taking shelter behind walls and fallen tree-trunks, until they reached the Sana-torium, where Carucci went to his room for a shave and a wash. They then pushed on through a gorge between the Mennola and Cupa-Cupeto down to the main road, where they were met by a captain of a field security section, who, waving his pistol and shouting incomprehensible words at the three Italians, ordered some nearby soldiers to arrest them.

In vain Gatti tried to explain; he was told to "Shut up". They were taken to a first-aid station, where, despite the pistol-waving captain, a kindly medical officer offered them tea and listened sympathetically to their story. Shortly afterwards the security officer stopped a passing 15-hundredweight truck and bundled them, together with another Italian youth of whom he was sus-picious, into the back of the vehicle.

They were driven into Salerno, firstly to the Hotel Diana, then to the prefecture, then to the town hall, and then back again to the prefecture. At each place they were questioned by British and American officers, but, although their tale appeared to be believed, no one seemed to have sufficient authority to order the security officer to release them. Finally they were taken to intelligence headquarters near Pontecagnano, where another officer who spoke good Italian told them not to worry; all would be well; his colleague who had arrested them was "a bit peculiar". They were forced to wait around without food or drink with the added excitement of a German air raid, during which they took refuge in a ditch.

At 2300 hours an interpreter arrived; the young Italian was taken off for interrogation, whilst Carucci, Gatti and Soffietti were joined by a young British lieutenant, who informed them that he did not speak or understand a word of Italian, although he stuck close to them, listening intently to everything they said. Then at about midnight, to their amazement, General Clark walked into the room. He recognized the priest, and Gatti explained to him in English what had happened and why they were there. Clark listened patiently and assured him he would speak out for them, but as they had come from what was virtually inside the German lines, at least one of them would have to be questioned, as they might have valuable information. Turning to the British officer, the commander ordered that the Italians should be given food, drink and cigarettes.

After what seemed hours to these tired and worried men, the young Italian emerged from the interrogation room under escort.

Excitedly he turned to Carucci, saying: "They think I am a spy. I'm sure they will shoot me. You must help me, for God's sake."

The chaplain promised to do all he could, and the protesting youth was led away. At a later date they heard he had been released.

Gatti was then taken before a group of intelligence officers and closely questioned. He was surprised to find that his interrogators knew almost everything about the hospital, including the names of members of the staff. They were even aware of the fact that he was in reality a lieutenant in the Italian Army. It was not until 0230 hours on the following morning that Gatti emerged to tell his companions that all was well; they had even been invited to spend the night at the headquarters before leaving. Carucci, thoughts for the safety of his flock uppermost in his mind, refused the offer, saying he wanted to go to Salerno.

A truck was placed at their disposal and a kindly soldier threw a box of compo rations into it. They went off into Salerno, Carucc directing the driver towards the Hospice for the Poor, where he knew some of the priests. The road leading to the building was blocked; reluctantly they left the vehicle, shouldered their rations and, stumbling over the mounds of rubble and slipping into shell holes, made their way up to the massive wooden door. They knocked and shouted for fifteen minutes, before a frightened priest opened the door a crack to ask who they were and what their business. Carucci called out his name, and they were at once admitted. The priest explained that, as it was rumoured that the Germans would come down from the hills to retake the town, he had thought they were an advance patrol.

Offered beds, they tried to settle down to sleep, but in spite of tiredness they were too worried by their thoughts and the noise of battle and spent most of the hours of darkness talking over plans for the next day.

*　　*　　*　　*　　*

Hit-and-run raids by the Luftwaffe continued all through 13th September. At 1440 hours, during a lull when no air-raid alert was in operation and the exhausted gunners were cleaning their weapons and taking well-earned rests, a guided bomb launched from maximum range screamed out of the sky to strike the cruiser *HMS Uganda*. The attacking plane was never even seen. The missile struck surely, penetrating through seven decks to explode beneath the ship, putting three engines out of order. Sixteen men were killed outright and seven wounded, a surprisingly light casualty list considering the damage the bomb caused. Thirteen hundred tons of water poured in through the huge thirty-foot split in her hull, but thanks to prompt action taken by the crew in shoring up threatened bulkheads, work carried out under appalling risks, the ship was saved. *HMS Brecon* was nearby and her log contains the following incident:

> Closed *Uganda* at 1530 hours and picked up a naval war correspondent, Ian Munro. He had no clothes or gear, as *Uganda* had just been hit by a rocket bomb just outside his cabin as he was packing. He was somewhat shaken.

Early next day *Uganda* was taken under tow by the tug *USS Narrangansett*; with an escort of two destroyers, she set off for Malta.

Within an hour of this attack the destroyers *Nubian* and *Loyal* were narrowly missed by other guided bombs, and to the naval commanders the situation was not quite as rosy as it had been. Two light cruisers were out of action, in most ships the ammunition supplies were running low. Commodore Oliver signalled his plight to Admiral of the Fleet Cunningham, who ordered *HMS Aurora* and *Penelope* to steam up from Malta. They joined the fleet at dawn on 14th September.

*   *   *   *   *

Early in the morning a planning conference was called by the General Commanding XIV Panzer Corps, where it was decided to launch a large-scale attack on the 16th, with the object of splitting the Allied forces into two groups and pushing them back into the sea.

The Hermann Goering Division was given Salerno as its objective and they would drive along the highway to Battipaglia to join the 16th Panzer Grenadier Division, plus 29th Armoured Infantry Division and parts of 15th Panzer Grenadier Division, who were ordered to simultaneously attack through the Gap to the Paestum area. Detailed instructions were issued to the German commanders, and in the following days troops and tanks were reorganised to fit into the plan.

On the northern beachhead boundary Colonel Bill Darby's Rangers had been fighting continuously ever since the 9th. By dodging here, there and everywhere, and working in small groups, they had led the Germans to believe that far stronger forces were operating on the Sorrento peninsula than was the case. When the Rangers finally moved into positions overlooking Castellamare and probed forward, they ran into stiff opposition. It was thought by the Wehrmacht that the Rangers were the spearhead of an attack through to Naples and the area was quickly reinforced. The Rangers, with indomitable courage and great elan, were quite capable of controlling the road and railway gap at Nocera, but they had neither the strength nor the weapons to advance; with a stronger German challenge, it began to look as if they might be pushed out. General Clark subsequently sent them on the following day reinforcements in the shape of a battalion of parachutists.

On the Rangers' right flank the Commando Brigade was still stubbornly clinging to the ground which they had initially captured. Despite occasional setbacks, they had stuck to it, although the force was by now very badly cut up. Dawn on the 13th saw yet another heavy shelling of Dragonea Hill, where Number 2 Commando was entrenched; a subsequent infantry/armoured assault broke through the thin line in several places.

Captain Brian Lees, *RAMC*, medical officer of the Commando, was tending the wounded in a small stone hut on the reverse slopes of the hill under pretty crude conditions. In the middle of an operation, when he glanced up to wipe the sweat away from his eyes, he saw through the open door the figures of several German soldiers. Hastily ordering the door to be shut, Lees told the patients and orderlies to keep quiet. There they remained for four hours, as hand-to-hand fighting went on around them, until the front was finally stabilised and they found themselves once more inside the Allied line.

Brigadier Laycock and his staff were fast coming to the conclusion that, if they were not soon relieved, there would not be any troops left to command. All they got from the Army was encouragement and congratulations, but precious little material help, except from the Gunners and the Navy.

On this morning General 'Ginger' Hawkesworth arrived at Vietri to see Laycock; hearing that the fighting up front had settled down, he suggested that he would like to speak to Lieutenant-Colonel Jack Churchill. Laycock thought it more than likely that Churchill would be sleeping after the battle, as he knew he was desperately tired. In the circumstances, he would have preferred not to disturb him. Using the simple Army code for ranks, he telephoned the battalion and enquired of the adjutant:

"I suppose Sunray is fast asleep."

"Oh no," was the reply. "He's standing next to me."

As Laycock passed the microphone to Hawkesworth, Churchill came on the line and with a roaring voice shouted to the Divisional commander: "This is little ray of sunshine speaking!"

His morale, humour and courage were an inspiration to everyone.

In the original party at brigade headquarters Laycock had included Commander Derek Wyburd, *RN*, who acted as a naval liaison officer. After a couple of days, he was recalled to his ship to join Captain Andrew's diversionary group of destroyers and *MTBs* that were operating around the islands to the north. The Commandos would have dearly loved to be part of this romantic force; Laycock had offered his services, only to be told he was more urgently needed at Salerno. It was with some good-humoured banter that he said goodbye to the naval officer. On 13th September the Navy occupied Capri and a headquarters was established in Countess Edda Ciano's villa. Wyburd despatched a signal to Laycock, who read it with amused chagrin.

OPERATIONAL IMPORTANT STOP HAVE CAPTURED LARGE SUPPLY KRUG VEUVE CLIQUOT STOP REQUEST BENEFIT OF YOUR EXPERT KNOWLEDGE STOP WHICH SHOULD I DRINK FIRST.

During that evening reports came trickling into Commando Brigade headquarters that the sound of large numbers of Panzers was being heard on the roads to the north. Laycock, who at first did not believe it, went forward to find out personally. The unmistakable sound of roaring engines and rattling tracks met his ears. More than anything else he feared a strong attack, as the Commandos just had not the weapons to deal with heavily armoured vehicles. From the nearest wireless set he contacted the divisional commander, who also would not believe the report and refused to do anything about it. Laycock and his men prepared for a last-ditch stand, quite convinced that this would be the last of their battles. The sounds increased; then out of the gloom shot a squadron of American tanks, which charged straight through the lines, completely ignored the Commandos and disappeared to the rear. Where they had come from or where they went, Laycock never discovered, but it was one of the most worrying days of his life.

* * * * *

American artillery began softening-up fire at 0545 hours and the infantry crossed the start-line fifteen minutes later. Their plan was to retake the hills at Altavilla, recapture the town and Hill 424. The assaulting troops of the 36th Division were 3rd Battalion 143rd Infantry, 1st Battalion 142nd Infantry and 3rd Battalion 142nd Infantry. The American attack had been launched in the face of the German offensive. In the early stages the attack went well with the capture of several hill features, including the high ground overlooking Altavilla. The infantry fought doggedly up the precipitous slopes in the face of severe shell fire, harassing machine-guns and countless snipers. By 0730 hours the 3rd Battalion 142nd Infantry neared the top of an unnumbered hill, but were then pinned down by artillery. A German counter-attack soon forced them off the heights, and from the lower slopes the Commanding Officer sent out a call for help. General Walker ordered forward the badly battered 1st Battalion 142nd Infantry, but it was cut to pieces by enemy shelling and was unable to go into action that day.

The brunt of the combined German attack fell on the American 36th and 45th Divisions. The main attack was launched about midday.

On the left flank the 3rd Battalion 143rd Infantry under Colonel Barnett, pushed its way up a ridge north-west of Altavilla and then planned an attack on Hill 424, but before they could start, units of the 15th Panzer Grenadiers stormed in on them from several directions; by the time the *US* troops received the order to withdraw they had been surrounded. The rest of the force retreated to La Cosa Creek.

Faced with this general withdrawal of his unit, General Walker went to VI Corps headquarters to report to General Dawley. After appreciating the situation, Dawley ordered the 36th Division to reorganise and defend the sector between the Calore and Monte Soprano, with La Cosa Creek as the front line. Walker recalls:

> The front assigned to me was about eight miles long. It was late in the day. The positions had to be reconnoitred and occupied at night. Previously I had been ordered to send the 141st *RCT* to the British Sector. I retained one battalion to outpost my southern sector. I had also been ordered previously to send the 1st Battalion 143rd Infantry to join Darby's Rangers (11th September) and I had been ordered to send the 2nd Battalion 143rd Infantry to provide a defence between the Sele and Calore rivers. The 1st Battalion 142nd Infantry, which had been driven off the hills at Altavilla the previous day, was in need of reorganisation, so at the end of 13th September I had available for the defence of La Cosa four battalions of infantry.
>
> I organised the front into three sectors and assigned a brigadier-general to each—Brigadier-Generals William H. Wilbur, Michael O'Daniel and Otto F. Lange. Since General Lange was still engaged supervising *Yellow* and *Blue* Beaches, I assigned Colonel Forsythe to the southern sector until General Lange could take over. I did this because the troops assigned to the various sectors, aside from the infantry, were not used to working together and I wanted everything done that could be done to meet a possible attack by daylight on 14th September.

The 45th Division under General Middleton was dangerously exposed in the Sele–Calore Gap, where the Germans launched the heaviest attack of the whole Salerno battle. The 79th Panzer Grenadier Regiment forced back the 1st Battalion 157th Infantry covering the Sele crossing at Persano, and followed this up swiftly with more tanks and infantry, hitting the 2nd Battalion 143rd *RCT* on both sides with two columns and thrusting down towards a burned bridge across the Calore.

By late afternoon the enemy were right in the Gap with strong defensive units out on their flanks to stop the Americans from cutting the lifeline. At 1830 hours fifteen Panzers were in close country on the north side of the Calore, near its junction with the Sele. For some reason the Germans then paused.

Clark, up in the front line at this time, was convinced that nothing could now stop a break-through. Yet the pause was long enough to allow the 189th Field Artillery Battalion under command of Lieutenant-Colonel Hal L. Muldrow Junior and the 158th Field Artillery Battalion, led by Lieutenant-Colonel Russell D. Funk of the 45th Division, to move into the end of the Gap near Persano on the south bank of the Calore covering the burned bridge. Realising there were few infantry ahead, both officers stripped gun crews to a minimum and sent the artillerymen into the trenches. Other officers and *NCOs* were hastily despatched to nearby roads to drag in any available soldier.

Clark in a nearby command post discovered that one particularly dominant hill was not included in the defence scheme, as there were no troops to spare for this purpose. He personally ordered a regimental band to be armed and sent there. Asked to name the hill feature and finding it unnamed on the map, Clark in honour of the fighting bandsmen decided to christen it 'Piccolo Peak'.

Panzers hidden in dense brush behind the burned bridge commenced firing at the guns and positions of the 189th Artillery Battalion with the obvious intention of softening the area up for an immediate attack. The moment infantry and tanks appeared on the road leading to the bridge, every single weapon in American hands opened up, the field guns firing at a tremendous rate of eight rounds per minute per gun, crews stripped and sweating.

The Germans at first refused to give. They kept pushing forward into a zone absolutely swamped by the American barrage. Their casualties were appalling; after several unsuccessful attempts, they wavered and began to retreat. The two field battalions saved the day, firing between them 3,650 rounds, added to which were another 300 rounds from the 27th Armoured Field Battery, which had arrived towards the end of the battle.

It was in this action that a famous American battle cry was born. As the German Grenadiers smashed their way through the defending *GIs* and stormed towards the gun positions of the 132nd Field Artillery, one of the battery commanders telephoned the battalion commander, Lieutenant-Colonel John N. Green, to ask what to do.

Colonel Green's grim reply was: "Put out local security, and if necessary *fight with the rammer staff*."

This was picked up by the soldiers and adopted as the unit battle cry, which became renowned throughout Texas.

In contrast to the behaviour of the gunners in the Gap, in another area a whole field battery left their positions and, finding a tank unit with the same intentions, grabbed lifts and started charging back down the rutted roads towards the beaches. General McLain of the 45th Division halted the column at a bridge; when he learned of their purpose, he blocked the road, saying:

"The fight's up there, not back here."

The men turned about and later fought well.

General Middleton, commander of the 45th Division, hearing reports of retreats in some places and rumours of re-embarkation, and realising what would happen if the bad news spread, issued the following order to his staff:

"Put food and ammunition behind the 45th; we are going to stay here."

In the early evening General Dawley got through to Mark Clark on a field telephone to describe just how critical the situation was. Clark acidly comments in his book: *it was the first word I had had that such a critical situation had developed at this point.*

Clark asked: "What are you doing about it?"

Dawley replied: "Nothing. I've no reserves. All I've got is a prayer."

And for Clark, or for anyone else for that matter, a prayer was just not enough.

Later on General Clark called a conference at Army headquarters at Paestum, which was attended by General Dawley and General McCreery. Things were far worse than they had been on the previous day. Although the British had stood firm, there was no question of a break-out: the beachhead was too narrow for proper manœuvre, and with Salerno port still closed and Montecorvino airfield unusable, they were bogged down and on the defensive. In the American sector things were even more critical, with the real possibility that the Germans would cut the bridgehead in two. Every soldier was committed to the line and reserves were still coming in. General Clark, with his staff college training very much in his mind, had now decided to keep his thoughts to himself no longer. Contacting Admiral Hewitt at 2030 hours, he urgently requested him to make plans to evacuate VI Corps in the south and re-land it north of the Sele to join X Corps, or vice versa. Admiral Hewitt did not like the idea, and his views were later shared by the British Naval Commander, Commodore Oliver. Strangely, neither McCreery nor Dawley nor any other senior Army officer were informed of Clark's plans.

An added pinprick, which drew justifiably acid comments from the Army Commander, was a *BBC* news broadcast, suggesting that

General Montgomery and the 8th Army were advancing rapidly northwards to relieve the 5th Army. The battlefront news was presented with a strong British slant, and the Americans felt they were not getting their share of publicity and praise, particularly in view of the heavy casualties they were suffering.

* * * * *

The only heartening news that day had come from General Matthew Ridgway to say that his paratroopers would be landing inside the perimeter precisely at midnight. Ridgway, whose division had suffered severely in Sicily at the hands of friendly gunners, had stipulated that all anti-aircraft fire in the Salerno area should cease five minutes before midnight and not start firing again until the last transport plane had left the area. Liaison officers were sent round to every single ship and shore position, ensuring that the order had been received and would be complied with.

At 2355 hours an utterly weird silence settled over the battle-field. For the first time in many days not a shell was being fired from land or sea. At Army Headquarters, and at every single command post, officers and soldiers stepped out into the starlit night; cocking their ears into the sky, they tried to pierce the darkness with their eyes. At the scheduled hour, the sound of heavy aircraft engines was heard: but it came from the north. The Luft-waffe, either by luck or because they had intercepted wireless messages regarding the airborne operation, came in exactly at the right time. For five minutes they circled the area, roaring up and down the beaches, bombing and strafing whilst the furious troops just had to lie down in the mud and take it.

Five minutes later, ten minutes behind schedule, the American Dakotas came over the beachhead. They made a magnificent sight, wing tip to wing tip, as they flew in groups of three in perfect formation. Then, as the lights flashed green in the fuselages and jumpmasters screamed "GO", two thousand men leapt from the aircraft doors and the sky was filled with the fluttering dots of white canopied parachutes drifting down into battle. Soldiers stood in their trenches cheering themselves hoarse. The paratroopers landed dead on the chosen dropping zones and moved swiftly into position near Altavilla. Their arrival was a welcome fillip to the morale of the troops and provided Mark Clark with sufficient reinforcements to hold the balance against increasing German pressure. The Germans were back in the dominating positions and had punched a hole in a vital area which needed strengthening immediately.

CHAPTER XIII

D-DAY PLUS FIVE

14th September, 1943

*B*BC News 2100 hours: "The Allies in the Salerno Area have lost ground to repeated and desperate German counter-attacks. Reinforcements have been arriving for the 5th Army. Two Panzer divisions have been identified among enemy forces."

This dismal announcement was enlarged upon by Radio Berlin, who claimed that Allied troops had been taken by surprise by tanks and motorised forces and that many Allied positions had become untenable. "Transport ships have arrived to take off the troops," the newsreader excitedly shouted. "The Allies are facing another Dunkirk!"

*   *   *   *   *

By now the Germans had five divisions in action and were full of hope that they would force the 5th Army back into the sea. Commanders were urged to keep up the pressure; in high Nazi circles communiqués were being optimistically prepared to announce that Allied Forces had been driven out of Fortress Europe and that the Axis still controlled the whole of the Continent!

Soon after midnight a Wehrmacht officer, who had watched the descending *US* parachutes, went off with a company in search of wandering groups of paratroopers. In the village of Penta they learned that some American soldiers had been there; he started a house-to-house search for them. The village consisted of only one street; the Germans thoroughly investigated every house, rudely turfing the few remaining inhabitants out of bed and threatening them with death if they concealed any Allied soldiers. They discovered nothing until they came to the last house in the row, which they found firmly locked, with complete silence inside. As two men rushed the door to break it down, several automatic weapons emerged from the windows. The attackers immediately tossed a dozen stick grenades through the openings and charged into the building, firing as they ran.

"Hands up," shouted the German officer and, flashing a pocket lamp along a short hallway, found himself faced by about ten bemused American parachutists, some of whom were wounded.

They raised their hands and at the same time there came a clatter of feet out of the back door, as another covey of paratroopers made good their escape to join up with their comrades. The German officer recorded how impressed he was by the American soldiers and their equipment. Each man was excellently armed with a tommy-gun, a revolver, three grenades, numerous fuses and a knife; they also carried a compass, silk maps, brass knuckledusters, cigarettes and a first-aid kit. Apparently many of these men talked when questioned, because later he wrote down the names of their units and their objectives.

*   *   *   *   *

Admiral Hewitt having received his orders to plan for re-embarkation of the troops on the previous evening, and his objections to Clark having been overruled, sent that morning for Commodore Oliver, who left *Hilary* and went over to *Ancon* in his launch.

Hewitt told him the plan. Code word *Sea Lion*, if issued, indicated the transfer of the American corps to the British sector, whilst *Sea Train* stood for the move of the British troops into the *US* sector. Oliver, who had no idea that the Army Commander was taking such a dismal view of the course of battle, was horrified.

"It just cannot be done," he responded. "Ships get deeper when being loaded and it would be impossible to get them off the beaches. It will be another Dunkirk. If you shorten the beachhead, the Germans will be within kissing distance and able to shell us from both flanks."

Hewitt listened sympathetically, but in view of Clark's determination was forced to reply: "Never mind, Commodore; you go and do it."

Oliver returned to his headquarters ship and explained the situation to his staff. To this day he recalls what happened. "They hooted with laughter and nothing was done about it."

He did, however, send a signal to McCreery, who had been kept completely in the dark over the project. Not surprisingly the corps commander was livid and agreed entirely with Oliver's views that it would be nothing short of a disaster if it was allowed to be carried out. He was additionally disturbed, as no mention of this plan had been made during the Army Commander's conference on the previous evening. McCreery told Oliver that he also had no intention of carrying out the orders.

Nevertheless rumours of this 'Dunkirk' plan did disseminate in certain circles and prompted some individual moves.

* * * * *

The 12th Air Support Control, an American unit under command of General Edwin House, which had landed on the previous day near Montecorvino, had been set up in an orchard. Having received news from Army Headquarters that the situation was going from bad to worse, General House was ready to evacuate his whole unit. The officers were sitting round a rough table having an open-air breakfast under the fruit trees, when a couple of officers from a sub-unit arrived and were invited to join them. Conversationally the general asked where their men were.

"Gee, General, they've pissed off," was the reply, with the added information that troops had retreated during a counter-attack.

With the news he already had General House addressed the group: "Boys, we've gotta get out of here."

Without delay, the whole unit, every man for himself, started packing: a stream of speeding jeeps was soon departing towards the southern sector.

Group Captain Jack Millar, *RAF*, attached to 12th Air Support Control, spoke to an airman. "Where is the camp commandant?" he asked, as he wanted to know the new location of the unit.

The man pointed to a revving jeep: "I guess that's him."

There was complete chaos; to make matters worse, all the unit signs pointing to the headquarters were left behind, and for days afterwards visitors followed them to a deserted orchard.

But not all American Air Control officers reacted in this way. House sent a message to his wings to the effect that he was retiring to the beaches preparatory to re-embarking on the ships. Colonel Hawkins, Commanding the 64th Wing, upon receipt of the signal, immediately replied that he intended staying put, and that it was safer close to the enemy than sitting on a beach under constant gunfire. He ordered his men to remain where they were; in addition, he took it upon himself to bring in some Spitfires to the air strips that had been newly carved out of the beachhead. These planes proved invaluable in close support of the infantry. Hawkins, soon to be promoted general, took the risk of incurring the displeasure of his seniors as, if any of the aircraft had been destroyed by enemy shelling on the ground, he would have been proved wrong and held responsible.

Another senior officer who had not been taken into Clark's confidence was Major-General Fred Walker, who has recorded:

> Clark became alarmed and ordered the Navy to be prepared to evacuate the 36th Division and attached troops from the beachhead. He never discussed his uneasiness with me, nor did he ever discuss with me the detailed dispositions of my troops and their missions. It is my opinion that his uneasiness, which unfortunately was transmitted to the Navy and the Pentagon, was due in great measure to his lack of knowledge of my detailed plans and dispositions for disposing of German tank attacks. My operations and intelligence sections kept VI Corps (headquarters) informed by periodic reports and VI Corps in turn made reports to Army, but such reports by the time they reached Army Headquarters were out of date, in the moving situation, and positions of troops posted on maps as a result of such reports were incomplete and misleading. The prisoners we took from time to time gave us a very good indication of what was brewing behind the German front, so that while the combat troops and my headquarters were concerned, they never did feel any cause for alarm.
>
> At another time Army Headquarters became apprehensive about its own security and I was directed to send one tank-destroyer company, from the 636th Tank Destroyer Battalion, and an infantry battalion to guard Army Headquarters. I was also directed to post one company of *TD*s to guard VI Corps headquarters. While I did not see any necessity for this, I took care of the directive by sending two platoons of tank destroyers from their positions on the front and posted my only reserve infantry battalion, one of those that had been previously mauled, near Army Headquarters and sent a company of *TD*s being landed on the beaches, to VI Corps. This directive did not weaken our defence to any appreciable degree, but it did indicate unnecessary alarm. The defences were ample without the company and two platoons of tank destroyers, and I had to give the mauled infantry battalions an opportunity to rest and reorganise.

General Walker is also critical of Clark for what he describes as unnecessary shelling of inhabited areas:

> General Clark informed me this day that the Navy was going to bombard Altavilla. At the time we were in a defensive position along La Cosa Creek. I did not see how the destruction of buildings and killing of civilians in Altavilla was going to help our situation. There were probably some German troops in the town but they would know

how to take cover and protect themselves as soon as the shelling began. A very few of them might become casualties. The greater part of the German force could be expected to be on the high ground outside the town. After the bombardment it would still be occupied by German troops.

My views were not requested and I did not volunteer to state them. Some days later I visited what was once the town of Battipaglia. It was a complete wreck. I was told that the Navy had had the principal part in its destruction. A town on a map makes an excellent target for any fire direction's centre. It can be hit every time and the flying debris and dust proves the fact. The observers and spotters who are directing the fire have a feeling of pride and accomplishment. Actually, such destruction added little or nothing to the improvement of the tactical situation. But it did great damage in the way of causing misery and loss of homes to the non-combatants and, in my opinion, was not justified.

Admiral Hewitt in the afternoon sent an urgent cable to Admiral of the Fleet Cunningham:

> The Germans have created a salient dangerously near the beach. Am planning to use all available vessels to transfer troops from southern to northern beaches, or the reverse if necessary. Unloading of merchant vessels in the southern sector has been stopped. We need heavy aerial and naval bombardment behind enemy positions, using battleships or other heavy naval vessels. Are any such ships available?

Cunningham received this message at 1500 hours. Within two hours he had ordered Admiral Vian to speed up the embarkation of reinforcement troops at Philippeville and to sail at once with *HMS Euryalus*, *Scylla* and *Charybdis* direct to Salerno. One hour later the captains of the mighty battleships *Warspite* and *Valiant*, anchored at Malta, were ordered to raise steam and with an escort of six destroyers report to Admiral Hewitt at the earliest. He also offered *Nelson* and *Rodney* if needed. Cunningham's decision was not taken without some apprehension in view of the danger of flying bombs and the possibility of losing these capital ships. But it was a risk that was well worthwhile.

Unfortunately a copy of Hewitt's message to Cunningham, received at Algiers, was handed over to General Eisenhower. Having been badly garbled in transmission, it gave the impression that Clark was contemplating the complete evacuation of Salerno. It was some hours before the Supreme Commander was satisfied that this was not the case.

On the previous day Eisenhower had told Air Chief Marshal Tedder to use the whole might of the North-West African Air Forces in direct support of the troops; the ground commanders with relief now saw a succession of bomber flights soaring over the area nearly all day long. Hasty briefing and an unfamiliarity with the ground on the part of many pilots led to several mistaken targets, and friendly troops were bombed and machine-gunned in error. But the weight of bombs disrupted enemy communications and so bemused the German troops that the Allies were able to consolidate their positions.

Kesselring and Clark both had anxious eyes and ears pointing in a southwards direction, waiting for the arrival of the 8th Army. For the Germans it was imperative that the 5th Army should be thrown back before a union was made, whilst Clark knew that if they did not join up in a few days it would not be possible to hang on even with additional forces. Yet Monty's troops were still nearly one hundred miles away. There was little fighting on their front, apart from patrol contacts. But the mountainous terrain lent itself to a policy of demolition; every valley, every stream was a barrier, across which bridges had to be built before the mechanised forces could advance—and the 8th Army relied very much on its vehicles.

Marshal Kesselring's memoirs reveal that on the 14th he received a message that troops of 76th Panzer Corps had actually broken through to the beaches in the American sector, and there were high hopes that the Allies would be thrown into the sea. Montgomery's cautious approach being a great help to him, he described the threat from the south as unformidable:

> The British 8th Army's dissipation of force, which we did not make the mistake of imitating, helped us considerably.

Alexander's despatches read:

> The 14th was the critical day and the attacks on all parts of our front were pressed with the greatest vigour. We suffered heavy casualties and lost ground in some places, but by the use of every remaining reserve and by employing administrative troops in the line the enemy was held. It was an impressive example of stubborn doggedness in defence, for the sea at our backs was very close and all the troops were exhausted by six days of uninterrupted struggle.

*   *   *   *   *

When General McCreery returned that afternoon to his headquarters near Pontecagnano, he found the camp in disorder, with men rushing around busily packing all their belongings in lorries. He asked his Chief of Staff what it was all about, and was informed that the headquarters was virtually in the front line and in grave danger of being overrun. McCreery pointed out that there was hardly room in the restricted beachhead to park a lorry, let alone put a corps headquarters.

"We stay here," he ordered. "And the defence section will keep us out of trouble."

Hidden in the olive groves just to the south of Faiano, the 2/7th Queen's under Lieutenant-Colonel 'Chippy' Block had clung on to their forward positions against repeated attacks. They had suffered the additional inconvenience of being directly under the Luftwaffe route to the beaches; pilots with bombs or bullets to spare often swooped down to relieve themselves of a load.

In the few days they had been there they had come to recognise a daily sortie by a flight of eighteen Mitchell bombers, which had been nicknamed 'The 18 Bus service'. On this morning they sat on the lips of their trenches looking at the white-starred planes and generally freshening themselves up. At first no notice was taken of the sudden whine of a falling bomb, but within seconds they realised that the bombs were intended for them, whilst the whole area was engulfed in a storm of explosions wrecking emplacements and wounding many men. Not unnaturally the troops were ill-disposed towards the American Air Force from then on, and even an apologetic note from US Air Command failed to clear away their resentment and subsequent fear of close-support bombing.

Near the hospital on Laughing Hill units had been withdrawn into a tight perimeter round the buildings. It was a two-battalion sector defended by the 2/4th *KOYLI* and the 16th *DLI*. This day was moderately quiet, apart from desultory shelling and mortaring. A patrol of 'B' Company was sent out to obtain an identification of the enemy unit opposing them. After a drawn-out struggle at a German position, they managed to bring back a prisoner, but in the confusion they had grabbed a man without his tunic, and all his papers were left behind. Under interrogation he refused to reveal who he was or where he came from; the patrol's efforts had been in vain.

*   *   *   *   *

Arturo Carucci, who records that he had had a pretty harrowing twenty-four hours after he had departed from the hospital, was very worried about the fate of his charges in the tunnel. Knowing nothing of events there, he was still under the impression that the Sanatorium remained a neutral zone. From the Salerno Hospice he set off on foot with a guide heading for the seminary in the hope of finding asylum there for his people. He was fired on by both sides as he ran, crawled and staggered along, whilst a few frightened civilians recognising him shouted out for news. He finally came across a patient who had left the shelter, who told him that the Sanatorium was a fortress, barricades blocking every entry and exit, guns positioned in the park and on every vantage point. From the tunnel came worse news of an epidemic breaking out, of hunger and disease and the absolute lack of hygiene. The medical staff feared that if the refugees continued to live in those conditions for much longer the situation would get completely out of hand.

Meeting several other members of the hospital staff and patients, who had decided to leave the tunnel, Carucci divided them into three parties, sending them off in different directions in the hope that one group might get through to the Sanatorium to help with the evacuation of the sick from the tunnel. The chaplain was also deeply worried over the presence in the chapel of a few consecrated wafers which he had left in the pyx on top of the altar. If these were desecrated, it would mean that the whole chapel would have to be re-consecrated, and he was determined to avoid this. At about 1430 hours he started to ascend the Laughing Hill, but there came a thunder of shots; with his companions, Lieutenant Gatti, Soffietti and the Senior Sister, he was smothered in dirt from exploding shells. Carucci had to give up the attempt and return to the seminary.

But some hours later a nurse, who had got through to the hospital, returned bringing with her the wafers. Carucci immediately had them placed on the altar in the seminary, and his beloved chapel was saved.

*   *   *   *   *

On the 56th Division front the Germans mounted yet another tank-infantry attack from Battipaglia. Forward units of the Coldstream Guards watched helplessly as one of their patrols was chased back into the lines followed by four packed enemy half-tracks, one of which broke through and finished up in the brigade headquarters area, where considerably surprised staff officers and clerks fought a lively battle before knocking it out. On the right of the Guards, the 167th Brigade, with the remnants of the 8th and 9th Royal Fusiliers and the Oxford and Buckingham Light Infantry, were thrown back by tanks along the east bank of the Tusciano. 'B' and 'C' Squadrons of the Royal Scots Greys moved up before dawn, creating sufficient havoc amongst the enemy to cause them to withdraw.

This part of the line was, however, very thinly held. At one stage General Graham told his Commander Royal Artillery:

"I have every rifle man in the line, even the men from the beaches. I have only one squadron of tanks as my reserve and the enemy is nearly through on the fronts of two battalions. What can you do? It is up to you, otherwise I've nothing but the worst happening to us."

The gunners responded magnificently. All the reserve ammunition was brought in from the shore; thirty-six heavy anti-aircraft guns were positioned to fire in a ground role. Although they had never practised it before, they were most successful, and at the end of the day the general commented:

"It was the guns that saved us."

Fusilier Needham had spent the night in the wood. At first light he crawled for half a mile with his group of wounded down a ditch towards a field, from which they heard German voices. They retired, but as they reached a road they were challenged by a German sentry. They ran as fast as they could, with the crackle of small arms and bullets whistling around them; they were between the lines and at last running in the right direction. Mortar bombs were falling around; then, to their chagrin, British troops also started firing at them. Needham was conscious of an explosion and felt himself tossed through the air. When he next woke up he was about to be loaded aboard a Bren-carrier; from the pain in his stomach, he realised he had been wounded again. The Bren-carrier rattled down a lane leading to the beaches, but had not driven far before hitting a mine: both tracks were blown off and the occupants hurled into the road. A passing lorry rescued them; they were later transferred to an ambulance, which took them to a casualty evacuation ship and thence to a hospital ship bound for Algiers.

As he lay on a stretcher, the Fusilier looked back over his recent days' fighting, recalling the things which have remained in his mind ever since. The salient points went through his head in quick flashes:

What appeared to be a complete lack of plan. We were never shown any details, only rough notes, and everyone thought the landing would be easy.

The way American soldiers appeared on the beach when we were under heavy fire; they were carrying weighty kit-bags, had no shovels, and told us that they did not expect any fighting.

The terrible scream of German dive bombers and my pleasure at watching one smash into the ground just in front.

Seeing a large factory disappear into dust, together with its German garrison as a broadside from a ship tore into it.

The hypnotic attraction of tracer bullets as they came towards me so slowly, suddenly to speed up and crack by.

The terror on an Italian farmer's face, as he cried and asked for help for his wounded wife. As I and another helped him he told us in broken English how both his sons had died in Africa. We took his wife into his house, and upon opening the bedroom door found a German officer on the bed, dead, with both legs blown off.

The good tempers and help given by other Fusiliers—to the extent of crawling under intense fire to help and to pass cigarettes and food.

How I missed a cup of tea and hot food.

The terrible smell of death—I can still smell this now!

Watching a man lying down with six bullets in his stomach, groaning in agony as he slowly died; I felt sweat all over me, even though it was cold.

How the time and days passed—it seemed all so quick afterwards.

For Fusilier Needham, Salerno was over.

By the evening, the situation on the Battipaglia front was much easier. It was therefore decided to transfer the 167th Brigade less the 9th Royal Fusiliers to bolster the positions in the north and they moved north of Pontecagnano under command of the 128th Brigade of the 46th Division. From the Hampshires they took over a 4,000-yard front, which spread up and down hills and was dominated by the enormous San Mango feature. The men welcomed the change of scenery from the mosquito-infested swamps of the plains.

The departing Hampshire lads had described the positions as "quiet". But just before midnight the enemy launched a surprise silent attack on White Cross Hill and the nearby Crag. The 1/4th Battalion Hampshires, who had not yet left the position, were overrun, together with their replacements. Luckily they were all able to slip across to White Cross Hill to join the 1/5th Battalion, who were then soon afterwards subjected to another silent assault. The troops had become so accustomed to thunderous barrages preceding all enemy moves, that it took them some time to get used to the change in tactics. These important heights, held for so long against heavy odds, were thus lost. A quickly organised

counter-attack by 'W' Company of the 2nd Hampshires with two
platoons of the 5th Battalion charged up White Cross and regained
the peak. But they suffered so many casualties in the process that
they had to be withdrawn at dawn; both sides temporarily contented
themselves with covering it with fire.

Time and again during the following days the troops were to
attack these objectives. Units became hopelessly intermingled;
at one time Lieutenant-Colonel R. Chandler, *CO* of the 1/4th
Battalion, found himself commanding seven companies of various
units. Once again the 46th Division line was in danger and the
Germans in positions overlooking the entire beach area. Some fast
thinking and action was required to stabilise the situation.

*   *   *   *   *

The Tactical Air Force played an important role on 14th September. Flying a total of 700 sorties, it struck at every conceivable
static and moving target. Wherever the Germans thought they
were safe, the airmen sought them out and pounded them. The
main weight of bombs fell on already battered Battipaglia, which
by the end of the day was merely a pile of smoking rubble. Only a
hundred years before the small town had been established after a
severe earthquake to house the survivors of other villages: yet it
was now a dead and abandoned city.

James Cooper, the *Sunday Express* War Correspondent, wrote:

> A new and gladsome sound today—the first roar of heavy bombers
> in big numbers as Fortresses, Bostons and Mitchells come in waves.
> Sailors run on deck to find new interest in the old scene of golden
> beaches fringed by orchards and with hills hidden by sirocco-borne
> mist.

But, above all, it was naval shelling that was causing enemy dismay. Wherever they moved, wherever they fired from, they were
certain to get in return a salvo from the ships' guns. The system
between the troops and naval forward observation officers with
direct wireless contact to the ships was by now working perfectly.
A battalion commander could call for fire support and was almost
guaranteed to receive it within a few minutes. Day and night, these
guns never stopped. On the night of the 14th General von Veitinghoff wrote:

> Our attack this morning pushed on into stiffened resistance; but
> above all the advancing troops had to endure the most severe fire that

had hitherto been experienced; the naval gunfire from at least sixteen to eighteen battleships, cruisers and large destroyers lying in the roadstead. With astonishing precision and freedom of manœuvre these ships shot at every identifiable target with overwhelming effect.

The history of the 16th Panzer Division records:

Wherever German units attacked on the 14th September, such heavy fire from the sea and air struck them that they were able to gain only local successes.

Nevertheless the 10th Army did not give up the fight. The remaining units of the 26th Panzer Division arrived from the south and one regiment of the 3rd Panzer Division from Rome. The Army decided to regroup its forces in order to launch further attacks on the 16th September simultaneously from the north and south to destroy the bridgehead!

* * * * *

General Mark Clark decided to go on a personal reconnaissance of the American front line. Having held a brief conference with General Dawley at 0700 hours, he drove off in his jeep along the dusty tracks just behind the forward trenches. He stopped and talked to hundreds of officers and men during the day; wherever he went, he noticed the fatigue of the troops and often the fatalistic air of defeat. Not many of the *GIs* understood the true situation and listened in wonder when the tall, gangling Army Commander said: "There mustn't be any doubt in your mind. We don't give another inch. This is it. Don't yield anything. We're here to stay."

At one point in the line he left his jeep and with his aide, Captain Warren Thrasher, climbed a small hill overlooking no-man's-land. There were no American troops forward of this position, but he did see a group of eighteen tanks infiltrating through the lines. He first assumed them to be American, but a hasty glance through his binoculars assured him they were German. Looking around, he saw there were no tanks or anti-tank guns to oppose them; if nothing was done, the armoured vehicles would be through the Allied front in a very short space of time. He ran down the hill back to his jeep, and personally ordered an anti-tank unit into the line: within a short time, the Panzers had turned tail leaving some burning wrecks behind. General Clark in his memoirs claims that if this attack had been backed it could easily have sealed the fate of the American beachhead and he criticised Kesselring for never using his six hundred available tanks in mass formation, instead of wasting them in piecemeal attacks.

Leaving this area, the Army Commander continued his drive northwards. Turning once again towards the front, he passed a column of speeding trucks, in which all the occupants were wearing gas masks. His first reaction was that they were attempting to avoid the heavy clouds of dust which hung everywhere, filling the lungs with every breath. His second thought was that maybe gas had in fact been used by the Germans. Stopping the next lorry, he asked the driver:

"Why are you wearing gas masks?"

"Gas!" shouted the driver, pointing his thumb backwards.

"Where is the gas?" asked Clark.

"Somewhere up front," came the muffled voice through the mask.

It was obvious to Clark that there was no gas; he ordered the men to remove the masks and return the way they had come. This false alarm, which spread right through the American sector, could have caused serious trouble if it had not been squashed at once.

One of Clark's calls was to the command post of the 179th Regimental Combat Team, which had been hit so hard on the previous day. To Colonel Hutchins, the Army Commander proffered congratulations, requesting the troops to hang on at all costs. The tired men nodded and said they would try. Hardly had the Army Commander's jeep disappeared when a heavy artillery barrage engulfed the zone; within minutes reports of fresh enemy tank attacks were coming in from the forward foxholes. There followed other assaults all along the line, and some estimates claimed that two hundred Panzers were used in a final effort to break through.

Within minutes shells from the Navy were landing in the midst of the tanks and amongst the advancing infantry. A company of Panzer Grenadiers facing the 179th *RCT* suddenly appeared to give up the fight; crawling out of folds in the ground, they came forward waving white towels and sheets on sticks. The Americans held their fire; then, at a range of a hundred yards, the enemy fell to the ground sending a vicious automatic fire into them. Cursing with rage, the *GI*s let loose with every weapon they could muster; within a few minutes they had killed forty Germans, whilst the rest scurried off like beaten dogs.

Eight Tiger tanks, which tried to rush down Highway 18 just above Bivio Cioffi, were all knocked out by infantry weapons and tank destroyers. 'A' Company of 751 Tank Battalion moved into the attack against a squadron of Mark IVs which had crossed the Calore; in the ensuing battle the Panzers got the worst of it and retired, leaving eight flamers for the cost of only one Sherman.

At 1300 hours more enemy tanks and infantry appeared north of
La Cosa Creek and came up against the 1st Battalion 141st Infantry
which had only just arrived by truck in the line. At first the situation was very confused; the new arrivals did not know the country
and were wandering around getting their bearings. Several tanks
did get through, but a quick call to the Navy resulted in their
destruction. Sergeant Edwin Yost of 636 Tank Battalion, commanding the self-propelled anti-tank gun 'Jinx' belied the name of his
tracked gun on this day. In the face of heavy high-explosive and
anti-tank shelling, he manœuvred his vehicle to the top of a ridge
from where he commenced firing at a mass of advancing tanks.
His first shot fell two hundred yards short of the target, whilst a
vituperative stream of words descended on the ears of his crew.
The second shot hit a tank. The third set fire to an ammunition
half-track. Then the accurate shells from an 88-mm. gun forced
him to reverse from the ridge, but he merely changed position
appearing in another spot to destroy within thirty minutes another
five Panzers.

During the day the divisional artillery regiments fired the highest
total for the whole of the Salerno battle; the 36th Division shot off
4,100 rounds and the 45th Division 6,687 rounds. Despite the
German pressure, the American line remained intact, and by dusk
the attacks were petering out.

*   *   *   *   *

Close inshore, the water and the beaches were still subjected to
heavy fire, whilst the ships in the bay were taking regular evasive
action from fighters and guided bombs. One of the latter struck a
merchant ship, the *SS Bushrod Washington*, setting on fire thousands
of gallons of petrol which formed part of the cargo. Captain John
Wainwright supervised the abandonment of his vessel and then
jumped overboard. He soon returned with a salvage crew plus an
armed guard, evacuated some wounded sailors who had been left
aboard and tried to fight the fires, helped by the salvage tug *Hopi*.
But shortly the fire got out of control; once again they had to
abandon ship. The vessel was a total loss.

During the night vital reinforcements began arriving by sea and
air. The main body in the shape of parachutists of the 509th Parachute Battalion, commanded by Lieutenant-Colonel Doyle R.
Yardley, dropped twenty miles behind the German positions near
Avellino, with the object of harassing enemy communications and

ausing as much trouble as they could. It was a bad drop. The pilots of the *USAF* transport planes despatched the men over an area of many miles; the whole countryside was littered with discarded parachutes and wandering groups of soldiers, who did not have the faintest idea of their whereabouts. Forced by the mountains to release the men at altitudes of between 3,000 and 5,000 feet only fifteen out of forty planes got to the right place; four hundred paratroopers were dropped anything up to twenty-five miles away, and many were captured.

On the German side:

An alarm was sounded in the bivouac area of 16th Panzer Division. "Paratroopers have landed at Montella!" Their intention was clearly to destroy the division's limited supply roads. It was a clear night. "Assemble!" Groups were formed. Sub-machine-guns and machine-guns were made ready for action. Lieutenant Köpke of the 9/64th and Lieutenant Krause of the 10/64th, who had been wounded, took command. In a night of hand-to-hand fighting, group after group of the enemy, some of whom had dug themselves in, were put out of action. Thirty-five men and one officer were taken prisoner; large quantities of high explosives and new types of rockets were captured.

A lieutenant of the 16th Reconnaisance Regiment wrote in his diary:

I was awakened by a violent shaking of my arm by a guard, who pointed to the sky. I was still half asleep but forced my eyes open and saw the amazing sight of 500 paratroopers at 150 metres swinging towards the ground. As it was bright moonlight one could recognise every white fleck in the heavens. Like cats the gunners sprang into their turrets and soon twenty machine-guns were firing at the descending troops.

Although in the end nearly eighty per cent of the parachutists returned safely back to Allied lines, the whole purpose of the operation was lost. Possibly a hurried briefing of the crews and the speed with which the operation had been launched were partly responsible for the ensuing chaos, but the landing of this battalion did not have the slightest effect on the Salerno battle.

General Walker, in his later comments on the action, writes:

General Clark directed the 509th Parachute Battalion to be dropped near Avellino on the night of September 14th to strike the German rear lines. Avellino was some twenty miles from Salerno. I was never consulted as to the advisability of this procedure. If I had been, would have recommended no drop at that time, for we were on th defensive and in no position to push forward to co-operate with th paratroopers. The parachute battalion was promptly dispersed an had no real influence on the situation.

A letter from General Eisenhower was waiting for Clark when h returned to his headquarters. It read:

> We know you are having a sticky time, but you may be sure tha everybody is working at full speed to provide the reinforcements you need. . . . In the meantime don't forget that we have an air forc that is more than anxious to do its full part in your support. I hop that your bombline will be drawn as accurately as possible along you front, so that our Air Force can continue to disrupt the force trying to concentrate against you.
>
> You and your people have done a magnificent job. We are all proud of you, and since the success of the whole operation depends upon you and your forces, you need have no fear that anything will be neglected in providing you all possible assistance.

The letter gave Clark a great uplift in his morale. Before going to bed, the Army Commander wrote a quick congratulatory note to VI Corps Commander, General Dawley:

> We have arrived at our initial objectives, our beachhead is secure. Additional troops are landing every day and we are here to stay. Not one foot of ground will be given up.

Not quite such a morale-raising letter as the one he had received from the Supreme Commander, but nevertheless it was congratulatory. It is surprising, therefore, to hear a few days later that Clark was thoroughly dissatisfied with his corps commander and sacked him on 20th September.

General Eisenhower, in his role of co-ordinator and co-operator, made a great point about the Air Force in his letter. Yet only a few days before the Army commanders and Air Force chiefs had been at loggerheads over the amount of fighter cover to be put over the beachhead, and it was only after several urgent pleas that the Air Force had agreed to keep it up to Army requirements.

Various claims have since been made, especially by the *RAF* and *USAF*, that it was the planes that saved the day. Yet German histories and diaries reveal that much of this effort was wasted.

Lieutenant Gunter Schmitz of the Pioneer Battalion 16th Panzer Division wrote:

> The bombing of the Strategic Air Force destroyed roads and railways, but we were always able to make a diversion or free the roads. The lack of railway transport was offset by the lorries, which we took over from the Italians after the capitulation: 16th Panzer Division had 600 of them. I don't know what it looked like in the hinterland, but in spite of the heavy bombing the ambulances, supplies and ammunition, and even the leave transports continued!

On the other hand, General Schmalz of the Hermann Goering Division recorded:

> Owing to the urgency of the occasion, the troops had to march up by day in the face of overwhelming enemy air superiority; there was no visible intervention by our own air force; for example, the Division found only two narrow mountain roads available, which were under heavy attack from the enemy air force and naval guns, along which to mount a counter-attack. . . . The enemy air force was unable to operate fully in low level attacks in the hilly country. On the other hand, its operation against our reserves was all the more effective.

For the first time it was true to say that the bridgehead was secure.

CHAPTER XIV

D-DAY PLUS SIX

15th September, 1943

" STIFF fighting continues in the 5th Army sector between Salerno and Agropoli. Determined counter-attacks have been carried out by both sides. In some places our troops have been forced to yield ground, but new positions are being consolidated and reinforcements continue to arrive rapidly. Support provided by naval aircraft is excellent . . . the 8th Army is within eighty miles."

Thus the *BBC* recorded the day's events.

*   *   *   *   *

As dawn rose on the seventh morning of the invasion, naval lookouts reported the presence of two large capital ships with an escort coming up fast from the south. Within a few minutes they were identified as the battleships *Valiant* and *Warspite*. By 1000 hours they were ready for action and took up station in the bay. A magnificent sight in their war paint, they had an air almost of disdain towards the lesser cruisers and destroyers already there. But for some reason the briefing of their gunnery officers took a long time and it was 1720 hours before a shot was fired, owing to delays in communication with *FOO*s.

Warspite, the grand old lady of the Battle of Jutland, was the first to go into action; her target was in support of the Americans. She fired thirty rounds of 15-inch shell into the Altavilla area, and excited radio operators signalled back that nineteen had fallen exactly on target. This was naval gunnery at its best. The battleships were shooting at ranges from 19,500 yards to 21,800 yards, and the effect of those heavy shells on the enemy emplacements was horrific.

General Alexander had arrived at Clark's headquarters, having sailed from Bizerta aboard a destroyer. He had consultations at all levels throughout the day and made some important decisions. The Army Commander painted a pessimistic picture of the situation, explaining to Alexander his plan for the evacuation of the American troops and their re-landing in the Northern sector. He listened to the arguments against this from Commodore Oliver and from General McCreery, both of whom insisted that such an operation would be disastrous. He also visited Dawley at VI Corps *HQ*. Having weighed all points of view, and with the knowledge of greater resources still untapped in the Mediterranean, Alexander made up his mind: he told Clark that the whole idea was to be scrapped and that he would do his utmost to bring in more air and sea power and to hasten the arrival of reinforcements.

A matter which Clark also discussed with Alexander was the conduct of the battle in the American Sector by General Dawley. Clark had come to the conclusion that Dawley was responsible for most of the errors that had been made, and was accordingly determined to make a scapegoat of him. Alexander, it was reported, was in full agreement that a change of corps commander would be for the better.

After verbal explanations, General Alexander went on a long tour of the battlefield accompanied by General Mark Clark and General Richard McCreery. They filled a jeep to overflowing: Alexander spruce and typically 'Guardee', with his clipped moustache and gently slanted peak cap; Mark Clark, tall and gangling, hooked nose and cowboy appearance; McCreery, all Cavalry and efficiency. One of their calls was at the headquarters of the 201st Guards Brigade. Alexander was pleased to see men of the Household troops, and urged them to hang on for a few more days. The battered Guards were in no mood for cheering speeches, but they knew they had no choice but to hang on or finish in the sea.

By nightfall General Alexander was feeling much more cheerful. Before leaving the beachhead, he signalled to General Eisenhower to the effect that, although he was not entirely happy about the situation, it was better than it had been twenty-four hours earlier. The troops were tired, but on the whole in good heart. He reported the emergency reinforcement programme had been put into operation and asked for the Army's gratitude to be passed on to the air forces and the navies for the great support they had given the soldiers on the ground.

Mark Clark was regaining some of his lost confidence, but he was not at all pleased to get a typically bumptious message from General Montgomery which, giving a résumé of his progress up from the south, ended with the request:

> Perhaps you could push out a reconnaissance along the road from Agropoli to meet my people, who have already started from Sapri ...
> It looks as if you may be having not too good a time, and I do hope

that all will go well with you. We are on our way to lend a hand, and it will be a great day when we actually join hands.

Clark, somewhat annoyed by the casual reference to sending out a reconnaissance patrol, responded:

It will be a pleasure to see you again at an early date. Situation here well in hand.

However, unknown to either Clark or Montgomery, contact was to come very shortly and from a most unexpected source. A party of war correspondents, accredited to the 8th Army, had got fed up with the slow progress and had decided to go out ahead in a couple of jeeps to see for themselves what was happening. This party, which included Alan Moorehead and Ronald Monson of the *Daily Express*, Evelyn Montague (*Manchester Guardian*), Ted Gilling (*Exchange Telegraph*), Eric Lloyd Williams (*Reuters*), Christopher Buckley (*Times*), Alexander Clifford and Captain John Soboleff, an Army Public Relations Officer, had set off on the previous day, leaving the 8th Army's forward patrols to the rear. Between them and the 5th Army were fifty miles of so-called enemy territory. The correspondents presumed that the withdrawing Germans would mainly use the inland road, so as to avoid the Americans at Paestum; their supposition was correct.

The night of the 14th/15th was spent in a small chateau near the town of Castelnuovo. The Chief of the Carabinieri, who had obligingly telephoned the next village to the north, had learnt that German armoured cars were still in occupation. Early on the 15th, the party again set off, picking up local guides to show them tracks and minor roads, thus managing to circumvent many demolished bridges. By the time they reckoned to be within fifteen miles of the nearest *US* outpost, they came up against a chasm on the opposite side of which was unmistakable evidence of recent American occupation. The edge was littered with discarded 'K' ration boxes and empty tins. After hours of frustration, they finally located a guide who revealed a wide-open road to the north; following the signs of American occupation rather like competitors in a cross-country paper chase, they finally turned one of the thousands of corners on a hilly road, and saw ahead of them an American half-track. The surprised crew, who were under orders to destroy every bridge and gully they could find, took them for Germans and came very near to firing on them.

The time was 1050 hours, 15th September, 1943.

There followed the usual handshakes and short speeches of congratulations, whilst the correspondents managed to convince the Americans that they should stop further demolitions, as the road to the south was free of Germans and any destructions would now be only to the detriment of the 8th Army.

At Army Headquarters the tired journalists were questioned by senior officers and by General Alexander about the type of terrain they had crossed and the exact route they had taken. Altogether the party had come through 120 miles of what was presumed by both armies to be enemy territory. Not unnaturally the correspondents felt that if an unarmed party could do this, there was no reason why properly organised and equipped units could not do better. Many army officers at the time, and later, spoke disparagingly about the feat, dismissing it as unimportant. The main lesson it should have brought home to the commanders was that they were too road-bound; if a vehicle could not get through, they generally gave up the attempt, instead of sending men on their flat feet to take over territory and keep contact with the enemy. In addition, several important bridges were destroyed quite unnecessarily between the two armies, delaying even further the eventual link up.

Strangely enough a very similar error was to prove fateful at Arnhem just over one year later, when Monty's troops again failed to follow a route up to the Rhine, which for several days had been used by unarmed jeeps and ambulances.

Rumours of the journalists' arrival in the beachhead passed from mouth to mouth, proving to be of tremendous morale value. Many soldiers were soon swearing that they had heard bagpipes and that the 51st Highland Division would shortly be there to relieve them. In fact another twenty-four hours were to pass before patrols of the British 5th Reconnaissance Regiment from the 8th Army were to join with American troops of VI Corps.

* * * * *

The 46th Division was to bear the brunt of the day's fighting in the British sector. All the way from the northern tip of the perimeter down to White Cross Hill the enemy had infiltrated and were still pounding away, trying to find a weak spot through which they could pour onto the beaches. The Germans were well aware that their time was running short.

During the afternoon the weight of enemy shells increased on positions occupied by the Hampshires, *KOYLI*, Leicesters, Durham Light Infantry, the 8th Royal Fusiliers, the York & Lancasters, the

Lincolns, the Ox & Bucks, and the men from these famous County Regiments cursed and spat at the thought of yet another day of sitting down and taking it. At dusk a very determined attack was launched in the Sanatorium area against the Durham Light Infantry and the King's Own Yorkshire Light Infantry. 'D' Company of the Durhams was overwhelmed on a pimple hill by Grenadiers of the 16th Panzer Division, and scattered in some confusion into another company's position. There the officers stopped and rallied the tired men. Two counter-attacks were sent in. The first was unsuccessful; then Major F. P. Duffy led his soldiers with fixed bayonets in a whooping shouting charge back up the hill, where the terrified Germans broke and ran.

The battalion's padre, George Meek, in retrospect, wrote of this night:

> They were queer times; on the evening of 'D' Company's bayonet charge we had a short service in the regimental aid post—the whole thing was unreal—the hymns, prayers and lessons were punctuated by insistent bangs which seemed to be right outside the door. Some irresponsible person looked in to say "Jerry's broken through" and almost immediately a quietness descended, as it seemed, everywhere, which was ominous. Men could be seen gathering kit together with no spoken intention, everything not being used was put in the truck, the light faded and the silence persisted.

Soon afterwards a slightly wounded German officer was brought into the aid post; in a truculent manner, he said that Rommel was organising an army in the north, which would push the British into the sea. A medical orderly blew a very loud and vulgar raspberry at these remarks; the tension was broken!

Other attacks followed during the evening on the *KOYLI* front and other Durham companies, but the news of the bayonet charge had spread and morale had risen to a new height; neither battalion gave up another inch of territory.

In the hilly terrain farther south troops crouched in their shallow foxholes under the fire of Germans newly entrenched on White Cross Hill. From time to time counter-attacks against the hill were launched from different directions, but none succeeded.

General Hawkesworth sent for the Commando leader, Brigadier Laycock, and told him that he wanted White Cross and the surrounding hills retaken. The Commandos were the men for the job: it should be done that night.

The position here was that the enemy, who had occupied the village of Piegolelli, had dug in on three hills: White Cross, Pimple and another, soon to be named 41 Commando Hill; they were grouped together north of the main road from Salerno to Battipaglia.

Allowed about one hour for planning, the Commandos formed up with only the vaguest idea as to where they were going and what the objective was. They were tired and had the feeling that they were being called in to do the Army's dirty work, as usual. The happiest were those accompanying a troop of Sherman tanks. Greatly pleased, they mounted the hulls with plenty of banter, shouting: "Lots of room on top, chum!"—"Sixpence for the front seats, threepence for the back." But the ground soon proved too boggy; one tank crashed through a bridge and two others stuck before they ever got into the hills. The swearing Commandos clambered off and walked forward, trying to catch up their comrades.

Number 2 Commando under Jack Churchill was ordered to advance up the thickly wooded valley, through the dense vines and other cultivation, and capture Piegolelli. The attack was to be carried out in the pitch dark; as the men and officers were all unfamiliar with the ground, it was not an easy task. Colonel Churchill, dividing his force into six columns of troop strength, told them to spread across the whole valley. To make the enemy think they were a much stronger force, he ordered them to shout "Commando!" at the top of their voices, which would also enable the columns to keep in touch. Churchill was at the head, waving a sword.

Setting a smart pace, his sharp eyes picking out every rock on the ground and every hazard along his path, the colonel soon found himself well ahead, having even outdistanced his escort, Corporal Fussell. First into the village, he moved stealthily along, keeping a wary eye on every shadow. He heard the sound of digging from the left; passing the first house on silent feet, he froze, seeing two cigarette butts glowing in a doorway. Slowly he crept towards the red dots, and soon recognised the outline of German steel helmets. He was about to pounce, when a villager came out of the house to ask the Germans in for a drink. Churchill waited impatiently for them. When they returned a few minutes later, they were faced by a fearsome figure waving a gleaming sword and shouting in appalling German "*Hande Hoch!*" which order they obeyed with startled rapidity.

Glancing around, the Commanding Officer saw a nearby mortar pit, with the crew evidently asleep round the weapon. By this time Corporal Fussell had caught up; telling him to guard the prisoners, he crept into the pit, kicked the mortarmen into wakefulness, and repeated his command: *"Hande Hoch!"* Four dozy soldiers stumbled to their feet and joined their comrades in captivity.

Handing over all prisoners but one to a passing group, they set off at a sharp pace deeper into the village. The German who was with them knew the passwords and the position of all the sentry posts. Overawed by the colonel's demeanour and probably fearful that he would be decapitated if he did not immediately obey every order, he found himself being trotted from one sentry post to another, shouting the password and seeing his unit captured one by one by the sword-waving English officer. Churchill personally captured thirty to forty men, including the occupants of a regimental aid post.

Captain Hemming of Number 4 Troop took thirty-four prisoners under similar circumstances; altogether the Army Commandos took 136 prisoners-of-war, more—up to this time—than the whole of the 46th Division combined.

From Piegolelli the troops set off towards Pimple Hill, which had been a constant menace to the defending infantry. Most of the enemy soldiers, hearing the constant repetition of "Commando—Commando—Commando" echoing up the hills from the valleys, stayed quietly in their trenches in the hope of remaining undiscovered or, after a few desultory shots, quickly retired farther inland. Reaching the objective virtually unharmed, the men turned about and repeated the process in reverse.

By daylight they had accomplished all they had been sent out to do and returned to their positions outside the village. Later General Hawkesworth asked Colonel Churchill why he carried a sword.

Churchill replied: "In my opinion, any officer who goes into action without his sword is improperly dressed!"

Faced with such a reply, the general was at a loss for words. Churchill was awarded a *DSO* for his distinguished conduct during this and subsequent actions.

*   *   *   *   *

As reports flowed into Supreme Headquarters from Naval, Army and Air Force commanders, for the first time General Eisenhower began to get a true picture of the situation. He wrote that night to General George Marshall in Washington:

> We are very much in the touch-and-go stage of this operation. We got the Italian fleet into Malta and, because of the Italian surrender, we were able to rush Brindisi and Taranto where no Germans were present. Our hold on both places is precarious, but we are striving mightily to reinforce. Our worse problem is *Avalanche* itself. We have

been unable to advance and the enemy is preparing a major counter-attack. The 45th Division is largely in the area now and I am using everything we have larger than a row boat to get the 3rd Division to Clark quickly. In the present situation our great hope is in the air force. They are working flat out; and assuming, which I do, that our hold on southern Italy will finally be solidified, we are going to prove once again that the greatest value of the three services is ordinarily realised only when it is utilised in close co-ordination with the other two. . . .

There spoke Eisenhower, the great co-ordinator, the man who was to prove time and time again in subsequent operations that, without close liaison between the three services, individual effort was always wasted when it came up against service jealousies and rivalries.

*   *   *   *   *

Meanwhile throughout the day Arturo Carucci and his companions had been seeking Allied Headquarters in order to plead that the patients and nurses be allowed to evacuate the tunnel, around which vicious fighting ebbed and flowed, to a place of greater safety. Accepting a lift from an Allied jeep, they drove towards Ponte-cagnano. The chaplain was horrified to see numerous dead civilians lying at the sides of the roads, victims of bombing or shelling attacks. The British headquarters had moved and they finally went back to Salerno to plead their case with the Allied Military Governor.

At the seminary Carucci lunched with the Archbishop of Salerno, where he was offered a new pair of shoes by an Italian soldier, shocked by the deplorable state of his clothes. The white cassock of the Sanatorium chaplain was stained with blood and spattered with mud; the soles of his shoes flapped loose from the uppers. He had the appearance of a foot-weary pilgrim, who had travelled thousands of miles seeking out a holy refuge. The care of his flock continually uppermost in his mind, he had in fact not rested since the invasion. He was a most devoted servant of God; his name and bravery were to be recognised and remembered by the people of Salerno for many years.

In the evening he managed to get a lift from an American journalist, who took him, Lieutenant Gatti, Soffietti and another priest to the town hall. Colonel Lane greeted them by kneeling down in front of the priests and asking for a blessing. He promised to do all he could to ease the plight of the sick people and nurses. This American colonel impressed every Italian he met; there was no doubt that he prevented Salerno from turning into a chaos of crime, rape, looting and general lawlessness. As they stood talking on the steps of the town Hall, eight German shells came screaming into the square killing several civilians, whilst the blast knocked over the small group, including the Military Governor, whose uniform was torn by splinters. He advised them to seek a place of safety and return at some other time.

They spent the night in the seminary, discussing the fact that, despite the promises and assurance they had received from the Governor and other senior officers, very little practical help had been forthcoming; they remembered all too clearly the reaction of one American lieutenant on the Government staff, who had responded to an appeal by saying:

"How can we be bothered with you people, when we cannot even fight our way out of Salerno?"

But something had to be done. Food was running short; the patients would die, if not from lack of nourishment, from disease which was rife in the unhealthy underground chamber. Dawn came, and there still was no answer to their problem.

*   *   *   *   *

The Germans had not yet shot their bolt. General von Veitinghoff, from his headquarters at Sant'Angelo di Lombardi in the Apennines, issued instructions for yet another general attack against the 5th Army perimeter. The 3rd Panzer Grenadier Division was hotly engaged north-east of Salerno at Sordina and was ordered to maintain close contact. At the same time, the tanks of the Hermann Goering Division were withdrawn from the Cava area and despatched farther south to San Mango, a large mountain dominating the whole area of the British sector.

General Schmalz prepared a new line of assault to include the defence of Cava and an attack on Salerno. The infantry were to gain the heights south of Sordina in a surprise night attack on the night of 15th/16th September, and push on to the sea. The Panzer group was to form up at daybreak and reach the sea from San Mango via Alfani, and there join with the Panzer Grenadier Regiment. Both groups would then re-form and recapture Salerno.

The 16th Panzer Division, which was also concerned in the forthcoming attack, found itself hampered by air and naval bombardment, as is revealed in their history:

On the morning of the 15th September, the division's positions came under heavy naval gunfire; low-flying aircraft plastered the

Battipaglia–Eboli road with bombs. Any attempt to attack or recon-
noitre was halted by enemy fire. Even those units that had dug in
suffered considerable losses.

The disengagement of the Stempel combat group, now without
the 1st Parachute Regiment Number 3, was delayed until the evening.
During the night it reached the 'Western Front' in the general line
from Battipaglia to a point two kilometres west of Persano, supported
on the left by the von Doering combat group. The assembly of other
units also was delayed by the hostile bombardment, with the result
that the attack could not be launched as planned at dawn on 16th
September and had to be delayed until 0900 hours.

During the night and early morning in the American sector
trenches were extended, barbed-wire barriers erected and large
minefields laid between the opposing armies. Artillery duels lasted
throughout daylight, whilst at night fighting patrols played cat and
mouse in the darkness of the hilly no-man's-land. Several times
during the afternoon *US* artillery batteries were ordered to cease fire,
to allow parties of German stretcher bearers carrying red crosses to
collect their dead and wounded.

At *Red* Beach a flying bomb hit the *SS James Marshall*, which was
unloading cargo alongside an *LCT*. A large number of merchant
sailors and soldiers were killed in the explosion. Many fires were
started; the crew and troops panicked and disappeared at a quick
trot up the beach. Salvage tugs came up swiftly, extinguishing the
flames within two hours. But then the crew could not be found;
they were skulking ashore with the obvious intention of staying out
of harm's way. Captain Jonathan Wainright, skipper of the *Bushrod
Washington* which had been wrecked on the previous day, volunteered to bring his crew on board the abandoned ship. They
successfully unloaded her, and the vessel was then towed to Bizerta,
manned by the volunteer crew. She finished up eventually in the
Normandy operations as part of the Mulberry Harbour.

During the day the 325th Glider *RCT* of 82nd Airborne Division
arrived from Sicily in the beachhead by *LCI*. They were put straight
in to thicken the line. The main units of the 7th Armoured Division
were also moving ashore, and Commodore Oliver, returning from
a visit to corps headquarters, remembers:

"How wonderful it was to see them with gleaming tanks and
polished equipment, after watching nothing but unshaven dusty
troops for days. It was a dose of salt to see them!"

D-plus six had been a day of small results but much preparation.

CHAPTER XV

D-DAY PLUS SEVEN

16th September, 1943

T HE *BBC* in London was broadcasting optimistic bulletins, which were described by one American officer as "Feed the public pap communiqués". The nine o'clock news on this day read:

"Allied Headquarters in North Africa announced this evening that the 5th Army has resumed its offensive from the Salerno bridgehead. The attack started at dawn this morning. German troops holding positions between the Sele and Calore rivers were driven back two to three miles and the offensive continues. General Clark has issued an order of the day congratulating the troops."

*   *   *   *   *

But at dawn that morning the Germans still had no intention of throwing in the sponge. General von Veitinghoff, as already noted, had decided to launch an all-out attack at both the northern and southern ends of the beachhead. During the night units of the 26th Panzer Division had taken over from the Stempel Combat Group north of Paestum. In the north the 16th Panzer Division, backed by parachute battalions, got itself in readiness in the Battipaglia area. Originally planned to go in at dawn, the assault had to be delayed owing to the confused fighting that had lasted throughout the night, following the arrival of the American parachutists around Avellino and the tremendous bombardment put down by the Navy in the early hours.

The 9th Panzer Grenadier Regiment, supported by a barrage from guns in the hills and from their heavy mortar companies, attacked the 56th Division south of Battipaglia. The 2/5th Queen's received the initial shock and the forward platoons were overrun. Smoke from both sides obliterated the countryside; men, coughing and spluttering from the sulphurous fumes, battled in the dark in hand-to-hand combat, throwing grenades at every figure that appeared through the mist. One section of the enemy regiment reached the railway line, where a German lieutenant courageously stood on top of a bank shouting and encouraging his troops to advance. Three Vickers machine-guns of the Cheshire Regiment, seeing him, switched targets, cutting him in half with a long burst of bullets.

An account of this action appears in the 16th Panzer Division History:

> The attack launched by the Panzer Grenadier Regiment Number 9 in the Stempel combat group area was stopped by the concentrated fire of the enemy. A fresh rain of iron descended upon the 16th Panzer Division, which was standing to, and particularly on the battle *HQ*. Communications failed; the enemy even used artillery against individual soldiers; fighter-bombers attacked individual motor-cycle messengers with machine-gun fire.

General Schmalz recorded:

> On 16th September the Panzer Grenadiers, who surprised the enemy, had taken the high ground without losses and had advanced to the heights west of I. Monti [round White Cross Hill]. They, however, encountered heavy artillery fire and a British counter-attack. Whilst the advance was still making good progress, two battalion staffs were suddenly knocked out in hand-to-hand fighting. The resultant confusion of the temporarily leaderless battalions brought the attack to a standstill. Owing to the unexpected intervention of a senior officer, the Panzer Grenadiers were despatched too soon. The planned support of the Panzer Grenadiers by the Panzer group failed to materialise and this attack also came to a standstill in the Alfani area.
>
> Though the attack as a whole managed to narrow the bridgehead, the enemy front was not breached and Salerno was not taken.
>
> The new positions gained were not favourable; they suffered seriously through artillery bombardment, but were nevertheless held until 21st September—the day on which the order was given to retire to the new 10th Army front.

The Royal Scots Greys, in position around d'Amore and Santa Lucia, were forced to withdraw, but 'C' Squadron subsequently launched a counter-attack at the crossroads south of Fosso to cut across the enemy flank towards Battipaglia. At 1100 hours the Shermans charged, led by Lieutenant Parker. His Gunner, Trooper McKenzie, sighted a Mark IV at 800 yards and knocked it out with his first shot, before the enemy tanks realised the Greys were upon them. The Shermans were surrounded by milling German infantry, and their machine-guns were in constant use on masses of men, as they fought through the enemy to close on the armoured vehicles. McKenzie hit another Mark IV at a range of 1,000 yards. Events were moving quickly; the opposing forces were hopelessly inter-mingled. A dozen Panzer Grenadiers took over an abandoned 3-inch mortar and turned the weapon on its former owners with deadly effect, until a platoon of Queen's assaulted, killing the enemy crew and once more turning the mortar on the Germans. On the left flank, another troop of Shermans, commanded by Lieutenant Howard, made swift progress, but somehow he misunderstood his orders and proceeded almost into Battipaglia, where his tanks faced vicious fire from several concealed 88-mm. guns. Two were hit and set on fire, and all the crews killed or captured.

Several days later Corporal Scott and Trooper Slade, who had been presumed dead, returned to their lines. They revealed that they had been interrogated at length by a Panzer Grenadier officer, who had been remarkably well informed about the regiment. One thing that had puzzled the Germans was the correct pronunciation of the Commanding Officer's name, Lieutenant Colonel Sir Ranulph Twisleton-Wykeham-Fiennes. As this had always been a matter for conjecture within the regiment, the two men admitted their inability to enlighten their captors!

By the afternoon the enemy had been pushed back and the line re-established in its original positions. But there was still no question of the British advancing.

*   *   *   *   *

In the 46th Division, General Hawkesworth again told the Commandos it was imperative that the village of Piegolelli and the nearby Pimple should be recaptured. At 0130 hours the tired and weary troops of Number 2 Commando moved off in spread-out formation under the light of a brilliant moon which outlined all their objectives. But since they had last been in the area a few hours before, the Germans had returned to make a determined resistance. The Commandos faced heavy fire from two directions. Rushing into Piegolelli, they became involved in hand-to-hand fighting. Every house, every street, had to be taken by brute force from the occupying enemy. Troops swore and cursed, stabbing and hacking with bayonets, knives and rifle butts; when ammunition ran out or weapons were lost, they fought on with their bare hands. They occupied the village, but against overwhelming fire and with insufficient strength, they could not get to the top of Pimple.

The 41st Royal Marine Commando was then ordered by the Army Commander to attack the hill. It had been originally intended that an infantry battalion with more men and weapons should carry out this task; at the last minute for some reason the plan was changed. The Royal Marines, decimated and down to skeleton size, were asked to fill the breach. The officers were tired and the men exhausted. Hasty preparations were made and a fire plan agreed with the divisional artillery. Just as they reached the start line near Piegolelli, a devastating barrage from our own guns came down on the unit, producing heavy casualties. No one ever discovered how this error occurred—probably a combination of tiredness and carelessness; anyhow, it resulted in stopping the Marines before they ever got going. The attack was called off, the main body returning to their old posts on Commando Hill. One troop, however, cut off and out of wireless touch, went on to move right to the top of Pimple. Leading this party was Captain John Parsons, who recorded his impressions:

I attended the briefing and returned to my troops. I found that the last few days of sleeplessness had at last taken their toll. By the time I had roused the men and we had collected our kit, it was nearly H-Hour. We fell in on the road beside the position and started the march to the start line, which was the main road running through Piegolelli. A few moments later we got to within about a hundred yards and saw that the village was a shambles. Artillery fire was falling on the road and the houses beyond. Commandos were strewn dead and wounded on the ground. Amongst them was the Second-in-Command, Major John Edwards, who, attended by a medical orderly, was lying mortally wounded. The rest of the unit was nowhere to be seen. I tried to contact the Commanding Officer on the wireless, but could get no answer. I had no idea where the other troops were, whether they had crossed the start line or whether they had not yet arrived. I assumed that the intense artillery fire, which was catching us in the village, was the result of a lucky guess by the enemy. We decided to press on, cross the start line and move in what we thought was the general direction of the objective.

As we dipped down into an olive grove, we were hit by the stench of dead Germans and passed several green and bloated corpses which shone grotesquely in the light of the rising moon. This was a perfect example of the 'Fog of war' and we felt terribly alone.

Reaching the bottom of the valley, we found two spurs that ran out at right angles and it seemed possible they would be occupied by the enemy. We halted briefly and sprayed the tops with machine-gun fire. The men, either through tiredness or perhaps because they had been shocked by the bombardment we had passed through, were sluggish in obeying orders; they did not seem to understand, and had to be coaxed and shouted at. The tops of the spurs were clear of enemy and, branching left, we went on for about a mile in what we thought was the right direction. The country got closer and we began to climb in the weak moonlight up a series of terraced slopes. We plucked grapes as we passed the vines and sucked them to quench our thirst.

After perhaps two hours we found ourselves near the top of White Cross Hill and were astounded to hear, above us, the voices of British infantry and the sound of digging. We never found out to whom the voices belonged, but suspected it was another German ruse. We crept stealthily and quietly on up the hill. Then a Schmeisser opened up with a long chattering burst. We froze and the bullets passed over our heads into the valley below. What was the gunner firing at? Had they heard us? It was yet another of those unexplained things which characterised this particular night attack.

Now we could hear the enemy laughing and talking in German. We moved cautiously, aiming to get a close assault position. The scouts reported that the enemy appeared to be in two groups about fifty yards to our front, occupying a position which covered about a hundred yards from left to right. We held a whispered council of war, brief orders were given and the troop attacked. A few Commandos fell as they charged, but we captured several German and Italian machine-guns. Most of the enemy disappeared from sight down a steep densely tree-covered hill. Quickly we took up a defensive position and reorganised. An enemy light automatic fired at us from a small hill about twenty yards to our left. We replied with some 2-inch mortars, firing *HE* low angle, and silenced it. It must have now been about three-quarters of an hour before dawn.

Dawn when it came was welcome because we could see where we were. For the next three or four hours the troop was subjected to a series of counter-attacks by green-faced German paratroops, and although these attacks were repulsed, each one took a heavy toll of casualties. At one stage the thick hedge to our front was set ablaze. We had to close up to get at some enemy beyond and one of my men was shot and fell into the burning bushes. We tried to drag him clear, but were driven off by heavy fire. Another man, weighing six-teen stone, tried to get a Bren-gun into position in this burning hedge, but he was shot from a flank and we could see the bullets ripping a furrow in his back, but we managed to drag him clear.

About 1000 hours, when our ammunition was running low, I sent a runner down the hill to the area of our original start line to get help. His orders were to get more ammunition and reinforcements if possible. He was not seen again, but an hour later our position was surrounded by a thick mortar smoke-screen, fired by Number 2 Commando to help us to extricate ourselves. By then our ammunition was about expended and the troops, by now down to about seven men, withdrew, using fire and movement, down the hill up which we had come, carrying our wounded. The Germans burst through the burning hedge just after the last man had withdrawn. After a long trek, we finally reached the headquarters of Number 2 Commando near Piegolelli and reported to Colonel Churchill. The rest of Number 41 Commando was still nowhere to be seen.

It was only then that I learnt that the bombardment, which had caught us on the start line and which had smashed our attack before it ever really got started, had been caused by our own artillery.

Perhaps my most vivid memory of this attack was the fog of war, the sense of being utterly alone and the gallantry of the men who doggedly hung on to what they had captured, although it must have been clear to all that our attack on White Cross Hill, without the remainder of the Commando, could be no more than a reconnaissance in force.

By midday the Germans, for the first time, had come to the conclusion that there was no longer any hope of throwing the Allies back into the sea. The 16th Panzer Division had been virtually shot to pieces. Nearly all communications had been shelled or bombed out of existence. The slightest move was noted by the Navy or by patrolling aircraft; lone messengers on foot or despatch riders were hounded by cannon and machine-gun fire from Allied fighters. Even so, the remnants of this fine division reorganised and prepared yet another counter-attack.

During the morning General McCreery set off from corps headquarters on a personal reconnaissance with a troop of armoured cars, which moved forward of Pontecagnano. He was under the impression that ahead of them was a reconnaissance screen. The narrow lanes bore evidence of the battles that had been fought there. Burnt-out tanks and wrecked armoured cars littered the paths and lay jumbled in the ditches. McCreery was standing in the open turret of a Dingo. At one spot, as they passed the exploded shell of a cottage, he was surprised to see an extraordinarily beautiful but grubby girl looking from a window and solemnly shaking her head at him. He hardly noticed it at the time. Some distance further on he alighted, told the drivers to find somewhere to turn round and went up a small rise to take a look at the countryside through his binoculars. When he next looked round he saw all the vehicles blazing and the crewmen, who had not been killed, running for cover. Enemy observers on Monte Stella and San Mango had followed them along the route, firing as soon as the small convoy had stopped. The corps commander, with the remainder of his personal staff, had to make a hasty and slightly undignified retreat on foot to their lines.

McCreery, cheerful and unworried as ever, remained confident that the troops would withstand the assaults, encouraged in his personal feelings by the knowledge that disembarking over the beaches during the day were several hundred men, who had been rushed from North Africa to reinforce the battle-weary battalions and make them fit enough for an attack through the passes into the Naples plain. In the afternoon, back at headquarters, he was visited by a senior staff officer, who said that his presence was urgently needed on the beach, where a group of seven hundred soldiers had staged a sit-down strike, refusing to join front-line units.

McCreery hastily drove in his jeep to the shore, where he found an appalling situation, exactly as described to him. A huge crowd of mutinous troops, surrounded by military policemen, was sitting on the sand. They had been warned of the consequences of a mutiny in the face of the enemy and had been clearly ordered three times to pick up their weapons and kit, but they stubbornly declined to budge. It was a tricky situation, for the men had already placed themselves in an inextricable position, from which there was no return. Legally they could be tried by court martial and sentenced to several years' penal servitude.

The corps commander decided to give them one more chance to try to avoid the inevitable. After a quick consultation with his staff, he drove his jeep close to the crowd and stood up, inviting the men to gather round and listen. He understood their main complaint was that, having been promised they would be rejoining their parent regiments in the 8th Army, at the last moment they had been switched to the 5th Army. He promised that as soon as the military situation improved he would hasten their return to their units, with whom they had been fighting for so long; but in the meantime they were vitally required at the Salerno front. He assured them that if they carried out their duties in a proper manner the whole incident would be forgotten and no one would suffer. Throughout his speech he was interrupted by catcalls and whistles, while many officers present urged that the whole lot should be placed under arrest, re-embarked and returned to North Africa for legal action.

When McCreery had finished, he advised the officers in charge to give the mutineers a chance to talk it over and the opportunity to change their minds. The corps commander left the beach, silently praying that his words would have the desired effect. Shortly afterwards, he was informed that, with the exception of 192 men, the soldiers had responded to his plea. The recalcitrants were formally put under arrest and sent back to Constantine where, after trial, 191 received sentences of five to twenty years' penal servitude.

This was a sad day for the British Army. Not unnaturally the whole episode was hushed up under wartime secrecy, and the complete story has never been told.

Subsequent reports claimed that the troops had a real grievance: having been promised postings back to their own units in the 8th Army, it was not until they were already at sea that they learned they were bound for Salerno. Many had voluntarily left hospital beds and foregone convalescent periods in order to return to their comrades. This view became commonly accepted; a lot of sympathy was extended to the mutineers, with adverse criticism directed at officers and senior commanders.

The true situation, as told to me by General McCreery, is somewhat different. A decision had already been taken in London by the Second Front planners that the 51st Highland Division and other units of the 8th Army were to be returned to Britain for training and reorganisation for subsequent use in the Normandy landings. This information, owing to bad security, had percolated somehow through all ranks, reaching the ears of the troops. Naturally for many of these men who had been fighting in the desert for three years it was tremendous news and "Blighty" was the uppermost thought in their minds. Soldiers in hospital recovering from wounds or convalescing were only too keen to quit their beds and return. Their chief fear was that if they remained in hospital they would miss the homeward-bound drafts and be transferred to other regiments for retention in the Mediterranean theatre.

Most of the troops involved in the mutiny were Scots. Men of the Cameronians; Argyll and Sutherland Highlanders; Cameron Highlanders; Black Watch; Seaforths; and Gordons—all of whom had fought well throughout the North African campaign. Amongst them were men who had won medals for bravery and NCOs of high repute. How then did it arise that these men of undoubted quality found themselves in the ignominious position of being branded 'mutineers'?

There is no doubt that the situation was wrongly handled from the start by bad, or inexperienced, officers at the base reinforcement centres in North Africa. Colonel Robert Ahrenfeldt, an Army psychiatrist, later investigated the case and described it as:

> A tragedy of errors . . . there was a complete absence of clear direction, precise information, or firm leadership throughout. There was a total disregard of well-established loyalties in experienced fighting men of previously high morale.

Doctor Ahrenfeldt came to the conclusion that the main cause of the trouble was one of loyalty to units; nowhere in his report did he put forward the idea that the real reason was that the men wanted to go back home with their regiments, and that the question of loyalty was bound up with the fact that their units were being sent back to the United Kingdom.

Blunder followed blunder. Before being put aboard a landing craft, the deserters were shepherded into a prisoner-of-war cage at Salerno, where German prisoners, discovering the trouble, jeered, hissed and booed at them. This was hardly designed to help the spirits of these already demoralised men.

At Constantine the mass court martial came to a close. Sentences were passed on a sullen crowd of prisoners, and immediately suspended.

It was then announced by a senior officer that they were being posted to the 8th Army, where it was hoped they would "retrieve their honour". He went on to rub salt in the wounds, by harping on their cowardice and disgrace, emphasising that the sentences would be reimposed for the slightest breach of discipline. His threatening words led to a widespread feeling of hopelessness and fear. Aboard the troopship taking them to Italy the men were kept in a separate mess deck, with the result that word got around the ship and no other troops would talk to them, except to pass insulting remarks. Their morale got lower and lower. Many later deserted and were sent to penal servitude in British prisons. Not unnaturally, when news of their treatment reached the ears of officers in the 8th Army, they became very hostile towards those who, in their opinion, had dealt very badly with the soldiers; they too became convinced that the true reason for their behaviour had been one of regimental loyalty.

General Montgomery later summed up the situation by saying that, although the men's action was quite inexcusable and could not be condoned in any way, when soldiers got into trouble it was nearly always the fault of some officer who had failed in his duty.

*   *   *   *   *

In the American sector there were certain signs that the Germans were pulling out. A strong patrol of the 505th Parachute Infantry set out from Monte Soprano, edging their way towards Rocca d'Aspide, eight miles south-east of Paestum, which they occupied before noon. A few desultory shells still burst around them, but in Albanella they could find only a small number of enemy, and a plan was made for another attack on that town.

The chosen unit was 504th Regimental Combat Team under Colonel Reuben Tucker, who set out in the early afternoon on a tough gruelling march across the hilly country from Tempone di San Paolo, moving into positions along the Albanella ridge. By this time it was obvious that a daylight attack was out of the question; a night assault by one battalion was decided upon. Hills 424 and 315 were the main objectives. As dusk came quickly down, the tired troops lay on the hard rocky ground to snatch a brief rest before the action, but enemy artillery ranged on them in their exposed positions. Hoping to avoid the barrage, the units decided to move forward, but it followed them, hampering considerably the advance; soon sections were out of touch and the attack became disjointed. The 1st Battalion, after a brisk fight, drove the enemy away from Monte del Bosco, but the situation was so confused that it was decided to bivouac there for the night and hope for better things in the morning.

*　　*　　*　　*　　*

Eighty-five patients and refugees were successfully evacuated from the tunnel on Laughing Hill and housed temporarily in the Pascoli School. The archbishop, to whom they had gone for advice and help, admitted that he had not enough food nor room for all, but offered a roof to Carucci and a few of the staff.

The Chaplain refused, saying that he must stay with his party. For the next few hours they argued amongst themselves as to where they should go to escape the war, finally agreeing on Soffietti's plan to go to another sanatorium in Naples. It was a long way, particularly for the sick, but Carucci told them it would be carried out by easy stages, via the coast road to Maiori and through Chiunzi and Pagani; there was no alternative, as the short route through Vietri and Cava was still in the hands of the Germans.

*　　*　　*　　*　　*

Field-Marshal Albert Kesselring at Frascati was studying the latest reports from the battlefront. These were almost identical, showing that nearly all units were frustrated in their assaults by the overwhelming weight of shells from the Allied ships. In the evening he had to come to the decision that he could do no more and *in order to evade the effective shelling from warships*, he *authorised a disengagement on the coastal front with the express proviso that the Volturno line, to which the* 10th *Army intended to fall back, must not be abandoned before* 15th *October*. But there was to be no headlong retreat; every hill, every bridge, every crossroad was to be held until the Germans found it convenient to retire, and at no stage did the Allies find it possible to advance according to their own plan. At the same time Kesselring called on the Luftwaffe to make a supreme effort to avenge the defeat, and the pilots' eyes all turned to the battleships *Warspite* and *Valiant*.

Warspite throughout this day had been supporting *US* troops who were trying to take Altavilla. Her massive guns had registered with deadly effect on every target called for by the hard-pressed American infantry. At 1427 hours, just as her gun crews had ceased fire awaiting fresh orders, and Admiral Hewitt was signing a signal authorising the battleships' release, a heavy air attack was launched. A group of five FW-190s launched four of the hated glider bombs. Two scored direct hits on *Warspite* with tremendous results, whilst two others burst very close to her hull. A vast cloud of yellow smoke rose from her funnels; every gangway and cabin was filled with the noise, smell and confusion of the explosions which ripped through her steel decks, killing and mortally wounding dozens of sailors. Immediate action was taken aboard the vessel, where rescue parties scurried around succouring the wounded.

The Commanding Officer of *HMS Delhi*, the anti-aircraft ship, recorded in his log:

> 1425 hours. Attack by five FW-190s—1 shot down by *Delhi* (pom pom)—this coincided with rocket bomb attack on *Warspite*. I was the first to observe these from my ship and after ringing down more revolutions observed the vapour trail of the three bombs at some 15,000 feet turn together into the vertical with the result known. *Warspite* was then some two miles from the shipping anchorage.

Captain Packer, *RN*, commanding *HMS Warspite*, received reports indicating that his mighty ship could still raise enough steam to get under way for Malta, but the battered boilers soon gave up the struggle; she had to be taken under tow by the *US* tugs *Hopi* and *Moreno*, and escorted by five destroyers and three cruisers. It was feared that another air attack would place the whole group in peril, but the Luftwaffe did not strike again. *Warspite* finally reached Malta on the 19th, where she was patched up and continued to give great service, particularly in the Normandy landings.

HMS Valiant came up from the southern sector during the afternoon. She carried out a short bombardment of nineteen rounds at targets in the Nocera area with only partial success, sailing for Malta at 1945 hours.

*   *   *   *   *

On land, at 1400 hours, advance patrols of the 8th Army finally made contact with VI Corps at the small village of Vallo, some fifteen miles south-east of Agropoli; this meeting, which should have marked the end of the operation, came rather as an anticlimax after all that had gone before. Within a few hours the Americans found the enemy withdrawing in order to avoid being trapped.

That evening an optimistic Army Commander sat down to write to Eisenhower:

> We are in good shape now. We are here to stay. This morning we have restored the salient between the Sele River and the Calore River. . . . I am prepared to attack Naples. We have made mistakes and we have learned the hard way, but we will improve every day and I am sure we will not disappoint you.

As an addition to his report, he also announced the first casualty list of the campaign. The British X Corps in eight days of non-stop fighting had suffered 531 killed, 1,915 wounded and 1,561 missing. The American VI Corps, with only half as many troops involved in the battle, had 225 killed, 835 wounded and 589 missing. It had been a heavy price to pay, a price that was to rise steadily throughout the Italian campaign.

CHAPTER XVI

D-DAY PLUS EIGHT

17th September, 1943

FOR home consumption, the *BBC* News at 9 p.m. reported:

"Troops of the 5th Army who launched their attack from the Salerno bridgehead yesterday, have retaken the town of Albanella. Our patrols got there soon after the original landings, but were driven out earlier this week."

Frank Gillard, the *BBC* war correspondent, recorded:

"There are promising signs that the Germans now realise the impossibility of sweeping us off the bridgehead. In the last twenty-four hours the enemy have been thinned out considerably, though a strong well-armed rearguard screen remains to cover the withdrawal and to prevent the Allies cutting off the Germans still remaining."

Major Lewis Hasting, the military commentator, after the news gave his views on what had been happening in the Salerno area. He had to rely on the official communiqués and any background information he could acquire in London. But as a propaganda broadcast it no doubt served its purpose. He said:

"The Germans chose to make a test case of Salerno. They concentrated every possible man and gun they could muster. And not only that; they made so sure of victory that they announced it beforehand. The people of the Empire and America will now recall with grim satisfaction the triumphant yelps of Berlin Radio when the struggle was at its height. 'Evacuation; Dieppe; Dunkirk', etc. . . . There was no surprise, everything was ready. General Alexander has told us that the German guns and mortars were a few hundred yards from the water's edge. The enemy had the best positions, the best observation and the heavier metal, and still with these odds against them, the Allied divisions have broken through the ring and are now driving inland."

Few troops in the Salerno bridgehead heard the broadcast and, if they had, not many would have agreed with this summary of the

D-Day Plus Eight

situation. However, it made good listening for the people at home and in America.

* * * * *

It was on the afternoon of this day that the German High Command's orders for disengagement reached the front line. In the south most units pulled out in the evening, leaving a strong rearguard slowly retiring to fresh positions east of Eboli. But in the north, which was the pivot of the whole operation, the troops stayed in the mountains and did not move for many days. The 16th Panzer Division history recounts:

> The retirement at 2200 hours was carried out without interference: even the rearguard were able to break away unmolested.

General Mark Clark's plans, as he passed from the defensive to the offensive, were exactly in accord with Kesselring's wishes. The 5th Army from Salerno commenced swinging round to the right in conjunction with Monty's 8th Army.

The Germans still controlled the situation and fought the battle exactly as they pleased.

Having flown from Algiers to Palermo, the Supreme Commander, General Eisenhower, with Admiral of the Fleet Sir Andrew Cunningham, embarked on *HMS Offa* and sailed to the beachhead for discussions with General Clark and other commanders.

On arrival, after a meeting on the headquarters ship with Admiral Hewitt and General Clark, he proceeded ashore to Dawley's corps headquarters situated in another of the many tobacco factories that dotted the plain. General Dawley was greeted somewhat coolly by the Supreme Commander and asked to give his account of the battle. Two jeeps, packed with 'top brass', then drove to Headquarters 36th Division, loaded with Generals Eisenhower, Clark, Dawley, Ridgway and Admiral Hewitt. Ike asked General Walker to give a brief description and explanation of the fighting.

The most vivid account of this meeting is given by General Fred Walker:

> I was asked to explain the situation, which I did in general terms. I noted that they were not paying much attention to what I was saying. When I finished General Eisenhower turned to Dawley and said, "How did you ever get troops into such a mess?" General Dawley's explanation showed that he was not aware of the pains I had taken to insure proper tactical control and co-ordination. His explanation was how it got to be, rather than that there was no mess

215

at all. I was about to add my own explanation when Eisenhower changed the subject. I thought that perhaps Eisenhower was displeased at the 'mess' and held Dawley responsible.

Later Generals Clark, Dawley, Ridgway and I, in two jeeps, went to Albanella to look over the ground where an attack was being planned on Altavilla. On the way out I rode with Ridgway. On the way back Clark asked me to ride with him and Dawley. Clark and Dawley got into an unfriendly discussion about something which I considered to be unimportant. In the course of his remarks Dawley intimated that he did not approve of some of the things Eisenhower and Clark had done and referred to them as "Boy Scouts". Clark became quite upset and remained silent most of the remainder of the trip back to my headquarters.

There, after Dawley and I got out of the jeep, Clark drove off in a perturbed mental state leaving Dawley with me. I wondered why I had been invited to ride with them, for I did not utter a word and no remarks were addressed to me. I thought that perhaps this might have been the real reason why Dawley was relieved.

I have learned since the real reason. General Alexander, on his visit to Salerno, had noticed Dawley's hands were shaking when he was explaining the situation and this caused Alexander to conclude that Dawley was too unsteady for combat command. As a result he recommended to both Eisenhower and Clark that he be relieved.

The 2nd Battalion 504th Regimental Combat Team hung on grimly in the face of increasing artillery fire on the northern slopes of Monte di Bosco. Its regimental headquarters, which had moved too far forward, found itself cut off and out of touch with other units. The 1st Battalion continued their efforts to move forward on to the hill south of Altavilla. An attack, preceded by a heavy barrage at 1100 hours, gained a few yards, but was then caught off stride by a counter-attack and pinned down. They spent the rest of the day and most of the night crouching in shallow fox-holes, with shells falling continuously on and around them. Again lack of march discipline in these troops resulted in severe privations, when fresh supplies of water could not be got to them.

The Germans were determined to obey their orders; nothing the Americans did, even with the massive weight of air and sea bombardment, could drive the enemy from their positions in these hills. The prominent and vital features 424 and 315 remained in German hands. Only in one area did patrols find space to move forward; that was at Altavilla, which to their surprise was found deserted late in the afternoon.

*   *   *   *   *

Carlo Carucci, the schoolmaster, in his village in the hills, could not understand the ebb and flow of the battle.

Mystified as to the Allies' intentions, in his diary this day he wrote:

> England and America rule the skies, but for victory troops are needed. If they think they can win the war with aeroplanes, they are wrong.

All day the air bombardment continued. Nothing was safe from the patrolling aircraft. Fighter bombers swooped on every living thing that moved. A peasant and his family with an ox cart loaded with personal possessions were blown out of existence. Burial parties in the cemeteries were machine-gunned as they interred their dead. Rumours flowed fast and furious among the peasants. Some said that Hitler had decided to strip all the other fronts, send a million bayonets into Italy and fight the Allies to a standstill. Others brought stories alleging that the King and Badoglio were in Sicily organising a new national army, that would fight side by side with the Americans and British and take part in the liberation of Italy.

With his thoughts on the history of Italy and the domination of Europe by dictatorial powers for so many years, the old schoolmaster added:

> England must make a great effort with men, and fight herself—not make, or pretend to make, others fight. If she wishes to win and not have in Italy another Dunkirk, England must remember that, although she ruled the seas in the fight against Napoleon, she could not prevent his domination of Europe for about twenty years. And does England now wish to draw things out for so long?

As the day progressed, it at last became clear to the Italians that the Germans were in part retreating. Fresh troops pitched their tents in a valley below Olevano, while German officers reconnoitred the village seeking places to mount their guns. But to the infinite relief of Carucci and his compatriots, the small bridge approaching the village was too narrow and weak to support the tracked vehicles towing the guns, which had to remain outside the inhabited area. Trucks and half-tracks, camouflaged with bushes and branches, ground up the hill roads towards the new delaying positions. A group of these troops stopped near Olevano asking what news there was on the radio, but without electricity the Italians were in complete ignorance of the situation. Subsequently, they learned that

the Germans planned to stay in the area until the 20th, and one *NCO*, pointing at a calendar, said:
"We leave here on this date, and not before."

In the archbishop's seminary above Salerno, Arturo Carucci, having at last gathered his flock of eighty-seven tubercular patients, nurses and nuns, moved off at 0900 hours to seek sanctuary away from the battle. They made a pitiful sight, pale-faced and haggard after their days of privation in the tunnel; dirty, unshaven, some limping and dressed in rags. Carucci, at the head of the column in his stained white cassock, looked like a latter-day saint. Preceding him was a man carrying an enormous Red Cross flag. Before leaving, they had knelt for the archbishop's blessing, and had all been presented with a rosary.

In Vietri, caught in the middle of a barrage, they sought shelter in the battered houses. Panic was always near the surface; it was with the greatest difficulty that Carucci and his nuns managed to keep control. After a while they rested on a beach past Vietri, where they commandeered a small donkey cart to carry their belongings and some of the weaker patients. As they progressed along the coast road, they were greeted by Allied soldiers who offered them cigarettes, sweets, chocolates and tins of food. By dusk the weary party was in sight of Maiori, where Carucci planned to spend the night.

At the entrance to the village they found their passage barred by an American road block, and were told by an officer they could go no further without authority from the Allied Military Government. A jeep was sent off to get the necessary permit; when it returned it was 2000 hours, curfew time. Permission to proceed having been refused, a Ranger officer told them curtly they must go back the way they had come. Argument was futile; with many of the party in tears, the column turned and set off along the same route. Then someone remembered a large cave down on the beach; slowly down a cliff-path they wended their way into a vast cavern full of tumbled slimy rocks and scuttling insects, from where they could see the guns of the fleet still roaring above the rustle of the waves. Convinced that most of the patients would die during the night, Carucci and his nurses busied themselves making the sick as comfortable as possible on the wet sand.

*   *   *   *   *

Nazi detachments in the village of Corpo di Cava arrested the Archbishop of Cava, Monsignor Francesco Marchesani, and the

Abbott Don Idelfonso Rea, informing the inhabitants that if there were any hostile acts against the German forces these two men would be shot.

*   *   *   *   *

At the front above Salerno, Allied troops got their first inkling of the enemy withdrawal from the sound of many engines revving up and the twinkle of lights on distant roads. The artillery kept up a constant fire at every sign. The Oxford & Buckinghamshire Light Infantry patrolled cautiously forward, returning with some equipment and several prisoners, one of whom was a unit pay clerk, captured complete with his money and pay books. They also found two 6-pounder anti-tank guns that had been abandoned at one stage of the battle. These were still serviceable, although the Germans had tried to wreck them by exploding grenades in the barrels.

The Commandos, who had been withdrawn to a reserve area about three miles out of Salerno, took up quarters in an empty farmhouse. Rest was the thing they needed more than anything, and many flopped down in a vineyard, sleeping where they fell. Captain John Parsons discovered a most inviting double bed, which he shared with his troop sergeant-major. It was comforting to find the area already occupied by a regiment of 25-pounders, but when they opened fire for a regimental shoot in the middle of the night the Commandos wondered if they had picked the best area. The sudden violent noise, after a few hours of peace, had a terrible effect on some men, who jumped up from the ground and ran around, shouting pitifully until they were stopped or realised what was happening. The Commandos had been used to their limit; no troops could have done more than they had accomplished.

In the area of White Cross Hill and Pimple the Germans would not give up. Many units tried to reach the top, but were forced off with terrible casualties; a prisoner declared that White Cross was occupied by over two hundred Panzer Grenadiers, with orders to fight to the death. Eventually a mortar battery was borrowed from the American Army; phosphorus bombs were continuously fired for five and a half hours on to the positions, until not a shot or a sound came from them. It was turned into a blazing smoking furnace, visible for miles around, and the stench of burning bodies was carried on the wind to the nostrils of those who watched.

The Scots Guards, still south of Battipaglia near the Tobacco Factory, were attacked several times by the 29th Panzer Regiment; at one stage 'G' Company was driven back, with the loss of an

219

observation post. A heavy enemy barrage accompanied this assault, and one salvo falling on an occupied house killed eleven Guardsmen and wounded nine others.

Major Jack Romerman, *USAF*, in charge of a ground control station, was informed that German 88-mm. guns from the Tobacco Factory were slaughtering the British troops who were attempting to advance. After consulting the Army commanders on the spot, he called up a flight of dive bombers, in circuit over the bridgehead; and despite the fact that our troops were within five hundred yards of the target, these fighter bombers successfully wiped out the battery at the cost of only a few Allied casualties.

A patrol from the 2/5th Leicesters, seeking prisoners north of Salerno, heard an organ being played in a village chapel. The sound of magnificent chords reverberated across the valleys, bouncing back off the hill until it multiplied like that of an orchestra; the obviously holy music formed a weird background to those Mid-landers at war. They crept forward, easing themselves into the village street, hoping the whole place had been evacuated and that the organist was celebrating with a recital. They neared the building, but as the first men stepped out of the shadows into the square, several German machine-guns opened up and the whole place became alive with men and shooting. The Leicesters retired according to orders to report the village still in enemy hands.

*   *   *   *   *

These were strange days and strange happenings. During that afternoon a German half-track, liberally decorated with red crosses, had driven into the forward positions of the 2/5 Queen's. The troops held their fire to discover that a German Army doctor had brought in a wounded British corporal, whom he wanted to hand over. Lieutenant-Colonel John Whitfield was suspicious of the reasons behind the visit. He did not believe it to be a simple act of kindness, suspecting that the Germans wanted to have a look around their positions. He ordered the medical officer and the vehicle crew to be placed under arrest, whilst he reported the capture and circumstances to brigade headquarters. The German doctor resented strongly what he felt was a breach of confidence, but he was retained all that night, until an order was received from divisional headquarters early the following morning with an authorisation for his release. Reluctantly Colonel Whitfield obeyed, and allowed the vehicle to drive back to enemy lines.

This incident is remembered also by Captain Eberhard Spetzler, commanding the 2nd Battalion 64th Panzer Grenadier Regiment:

On the evening of 17th September, an English reconnaissance patrol was forced back and they left behind a wounded soldier. He was badly shot in the stomach; we dressed his injuries, but as we were about to retire according to orders the doctor said that a long truck journey would kill him. We decided to put him in an ambulance and, with the doctor carrying a white flag, they drove across to the British lines. The English were hospitable to the crew, but would not let them return for two days, when naturally they had some difficulty in finding the unit. Such an exchange of wounded would have been impossible on the Russian front.

CHAPTER XVII

D-DAY PLUS NINE

18th September, 1943

THE opening bars of Beethoven's 5th Symphony, with its staccato 'V-sign', brought the news from London:
"The combined growing pressure of the 5th and 8th Armies has begun to force the Germans back from the Salerno bridgehead. At the southern end the 5th Army has pushed some twelve miles inland and gained more elbow room by taking the small town of Rocca d'Aspide. The Germans are easing their pressure, though we're not allowing them to break off contact. An *RAF* Spitfire landed at Montecorvino airfield with engine trouble while shells were still landing and was repaired under gunfire. The German Overseas Military Commentator declared that it was only because of the British Navy that the Germans failed to drive us back into the sea."

Sertorius, the popular military reporter on Radio Berlin, had actually broadcast during the day the following message:

"With the landing of strong British forces the battle south of Naples has entered its second stage. That the first stage did not end in the throwing out of the American 5th Army is probably solely due to the British Navy, which, after the rest of the Italian Fleet had ceased to exist, had used all possibilities to intervene in the battle. It was only due to the fact that in the critical hours of Wednesday countless British naval guns, including those of the highest calibre, threw an impenetrable curtain of fire around the town of Salerno, and over the Americans concentrated on the coastal road south of Eboli, that the ragged divisions of General Clark were able to escape being thrown into the sea by the German Storm Troops. Thereby the Allied Command won time to draw up their confused formations in fresh order, and with the help of troops hastily landed, to stiffen their spirit."

*   *   *   *   *

During the night most of the German front line units had with-drawn to prearranged positions in the hills. Looking back over their shoulders, they saw a curtain of fire still descending on their abandoned trenches and strong-points. A German officer wrote:

> One last look at the Gulf. Down there we could still see, on the right in the mist, the towers of Salerno; in the centre the gleaming grey strip of Montecorvino; the asphalt highway and the railway with a loop near Battipaglia. Eboli down in the plain—and in the distance the sea. A warm wind blows up from the shore, taking no heed of the fresh graves lying in the shade of the olive groves.

Within the Allied lines it was not appreciated for some hours that the enemy had withdrawn so swiftly. Just after dawn a flight of Mustangs screamed in from the sea to dive bomb the Battipaglia Tobacco Factory. A strange silence followed the attack, with none of the customary sporadic firing which usually chased the planes from the German positions. A patrol from the Scots Guards reported back that they thought the Tobacco Factory had been evacuated. The commanding officer immediately ordered a probe into the area, making preparations to follow it up if the news proved correct. A Bren-gun section of the Coldstream Guards, asked to protect the right flank of the move forward, was commanded by Lieutenant Christopher Bulteel, with orders to shoot any Germans seen escaping over the nearby barrack wall.

Carefully the party crept along a stream bed, until they reached a broken bridge: there was a gap of stringy grass, some twenty yards wide, between them and their objective. They doubled across, fearing that any moment they would be shot down by a hidden sniper or machine-gun. Nothing happened. They were alone, surrounded by an uncanny silence accentuated by the fact of having lived for nine days in the midst of constant bombs, and the unceasing racket of mortar and machine-gun fire. Bulteel edged along the wall until he found a gap caused by a shell; peering carefully through, he saw the huts and surrounding area empty. Hopping through the hole, they charged into the nearest building, finding it abandoned and filthy. Suddenly remembering warnings of how the Germans booby-trapped everything when they retreated, the Coldstreamers decided to withdraw, leaving the official capture to the Scots Guards. Shortly after, they saw a patrol of Scots Guards gingerly creeping through a battered orchard, and an officer asked: "Is it all clear?"

During the afternoon the whole of the Guards Brigade advanced across countryside totally devastated by the completeness of war. Hardly an inch of the roads they marched over was free from pitting caused by shells or bombs. Every building had been demolished and the tattered remains of household goods were strewn over hedges and ditches. Dead cattle, bloated and horrible, with legs sticking straight and stiff into the air, lay side by side with dead German and British soldiers. Dozens of bodies left unburied for days were in the last stages of putrefaction; the revolting smell filled the nostrils and crept on to the skin like an evil clinging cream. Burnt-out tanks still smouldered, and charred bundles were all that remained of the men who had crewed the vehicles. Most of the trees were stripped of all foliage, the fallen fruit of oranges, lemons and vines adding a bitter sickly sweetness to the foulness of the air.

The troops trudged stonily through this carnage and, having occupied Battipaglia, cheerfully dug in with the hope that the Germans would keep on retreating and that their nine-day nightmare was over. At one platoon position, a batman scavenging in a battered farmhouse set up a tea-table, adorning it with a dainty pink tablecloth with beads and lace and garishly decorated glasses, and invited the officers to tea. Most of them, taking one look at the fantastic sight, politely declined the invitation!

But for the Guardsmen it was to be only one night of peace. Within a few hours they were to be switched to the north of the beachhead to lead an assault through to Naples.

Advances were also made on White Cross Hill and Pimple. Patrols probing forward found no resistance; when they finally reached the tops, they were met with the sight of mounds of dead bodies, both British and German, some still burning, others horribly mutilated, the earth pitted and scarred over every inch. It was an empty victory for these men, who had fought courageously for so many days, to find their objectives a completely dead world.

But in the Salerno area the Germans were not yet prepared to evacuate their ground. The Oxfordshire and Buckinghamshire Light Infantry, the Yorks and Lancasters, the Leicesters and the Durham Light Infantry found solid opposition whichever way they turned, the defiles leading north of La Molina Pass and Ponte Fratte being still strongly held by German infantry and well covered with artillery.

* * * * *

Arturo Carucci with his band of patients and nurses awoke in the cave on the beach as the rays of the sun poured in amongst the rocks, glittering and playing on the gentle waves that lapped the seashore. Once again they set off towards Maiori, breakfasting on the way off grapes and oranges that grew in profusion at the road-side. This time their reception was a little kinder; they were allowed into the town, and although the American town commandant did not greatly approve of their efforts to go through the lines towards Naples, he did not order them to stop. They plodded forward, but were soon in the midst of a battle, and finally returned to Maiori in the hope of getting to Naples via Sorrento.

In the village of Olevano the elder Carucci had stood most of the day watching German troops marching through, followed by convoys of vehicles, still singing their martial tunes and still in great spirits, despite the retreat. Other refugees who had come up during the night from Battipaglia had told him what life was like in the battered, deserted town. Over three thousand people had made their homes in the Grotto di San Michele, taking sanctuary around the altar rails in the pious hope that Saint Michael would protect them.

During the afternoon Allied guns turned on Olevano, seeking out the retreating Germans. Many of the troops broke into houses and, threatening the occupants with death, helped themselves to any food they could find and whatever took their fancy amongst prized household possessions. Two soldiers with stolen food, forcing their way into the courtyard of Carlo Carucci's house, ordered a meal to be prepared for them. There were twenty Italians in the yard; Carucci was tempted to suggest that the two soldiers be attacked, killed, and their bodies thrown down the well. He thought of how, after the war, he and his comrades would be praised as patriotic fighters; but in his diary he admits that this did not happen, because everyone, both men and women, was too frightened to take any action, although they outnumbered the soldiers ten to one. While the meal was cooking, the soldiers joined others at the village fountain, where, stripping off their clothes, they washed naked in the water, whilst women ran away shrieking, outraged by such immodesty. Having eaten their meal, the troops passed on, leaving the villagers unmolested.

*   *   *   *   *

Landing craft and barges were still coming into the beaches at regular intervals, and this day saw the arrival of the 59th General Hospital. It moved into the Mercatello school, which was evacuated by a bevy of war correspondents, who had made it their temporary home.

Commanding the hospital was Lieutenant-Colonel J. C. Watts, *RAMC*, who was surprised to find a regimental aid post within a few hundred yards, with several batteries of 25-pounders and American 105 mm. guns blasting away from positions in a nearby field. It was hardly his idea of a suitable location for a general hospital.

The hospital was a mixture of American and British surgical teams. Watts was astounded when, on being introduced to the steel-helmeted medical officers, he discovered that some of them were women. British *QAs*, arriving much later, were very chagrined to find they had been beaten to Italy by American nurses, but War Office policy was never to allow female nurses in the front line, whilst the Pentagon believed it was very good for the morale of the wounded to be looked after by them.

* * * * *

James Cooper of the *Sunday Express* reported that several vessels were leaving the area, as in some places the German forward positions were out of effective range of the guns, commenting at the end of his despatch: *We made a tortoise-like start, but we are now hunting the hare.*

John Redfern of the *Daily Express* wrote in his diary:

> Today the world seemed much brighter. I went out and saw German shells landing a couple of fields away. The news appeared to be much better. This afternoon, walking up this road, I reflected on the change in general mood. I was pulled up short when I passed the hospital and saw stretcher-bearers bring out two corpses for loading in a van. They were covered with blankets fastened to the stretchers by string brought across at the neck, waist and feet. The effect, save for their blanketed faces, was that they were cowled friars. I noticed one of the ambulance men turned up his nose as the stretchers came round to the waiting truck. Two girls stood watching for a minute— and then, when they realised the stretchers held corpses and not wounded, they went on, not visibly affected.

* * * * *

Throughout the night alert infantrymen of the 45th *US* Division had listened to the roar of engines in enemy-held territory. As dawn broke, forward artillery observers and lookouts saw a huge cloud of dust rising from the many valleys ahead of them as tanks, trucks and gun limbers withdrew. Patrols that went out found they had much greater freedom, although still harassed by enemy guns. Other groups were hastened forward to keep contact with the retreating enemy, but could not reach them. By early evening they occupied a tobacco factory, followed at midnight by the 157th *RCT* entering Persano.

The 3rd United States Infantry Division, commanded by Major-General Lucien K. Truscott, having sailed from Sicily, arrived off the bridgehead during the day and started disembarking over the beaches, ready to take over positions in the front line.

All along the Allied front troops were beginning to feel that they had at last got on top of the situation. In the south the Americans were regaining their cocksureness; moving into country less ravished by war considerably raised their morale. But for the British in the north there was still to be a lot of hard vicious fighting before the two main passes into the Naples Plain could be forced and the mass of tanks used to full advantage.

CHAPTER XVIII

D-DAY PLUS TEN

19th September, 1943

T HE *BBC* reported news from the Italian front to be scanty.
"But what there is, is quite good. The 8th Army continues to advance at a rapid rate and the 5th Army is still
pushing forward. We have occupied Altavilla and Battipaglia."

*   *   *   *   *

The 2/7th Queen's at dawn were waiting to go into a fresh attack
at Torello. For fifteen minutes before the assault a mixed barrage
of shells from a cruiser, a 25-pounder battery, a platoon of medium
machine-guns and six 3-inch mortars pounded the German positions
in and around the area. 'D' Company, commanded by Captain
Oliver Scammell, moved forward at a walk as close to the screaming
shells as they dared; as the shells and bombs lifted, they broke into
a run, with only a hundred yards to cover before reaching the top
of the enemy trenches. Bewildered and dazed, Panzer Grenadiers
peered from their holes, whilst sporadic fire broke out at the charging troops. Soon grenades were being thrown backwards and
forwards, but the Queens' men would not be stopped, and shortly
the surviving Germans broke off the fight and retreated. A lookout
was swiftly posted at the top of the Torello Church-tower; the
company started to dig in.

A sniper from a nearby hill shot down six soldiers as they were
digging and unable to reach cover. Two men from a rear position,
seeing their comrades dropping, ran with a stretcher through a
hail of bullets to take them back to the regimental aid post. Private
Jack Redman and Private Ronnie Adams, although both wounded,
carried out this task with complete disregard for their personal
safety. Redman was subsequently awarded a Military Medal, but
his comrade Adams died shortly after.

The Germans were not yet prepared to give up completely in
this region. Troop carriers and tanks came rolling into the village

backed by artillery and air bursts, which sprayed the entire area. The ghostly knell of a bell was added to the roar of battle, as shrapnel penetrated the church-tower, tolling the bell as if for a funeral service. The situation, which looked as though it was going to turn in the German's favour, deteriorated even further as the artillery, which had supported them in the attack, switched to a prearranged defensive fire task, many of their shells landing amongst the Queen's. Faced with heavy armour, and having no anti-tank weapons, Captain Scammell had to order a retreat behind the main defensive line. The company suffered six killed and twelve wounded, but although at first their withdrawal looked like a local defeat, it did in fact have considerable bearing along the front, as the Germans, fearing a stronger attack, switched important reinforcements to this part of the line, making it easier for flank units to advance.

*　　*　　*　　*　　*

After the capture of Battipaglia and the Tobacco Factory, the Guards Brigade were now transferred from the central front to take over the hills immediately north of Salerno. General McCreery had made his plans for the break-out to Naples. The first assault was to be carried out by the 46th Division up Highway 18 towards Nocera and Pagani. In the initial stages, troops of the 56th Division were to hold Route 88, going due north from Salerno towards San Severino and then, switching to the offensive, the Guards were to attack through them towards Naples.

Roused after a good night's sleep, the Guards soon guessed that the battle situation must be easier, as they were greeted by sergeant-majors and officers, who cursed them for being untidy and scruffy. A certain amount of the day was spent cleaning up; if it had not been for fresh orders to move, many of them felt they would have shortly been again attending drill parades. The journey from Battipaglia to the outskirts of Salerno was by three-ton truck, much to the soldier's joy, who were delighted to take the weight off their feet for the first time in days. As dusk was falling, they started trudging through the derelict town. The streets were tumbled with wreckage and filled with a grave-like silence. Not a sound, not a voice came from any of the houses, no crying babies, no scrounging snotty-nosed kids; everything appeared dead. It was an awe-inspiring sight for these men, few of whom had ever seen a town quite so badly wrecked. Broken telephone wires and electric cables festooned the buildings, trailing pointlessly nowhere. The air was full of acrid dust and the pungent smell of filth, broken sewers and rotting bodies. Every pole bore a unit sign or an arrow, pointing to Allied Military Government Headquarters and first-aid posts, whilst others in Italian led to civilian labour centres. Military Policemen with the unenviable task of directing traffic from the middle of much shelled cross-roads, urged the marching men on and cursed at drivers who tried to break through the files.

The Guards took over from the Durhams, the Foresters and Leicesters, who could not disguise their pleasure at being relieved from that hotly contested zone.

At the Sanatorium the stocky Geordies quickly showed their positions to the Guards and hurried away. They had scarcely left the park when a party of thirty German *SS* troops carried out a surprise attack against the main hospital building and obtained an entrance. The Guards, unfamiliar with the layout, were at some disadvantage. In the pitch black of the corridors and wards the opposing troops fought hand to hand, slipping and sliding on the marble floors. Barricades of beds and mattresses were erected in the passageways where soldiers, finding it impossible to recognise friend from foe, fought almost by smell or sixth sense. But many shot down comrades in the confusion. Eventually the British were forced out, withdrawing down the hill towards Salerno. For a few hours the Germans were again to have command of the Laughing Hill, with a first-class lookout over the whole of the valley and the bay and a convenient entry into Salerno.

The Coldstream Guards set up their battalion headquarters at the outskirts of Salerno, and positioned the companies further north. An officer of the regiment was approached soon after their arrival by an Italian youth, who, speaking a little English, indicated that he would like to join a fine unit like the Coldstream. He was light-heartedly told he would have to get a short back and sides haircut before they could even entertain the idea and, if he found a barber, they would themselves welcome a visit from him. Much to their surprise, he returned shortly with a hairdresser who was set to work, albeit much against his professional instincts when ordered to perform Guards' cuts.

The youth, highly pleased about the way he had carried out his first order successfully, explained that he still wished to join the regiment, as he had a girl friend in Naples he badly wanted to see. After much insistence, he was appointed unofficial interpreter to the battalion. The next of his jobs was to find some eggs and fruit and, if possible, some fresh meat; giving a comic opera version of a Guards' salute, he trotted off into the town. Not long afterwards, he was back with three women, a canteen of cutlery, silver vases and a large box of groceries and food. The four of them cleaned out a room and laid a table complete with napkins, flowers, finger bowls and even a centre piece of artificial roses. The officers dined at 9 p.m., waited on by the improvised staff, and by 10.30 p.m. the ladies had cleaned up and departed with their belongings. High praise was given to the Italian boy, and promises made that he could stay with the regiment. Later that night the German artillery put down a highly uncomfortable ten-minute barrage of very intense and accurate shelling. The youth was never seen again; he had no doubt thought discretion the better part of valour: safety lay in a Salerno cellar, and his girl friend in Naples could await better days.

*   *   *   *   *

The Commandos were out of the line and finding some relative peace near Piegolelli, apart from occasional mortaring. One morning, after a particularly prolonged bombardment, one of the biggest and toughest men in the Royal Marines suddenly began to weep, trembling and crawling about on all fours. Previously he had always been in the front in every attack and a great morale raiser to all around him. Nowadays his actions would be put down to 'battle neurosis' and given treatment in hospital. On the hills of Salerno, his behaviour was a mystery to everyone in the unit, although they did realise that he was a man who had just come to the end of his tether after nine days of non-stop fighting. Not surprisingly, he was soon back again with the Marines, having recovered after a few days of quiet and rest in a rear area.

Behind the enemy lines long columns of vehicles, tanks, tracked carriers and marching men continued to move northwards to their new front. A German diarist, taking time off to reflect on the Battle of Salerno, wrote:

> Though victory was denied, the 10th Army and its divisions had registered a defensive success under difficult conditions, with almost no air support and under fire of a strong fleet and a powerful air force. The enemy had hoped that German resistance would quickly collapse, under the shock of the Italian betrayal and the landing, and would permit him to advance rapidly northward. This would have cut off the German forces in Calabria. Instead, he was forced to fight a tough opponent for every yard of territory and use up valuable troops in a minor theatre of war.

These claims of limited success were not without foundation. The 16th Panzer Division had fought an extremely good battle, at first all alone and then side by side with the reinforcements. Between 9th and 20th September, this division took 2,500 prisoners, destroyed 63 tanks, shot down 36 aircraft, captured 49 guns, 44 mortars and 68 vehicles of all types.

*   *   *   *   *

For the Italians, 19th September was not a very pleasant day. Quite justifiably, the Germans blamed to a large extent their former allies for the predicament in which they found themselves; as a result officers and *NCO*s were apt to turn a blind eye on their soldiers during the withdrawal.

At Olevano seventy-year-old Carlo Carucci found his village full of Germans who were preparing to pull out on the following morning. The troops were looting freely. At one farm they commandeered two horses and a cart; from other houses they took olive oil, salami, linen and silver. They even rifled money-boxes, thrusting bayonets into mattresses in their search for valuables. In the small village square a parked lorry was soon loaded with loot. From the backyard of the house owned by Don Gaetano de Sio, an old and sick man, some troops captured five scraggy chickens that had survived the battle. They threatened the old man, who protested violently and would not go away. One of the soldiers finally produced a large pair of scissors and, in front of the old man, snipped off the heads of the hens, which fell into the dust. They then turned on their heels and walked away laughing.

Everyone in the village scurried around, burying and hiding precious belongings in the hope that they would escape the vigilant eyes of the looters.

An American trooper of the 45th 'Thunderbird' Division, advancing near Eboli in the afternoon, came upon the dead body of a German clasping in his lifeless hands a letter he had been in the process of writing when death had struck him. He had written:

My Dearest little wife,

You will be amazed to read about our bitter fighting in the Eboli sector. Casualties are ever increasing. To add to the terror, the enemy air forces are bombing us relentlessly and atrociously, and with all that an uncanny and perpetual artillery fire is scoring hits. Our fight against the Anglo-Americans requires more strength from us than our fight against the Russians, and many of us are longing to get back to Russia—even longing for conditions as they were at Stalingrad.

The Oxford & Buckinghamshire Light Infantry now found themselves in a quiet zone near Salerno; with their battles over for the time being, they looked forward to rest and a bit of peace. But as soon as they came out of the line into the flat marshes, malaria struck the battalion; despite copious supplies of mepacrine tablets and nets, the mosquitoes feasted on their blood, causing a large number of casualties.

Just about this time a corporal and eleven men reported to battalion headquarters. They had been left behind in hospital in Tripoli when the unit sailed for Italy. As soon as they were sufficiently recovered the corporal had arranged a lift for them aboard a destroyer to Salerno Bay. Unfortunately they landed in the 56th Division area during a sticky period and were sent to local units. Seeing General Graham one day, the corporal bravely stepped forward to tell the story of their hitch-hike from North Africa, and the general, admiring their pluck, promptly sent them off to their own regiment.

The newly arrived troops of the 3rd *US* Infantry Division took over from the 56th Division and from the badly battered 36th Division. In the evening they were advancing through the ruin-encumbered streets of Battipaglia.

On the extreme right flank the American troops occupied Eboli after slight resistance.

The 169th Queen's Brigade were relieved during the afternoon by a brigade of the 7th Armoured Division and retired to an orchard near Faiano. Their account summed up the situation for everybody.

The Salerno bridgehead was firmly in Allied hands. The Germans in retreat. The evening mail arrived and they had their first real sleep for eleven days.

Chapter XIX

D-DAY PLUS ELEVEN

20th September, 1943

To all intents and purposes this twelfth day saw the end of the Battle of Salerno.

From London at 9 p.m. the *BBC* broadcast:

"The pace of the enemy's withdrawal in the Salerno area has quickened. We now hold all the high ground at the southern arm of the Bay of Naples. . . . It is now known that the Germans suffered quite badly in the recent fighting on this front . . . their losses include at least forty tanks; and while their hitting power remains formidable, at present they are offering what is officially described as decreasing resistance . . . they are giving ground slowly north of Salerno."

*   *   *   *   *

This morning (wrote Carlo Carucci in his diary) not a German was to be seen in Olevano and the surrounding country. The news spread and there has been much rejoicing. It reached the caves and many people have come down, poor, thin, their donkeys loaded with what they had taken, cows, horses, etcetera. With difficulty they have told of their sufferings. Here and there along the roadsides and lanes things taken by the Germans, and then abandoned, have been found, and the people have suspected robbers and spies amongst the villagers, and voices have been raised. But there is still artillery fire and planes are going overhead to hit the Germans on the Acerno road and we can still hear the noise of the bombs.

Some time later he again noted that Allied troops were marching through the village and presumed them to be British. He was most surprised when the seventy-year-old village postman came to tell him that they were American, some of them coal-black negroes.

Like most Italians whose hearts had not been in the war, Carucci expected the invading troops to forget the past and treat them as comrades in arms and allies. He expressed great disgust in his notes over the arrogance of many British units and quoted an example of an

English captain, who, having removed an electric cooker from a house in spite of the owner's protests, then gestured with his feet indicating that he and all his compatriots should be trodden into the ground. 'Will they treat us as vanquished?' Carucci asked himself. 'Let us hope not. I especially think that the Americans will not do it and—dare I add—will not permit it?'

The hopes of these Italians rose and fell according to the troops they met and the way they were treated. Many of the British were harsh towards the local inhabitants, whilst the Allied Military Government upset feelings by interfering in local affairs, sacking officials who were thought to be Fascists and replacing them with men of their own choosing. Lots of Italians took the chance to pay off old scores by reporting past incidents or inventing some to enhance their positions.

AMGOT officials who enquired about grain supplies were immediately suspected of intending to commandeer all food, when in fact they were only trying to estimate the amount of stores necessary to keep the population from starving.

The generosity of the Americans overwhelmed the villagers. Bars of Palmolive soap, unseen for years, became valuable barter materials. Carucci's wife, delighted with two bars of green soap, brought out from the cellar her one and only bottle of champagne, presenting it to her liberators. One woman in Olevano, whose house had been sacked by the retreating Germans, was adopted by a group of *GIs*, who supplied her with all the necessities of life and not a few luxuries.

They are very correct (wrote Carucci). Quite different from the idea I had of Americans. If they are mostly like this, I believe that they will be able, in view of the richness of their soil, to head tomorrow a large part of the world's population. Posterity will see.

Carucci suspected a lack of fellowship between the British and *US* troops. With the kindness and sympathy shown to the Italians by the Americans, he penned the following lines:

They feel they are nicer and, I should say, more powerful than the British. It really seems that there are no kind feelings between the two brother nations and—if I am allowed to prophesy a bit—America wants and perhaps will succeed in obtaining superiority over the British. Should this happen, such superiority will not only be over England; it will be over the whole world. And then farewell to the hegemony of the European people! On the other hand, it does not seem that America could create a new civilization; she may be able to dominate the world with dollars, she might put science to better profit, but she will not rule it with the power of genius. And, anyway, it does not seem that she is thinking of weighing others down with her power. The great creator of civilisation was Europe, and Italy always had an important place in it. I do not believe that such strength is exhausted. With this wish I shall terminate this diary, written from day to day, in the midst of terrible anxiety, fright, dangers, as it came to me and only as a personal record and memory.

* * * * *

North of Salerno the battle was raging with unabated fury. The Guards Brigade found that the change of scenery had not led to a relief in action. The Coldstream Guards, still smarting from being forced out of the Sanatorium, planned a fresh attack on the main building. The tired men formed up at the bottom of the Laughing Hill, waiting for an artillery barrage to lift before they advanced up the terraced slopes and through the neglected vineyards. The *SS* troops between the stone walls ducked their heads, as the shells screamed nearby, but kept wary eyes on all approaches. In the late afternoon the Guards started up the hill in a spread-out formation, walking calmly with fixed bayonets, awaiting the order to charge. Men fell in their tracks as Spandaus ranged the slopes, but the line closed on the gaps and continued its approach as if on a parade ground. Fifty yards from the hospital, Lieutenant Michael Howard gave the order to his platoon to charge; only then did the khaki line break into a trot and with warlike yells rush onto the enemy positions.

Thirty *SS* men had taken the building—only sixteen escaped from it alive. Short of ammunition and out of touch with their head-quarters, they retreated slowly and bravely, fighting across the park, using every tree, every fence, every boulder as a firing position. Carrying wounded comrades on their shoulders, they staggered desperately to escape from the encircling guardsmen. As the Cold-streamers pushed through the park, they found the scattered bodies of many German soldiers; one lay on his belly riddled with bullets, surrounded by empty magazines, with his finger still on the trigger of a Spandau. Dead British troops were mixed up with the enemy; the flowerbeds, the summerhouses and walks were littered with empty ration and ammunition boxes, discarded grenades, wrecked wireless sets and even burnt-out vehicles.

But the advancing Guardsmen were soon stopped by a stony defence short of Fratte, where they dug in amongst the rocks. Some of the heaviest enemy shelling of the Salerno battle then followed. The Germans were determined to slow and control the pace of their retreat and the Allies' advance until they were ready to face the enemy again on ground of their own choosing. Lieutenant Christopher Bulteel with the Coldstream Battalion wrote:

Below us to our right lay the hospital in which Number 4 Company lived. To close a gap, we sent down a medium machine-gun under Corporal Blackham, with rather vague orders to shoot if he saw a target. There were plenty of targets, and as the morning advanced he fired several belts of ammunition. The Germans did not like this and soon a gun began to range. Suddenly a salvo came over and the machine-gun post had a direct hit. A man was killed, I think; Corporal Mountford and a Guardsman were wounded. A stretcher party of four men went down to pick up the Guardsman and brought him to the top of the hill. Again came the agonising scream of close shells, which burst around the stretcher party. All were killed except old Crowe, who was badly wounded.

Corporal Blackham reached me with Standley and told me Corporal Mountford was still down there wounded. Sergeant Glover dashed downhill and pulled him out, as another salvo of shells crashed down. I ran to company headquarters which seemed to be hit, but they were all right, though all very frightened. They were in a tiny white hut perched on the slopes, with solid rock and no slit trenches. It was suicide to stay there, for in a few minutes another salvo landed all round us, blowing us about, but still hitting no one. We crawled out of the hut and lay in a line against the side of a low rock wall. The pounding went on mercilessly. On the forward edge of a feature, where John Hamilton's platoon was that day, things were pretty sticky too. The cry came for stretcher-bearers. All were dead. Mervyn Griffith-Jones and I and two Guardsmen crawled forward, Mervyn leading, pulling the stretcher after him. We found poor Sergeant Newman with a tremendous hole in his thigh, and put him on the stretcher. Stoneman, with a small wound in his calf, was walking about as if he were hiking on Snowdonia. I helped carry the stretcher for a yard or two, but my broken wrist would not stand the strain and someone else had to take over. They got the wounded man back, through Mervyn's courage.

I went to my platoon and helped the wounded. Corporal Mountford had a hole right through his neck from front to back, but was talking, somewhat incoherently, and not bleeding overmuch. He survived to receive the Military Medal. Guardsman Flynn had a foot almost detached from his leg. We bandaged him with splints and I gave him some precious morphia. And the shells came and burst around us, all that terrible day.

Two officers of the Scots Guards, Lieutenant Elliott and Lieutenant Fraser, who had been missing for a week, presumed captured, managed to escape and return to the British lines. They had both sprouted very un-Guardsmenlike ginger beards. They described the feelings of their captors as confident that they would still win the war. Most of the troops had been in Russia; nearly all the cooks and orderlies were Russians captured near Stalingrad who, offered the choice between a prisoner-of-war camp or fighting with the German Army, had chosen the latter and were perfectly happy in their new role.

* * * * *

Although a few more days were yet to pass before the British divisions would advance through the defiles to the Plain of Naples, Salerno was now considered safe and the situation completely under control. There was still much fighting ahead for these men of the 5th Army and some hard campaigning under the filthiest of conditions, but the Battle of Salerno was virtually over.

A reflection of this confidence was an order issued to all Services: *Treat the Italians with watchful courtesy.* This was interpreted light-heartedly by some *RAF* officers to mean: "Give 'em a drink, but don't leave the bottle!"

There were general advances in the centre and southern sectors of the front. The 45th Division moved into the high ground south of the River Ofanto near Sant'Andrea di Conza and Teora. Their route was covered with thousands of mines; every bridge and culvert had been demolished by the retreating Germans. The reconnaissance troop made contact with 8th Army units.

The 3rd Division, after a dawn attack, moved into mountainous countryside that to many of them was reminiscent of the Rockies. The area was criss-crossed with steep-sided wind-swept canyons; in some places cliffs over a hundred feet high assisted the Germans in delaying the Allied advance. With little opposition, the troops pushed on until they reached a bend in the river two miles south-west of Acerno, where the road crossed a sixty-foot deep gorge in a single arch which had been destroyed by the enemy. On the opposite side, well sited and dug in, stood the 9th Panzer Grenadier Regiment in well-nigh impregnable positions, determined to delay the advance for as long as possible.

There was no doubt that Salerno was safe. But the optimistic forecasts of the Allied Command that, once a bridgehead was established, all German forces would withdraw to Northern Italy, was proved completely and utterly wrong. Kesselring, who until now had been out of favour with Hitler, was suddenly returned to the bosom of the Fuehrer, who had been delighted by the gallant fight put up by Kesselring's army, and found that his plans for defending Italy line by line were approved. The Field Marshal was once again in command of all German troops south of the Brenner Pass and was able to put to the test his theories of using Italy as a killing ground. How well his troops fought, and the bitter opposition which faced every step forward taken by the British and Americans belongs to other books and other campaigns, but the cost to the Allies was enormous and there will always be argument as to the wisdom of committing so many men into a blood bath that in the end had very little connection with final victory.

*　　*　　*　　*　　*

General Fred Walker returned to his headquarters from an inspection in the afternoon to find a note on his desk:
Goodbye to you and your fine division. Mike.
This puzzled him.

I could make nothing out of it (he wrote) other than that Dawley had been relieved from his command. I was distressed. I wondered why he had been relieved. A day or so previously he had shown me a letter of commendation he had received from General Clark. I searched back over the Salerno operation for some possible clue. I found many tactical mistakes, of a minor nature, by troops of my own command. For these I, not Dawley, was responsible. At no time had General Clark or General Dawley made any criticism, to me personally, of my conduct of the operations.

Mr. Winston Churchill sent a message to General Mark Clark:

Accept my hearty congratulations on the hard and brilliantly conducted battle which you have won on the beaches of Salerno, in which British and American soldiers have shed their blood together and not in vain. Every good wish for further successes.

General Eisenhower was also to receive from the same hands a note reading: *As the Duke of Wellington said of the Battle of Waterloo 'It was a damned close-run thing' but your policy of running risks has been vindicated.*
General 'Dick' McCreery, responsible more than any other man for the success of the battle, through his leadership, drive, tenacity and cheerfulness, remembered his troops and issued an Order of the Day:

After ten days of heavy fighting, X Corps has forced the enemy on to the defensive and on our right he is carrying out a big withdrawal. The enemy's objective was to drive us back on to our beaches. For this purpose he concentrated against us the 16th Panzer Division and elements of four other divisions. He has failed, thanks to the courage, endurance and splendid fighting spirit of you all. You have inflicted very heavy losses on the enemy, and he has lost much equipment. We will now turn to the offensive in conjunction with the *US* Rangers on our left, who have harassed the enemy continually in very hilly and mountainous country. Once we have the enemy on the run we will keep him moving. I wish to express my grateful admiration and thanks to all officers and men of X Corps for the fine fight you have put up throughout this operation in widely varying and difficult country.

British casualties from D-Day up to the 20th were recorded as a total of 5,211 killed, wounded and missing.

* * * * *

At last, with the advance into less damaged areas, the troops began to receive some of the benefits of their role of liberators. They were fêted in village after village with fruit, flowers, vino and kisses. In one small town a startled Fusilier saw a middle-aged woman rushing towards him, her arms outstretched, and in a voice born and bred not far from the Old Kent Road she welcomed him:

" 'Ullo, ducks, ow are yer? Let me shake yer bleeding 'and."

As for Arturo Carucci, the chaplain of the Sanatorium, having got himself and some patients as far as Amalfi, he decided, now that the battle had passed, to return to the Laughing Hill. The Americans packed them into lorries and the pitiful weary crowd went back the way they had come, to the wrecked building, that had once been the pride of the hospital staff and of Salerno town.

Carucci's diary reads:

As Salerno appeared, our eyes all turned to the Laughing Hill, from where a tall column of smoke was rising. No one dared put their thoughts into words: 'Is the Sanatorium on fire?' We reached the road leading up to the hospital. At the foot of the hill lay an English tank, burnt and buckled; higher up piles of shells; scattered across the road were bullets and unexploded bombs and empty brass shell cases. In the yard, just outside the gatekeeper's lodge, we saw another burnt-out tank and nearby the body of a dead British officer. The walls of the building were full of enormous shell holes; the tiles on the roof had slipped and in places cascaded to the ground. The watch-dog, still tied up to the lodge, was dead, full of shell splinters.

From the Fratte Tunnel came the hundreds who had lived in its unhealthy shelter for nearly two weeks. They were half-starved wraiths, worn out mentally and physically.

I made a rapid survey of the premises: the Sanatorium was riddled with holes; not one department was intact; the chapel in ruins, having been hit by two shells; the doctors' quarters and the nuns' apartments a mass of rubble, fallen walls and overturned furniture. In the various wings there were still barricades, artillery shells, bullets, hand grenades and a nauseating stench.

With much shrugging of shoulders, they started the long hard struggle to bring the Sanatorium back to life. As Carucci went out to get some belongings, a convoy of trucks towing guns pulled into the yard. Nervously he approached an officer:

"*Encore la guerre?*"

"*Non, monsieur,*" replied the officer. "*Pour Salerno la guerre est finie.*"

EPILOGUE

A ND so the spring tide of war that had flooded and engulfed Salerno and the surrounding villages, farms and hamlets in a torrent of blood and misery receded, leaving behind it the flotsam and jetsam of a storm that with fire, bullets, shells and bombs, had purified and cleansed the land from the evils of a dictatorship which, although in some ways of good intent, had brought with it all the penalties accompanying an egotistical, ambitious individual.

From the caves and tunnels, from the trenches and cellars, came forth the shocked inhabitants to gaze at the wreckage left behind by the holocaust of opposing armies and the sacrifice of their homes and belongings made by the fortunes of war.

The flotsam was the wrecked homes of the people, the ruined fields of the farmers, the broken roads and bridges and the injured bodies and minds of the population who had endured and suffered a war not of its own making.

The jetsam was the rubbish and waste in lives and materials left behind by both vanquished and victors in their haste for escape or pursuit of success.

Peasants took up their tools again to put order into the vineyards and the lemon groves. The bricklayers and masons mixed the mortar and hewed the stones to bring warmth and dryness back to the homes. The children played wonderingly in burnt-out tanks and made mock battles in the trenches and dugouts so easily transformed from battlefield to playground.

And the seeds of war continued to blossom and kill. As the ploughshares turned up a mine, the fragments exploding amongst animals and humans would complete its manufacturer's purpose. Lads seeking rope for a game would pull a trip-wire and the innocence of childhood would be blotted out. Peasants who burned wood gathered from ruins would be showered with hot embers, as a hidden bullet or grenade exploded on the hearth.

Travellers seeing a protruding foot or rotting skull would either turn away and, crossing themselves, hurriedly pass by; others, with tidier minds, would pour a few handfuls of earth over the remains and, again crossing themselves, hasten on. It was none of their business. It was not their war. It was not their husband or son. It was not even a distant relative or a friend. It was a stranger from a distant land—an enemy or ally, a foreigner.

But there was one amongst these people who saw and sorrowed, whose conscience rebelled against the indifference and the callousness of war and its aftermath. This was a simple woman, a woman of the people, the owner of a small general shop in the village of Cava de' Tirreni. On the road from Salerno to Naples, it is a labyrinth of arches and covered passages, mostly paved in cobblestones.

Lucia Apicella, known as Mamma Lucia, has unwittingly relived the Greek legend of Antigone: the woman who went out to the battlefield to bury the dead in defiance of King Creonte, who had decreed that the dead should be left where they had fallen and abandoned to the wolves, the rats and the crows. For her crime she was imprisoned in a tomb, only to be kept alive and fed, so as not to entice God's wrath.

In 1946 Mamma Lucia was fifty-nine years old. Her family had been spared from personal sorrow during the war and her two stalwart sons had returned safely home. It was in May of this year that she started her work of disinterring corpses from battlefield graves and placing them in caskets in a chapel.

There are those today, in the environs of Salerno, who swear she was sent a vision by Saint Giacomo Minore, after whom is named the small church at Cava. There are others who go even further, and predict she will be another sanctified Lucia—St. Lucia of Mercy.

Mamma Lucia had seen and been appalled at the destruction wrought by war on her homeland and the casual way in which bodies had been left unburied and forgotten. She thought with pity of the mothers and fathers of these soldiers who lay as unknown corpses, and she hoped that she could at least give them the burial they deserved and satisfy her deep religious conscience.

One morning she went to an abandoned temporary cemetery to start her work of rescuing the human remains and caring for them, as only a mother could. The cemetery was a mass of leaning twisted crosses, stuck into shallow graves, which had been ravaged by animals and in some cases by human vandals. Tall, solemn, humbly dressed in black, she bent her knees and back, as with work-worn fingers she searched and dug between the stones and weeds hiding human remains. She was not interested in the nationality of the dead. German, English, American, Moroccan? She answered only the compassion of her heart. For many days she concentrated on the cemetery, exhuming and re-burying the dead. Often she was able to identify a body from a disc or from sheets of putrefying writing paper found in a pocket. Nearly always accompanying her was her small niece, who followed, holding a small bunch of flowers, the sort of blossoms that no one bothers to gather, the blooms that get trodden on by passers-by. Mamma Lucia, tall and angular, dressed always in black, the small child all in white; and as the elder discovered a body, the child would lay her poor flowers in the midst of the bones.

When she had tidied the cemetery, Mamma Lucia extended her search and began roaming those areas where she knew fighting had taken place.

On 16th July, 1946, she visited a cave not far from Cava, set amongst tall shadowy pine trees. The interior was dark and sombre, with an air of mystery enveloping it. Accompanying her this time was a cousin, Carmela Pesaro; they had taken with them a small handcart. She crossed the threshold of the dark cavern and found there a charnel house, with the bones of fourteen soldiers, unburied and wrapped in decaying uniforms. They were Germans; it was easy to see how they had died from the stains on the clothing. Regardless of the stench and rottenness, she gathered armfuls of bones to carry them outside, where she washed and cleansed them, before placing them on the cart. Back at the village church, the priest was glad to recite the De Profundis and to arrange for their proper interment.

Some time later Mamma Lucia extended her work to Montecorvino. In the trenches and gun emplacements she found eight more bodies, unburied and exposed to the elements. By now the church authorities for some reason would not co-operate with her; so with her own money she bought zinc boxes and kept them in a special room in her home.

On the following morning she returned to the Montecorvino battlefield. As she was climbing a hill, some peasants working on the lower slopes shouted out a warning to beware of unexploded bombs. "Don't worry," she cried, "nothing will happen to me." On the brow of a hill she came upon a mound of stones supporting a cross, made of weather-worn branches. With caution she removed the stones one by one, finding under them a haversack of rusting hand grenades. Under the bag was the usual pitiful heap of mouldering bones. That day she returned to Cava with the remains of sixty soldiers.

On her daily self-appointed task she met with sarcasm, kindness, incredulity, rudeness and even official obstruction. Once on a hot summer's day she asked some farm workers for water. They mocked her with taunts and refused. She worked on under the blazing sun; her harvest for the day was so great that she had insufficient boxes for the bones. A few men and women nearby advised her to leave the rest until later, but she answered that the dead must wait no longer. She ripped off her outer skirt and used it as a wrapper. The peasants, abashed by her action, went to their homes, returning with wine, water and clean cloths.

Shortly after, she received a letter from the Mayor of Monte-corvino, ordering her to stop interfering with the battlefield graves. She felt she could not give up and for several weeks spent her time visiting the authorities, until written permission to continue was granted.

She immediately took up where she had left off, but was stopped on the first day by two policemen. "You are arresting me, because I'm simply a woman," she said, "who has thought of the dead who were abandoned. Far away in other lands lie hundreds of Italian soldiers, with whom nobody can be bothered. If I didn't have sons who would get anxious, I would let you arrest me, so that others might know that a woman was imprisoned because she was trying to give a safe resting-place to the remains of those killed in war. Here is my permit; now please let me get on with my work."

That same evening Mamma Lucia realised there was no more room in her house. She decided to take some of the caskets to the chamber at the top of the steeple of the Cava Cathedral. Avoiding the verger, weak with fatigue and fright, she crept up the criss-cross of ladders carrying the boxes. But as she descended the steps, she was greeted by the verger and ordered to remove the boxes. Again it was necessary for her to plead with the authorities; finally she was allowed to lay the caskets in the tiny church of Saint Giacomo Minore, close by the Church of Purgatory. With priestly blessing, the villagers now came to see and soon returned with flowers, candles, tears and prayers. There seemed to be always someone in the church, praying for the dead or for the mothers. The idea, the pity behind Mamma Lucia's plan appealed greatly to women, who could understand the grief of a mother who did not know where her son was buried.

Eventually a German War Graves Commission was formed and came to Italy to set up official cemeteries. A representative called at Mamma Lucia's home to tell her that the caskets would have to be removed. The night before they were taken she spent in the church praying with those to whom she had given a decent burial; on the following morning, when trucks drove into Cava, the villagers turned out in their Sunday best to throw flowers into the vehicles, some even kneeling in the dusty street to pray. Other bodies were collected in this way by the American and British authorities. But her search did not end. She still toured the countryside, either following evidence sent to her by local people, or searching battlefields on her own.

One day she climbed the bomb-pocked St. Liberatore hill, and found amongst the craters, crosses and mounds indicating more uncared-for bodies. There was infinite peace on the hill; only the sighing of the wind as it bent the trees. She was walking slowly towards the graves, when a rope swinging from a branch brushed against her head. She looked up following its strands, and noticed it went to a nearby cross. She reached up to grasp the rope, but some peasants, who had curiously followed her, cried out:

"No, Mamma Lucia! Do not pull it—there are mines up here!"

She turned towards them: "You may well be right, but under that cross is a soldier. Go away; I shall manage on my own."

Mamma Lucia lay full length on the ground, her face brushing the grass. Grasping the rope, she pulled with all her strength. There was no violent explosive blast, only a sharp blow on her head, as a skeleton tied to the end of the rope came falling out of the tree.

Had he been a prisoner hanged by his foes? Had it been tied there by some macabre humorist? With her head ringing from the blow, Mamma Lucia clasped the dry bones and put them into her handcart.

Close by this spot she found a stone, carved perhaps by the dead man's comrades, with the inscription: "O wind of the Tyrrhenian sea, you who know my name, kiss my distant mother for me."

It was not long before the news of Mamma Lucia's devoted task spread beyond the confines of Salerno. A journalist after a good story wrote her up in a Rome newspaper and letters started arriving from distraught mothers in foreign countries. One of these was a cry for help from Frau Thea Schafer in Germany, who sent a map of the place in which her son was reported buried. It was a vegetable garden behind a large farmhouse along the road from Cava to Nocera.

For days, forgetting meals and avoiding rest, Mamma Lucia searched the garden, moving masses of earth in her quest, until she came upon the last mortal remains of Private Louis Schafer. At her own expense, she travelled to Germany and delivered a casket to the mother. This was the first of many similar requests; eventually the old woman recovered a total of seven hundred bodies of German, British and American soldiers, which were either delivered to the proper authorities or sent to their families.

One morning, returning from yet another search, she was greeted by her nephew Vincenzo, excitedly waving a piece of paper:

"Mamma Lucia, look, look! A message has arrived, saying you have been awarded the Gold Medal of Kindness. Isn't it wonderful!"

"Why?" she asked.

"What do you mean? It's a great honour for you . . ."

"I never looked for any reward for what I've done. I have simply carried out God's will. How do you expect me to be interested in a reward?"

The peace of Cava was soon shattered by the arrival of journalists and photographers, who, hearing of the award, had come from Rome and Naples, even from Milan, to tell the story of the "Miracle of Kindness". Receiving them, in simple terms she told of her work.

On 13th December, 1951, accompanied by her sons Vincenzo and Antonio, and the Mayor, she left the cobbled village streets and the many-coloured roofs of Cava and went to the bustling, noisy capital, so different from the quiet haven of her home town. In Rome they were taken to Palazzo Marignoli, where representatives of the Pope, the Government and foreign diplomats were assembled to greet her.

At the age of sixty-four Mamma Lucia was still tall and unbent, in spite of her labours. Her eyes were then, and still are today, black and piercing, and her features sharply outlined, with a powerful nose below a sweeping forehead. Her hair, with only a touch of grey, was harshly drawn back to a bun. Her hands bore the marks of her dedicated toil, and in her austere ankle-length black dress she had something of the appearance of a nun, whilst the contentment of her face was reminiscent of a Michelangelo painting.

As she walked into one of the palace salons, those gathered to greet her rose to their feet. The Mayor of Rome went forward to kiss her, followed by the German Ambassador, Herr von Brentano. Then the Secretary of Pope Pius XI, pinning on her bosom the gold medal of virtue, requested her to say a few words. Mamma Lucia could only find the strength to utter the sentence: "No more war."

Epilogue

Some time after she received a letter from Doctor Adenauer, the West German Premier, thanking her for her work on behalf of the German nation.

Home to Cava she went and slowly her work ended. There were no more graves; most of her caskets had been sent to the mothers and the remainder reinterred in official war cemeteries.

Peace and quiet returned to Mamma Lucia and to Cava de' Tirreni. Every afternoon at the same time the figure of Mamma Lucia may now be seen walking down the village street carrying the key of the Church of San Giacomo Minore, which she will then open and will be followed by villagers who come to pray in this sanctuary which the bishop has entrusted to Mamma Lucia's care.

A NOTE ON THE SOURCES

As I explained in my preface, practically all the source materials for this book were provided for me by the generous co-operation of hundreds of participants from all sides of the battle.

In the course of my seven years as the Military Critic of the *Daily Express* I read countless books in which there were passages relevant to the battle I have sought to describe, but in view of the vast number of these volumes it would occupy pages of this book to list all those that had some reference to the topics I have dealt with. I will therefore only mention the chief of those from which material has been used in the preceding pages. These are, *La Battaglia di Salerno* by Carlo Carucci, *A Salerno nell'infuriare della Battaglia* and *Lo sbarco anglo-americano a Salerno* by Arturo Carucci, *The Road to Rome* by Christopher Buckley, *Calculated Risk* by General Mark Clark, the Memoirs of Field-Marshal Kesselring, *The Campaign in Italy* by Eric Linklater, *Sicily, Salerno and Anzio* (Volume IX of the History of U.S. Naval Operations) by Samuel Eliot Morison, *History of the 16th Panzer Division* by Wolfgang Werthen, and many Regimental Histories.

INDEX

A

Adams, Pte. Ronald, 228
Adenauer, Dr. K., 248
Ahrenfeldt, Col. Robert, 210
Alexander, Gen. Sir H., 8, 33, 35, 36, 38,
    39, 43, 45, 55, 118, 140–141, 143, 155,
    157, 158, 180, 192, 193, 195, 214, 216
    Rules out evacuation plans, 193
    'More cheerful' signal to Eisenhower,
    193
    Recommends relief of Dawley, 216
Altavilla, 121, 126, 151, 152, 154, 170, 171,
    174, 178, 192, 212, 216
Alvensleben, Maj. von, 21
Anderson, Ensign George, 53
Andrew, Capt. C. L., 39, 169
Ankorn, Col. Charles, 153
Apicella, Lucia, *see* Mamma Lucia
ARMIES
    5th Army, 7, 8, 30, 38, 43, 45, 55, 141,
    142, 156, 158, 174, 175, 180, 192, 194,
    200, 202, 208, 214, 215, 222, 228, 238
    8th Army, 32, 35, 48, 57, 58, 75, 80, 142,
    143, 174, 180, 192, 194, 195, 208, 209,
    210, 215, 222, 228, 238
    10th German Army, 58, 212
Asa (river), 57, 73, 128
Aston, Michael, 9, 157
Avalanche, Operation, 7, 8, 26, 36, 37, 38,
    41, 163, 198
Avellino, 48, 148, 188, 189, 202

B

Badoglio, Marshal, 17, 19, 27, 32, 33, 43,
    217
Barnett, Col., 170
Barron, Lt.-Col., 121, 151
Battipaglia, 8, 17, 44, 48, 49, 56, 57, 73,
    86, 93, 96, 99, 100, 103, 104, 106, 108,
    109, 122, 123, 133, 147, 149, 154, 160,
    179, 182, 184, 185, 197, 201, 202, 203,
    204, 219, 223, 224, 229, 233
Bedell-Smith, Lt.-Gen. W., 43
Bell, Maj. Richard, 149
Bellassis, Lt.-Col., 97
Bizerta, 37, 41, 43, 64, 201
Blackham, Cpl., 237
Block, Lt.-Col. A., 71, 72, 99, 181
Braham, Capt., 87
Brentano, Herr von, 247
Brinkenhoff, Maj., 79

Brock, Lt. Jerome, 83
Brooke, Gen. Sir Alan, 35
Bryant, Arthur, 36
Buckley, Christopher, 194
Buffell, Sgt. G., 67, 97
Bulteel, Lt. Christopher, 9, 88, 89, 103,
    104, 109, 223, 237
Burke, CSM T., 72

C

Calore (river), 119, 120, 124, 126, 128, 153,
    154, 159, 171, 172, 187, 202, 213
Canaris, Adm., 20
Carpenter, 1st Lt. Claire F., 77
Carucci, Arturo, 15, 17, 82, 100, 101, 116,
    117, 139, 140, 143, 144, 164, 166, 167,
    181, 182, 199, 211, 218, 224, 240, 241
Carucci, Carlo, 18, 164, 217, 225, 232, 234,
    235
Castellano, Gen. G., 32
Cava de' Tirreni, 94, 112, 122, 137, 200,
    211, 243–248
Cavallero, Marshal Count, 20
Chandler, Lt.-Col. R., 73, 185
Churchill, Lt.-Col. Jack, 60, 113, 114, 169,
    197, 198, 207
Churchill, Maj. Randolph, 114
Churchill, Lt.-Col. Tom, 114
Churchill, Winston, 16, 34, 35, 49, 239
Clark, Gen. Mark W., 8, 9, 29, 38, 40, 41–
    43, 47, 48, 50, 55–56, 83, 101, 102,
    116, 117–118, 127, 130, 140, 141, 142,
    154, 155, 157, 158, 166, 168, 172, 173,
    174, 176, 178, 179, 180, 186, 187, 189,
    190, 192–194, 199, 202, 215, 216, 222,
    239
    Gets command, 38
    On Dawley's appointment, 38, 56
    No bombardment decision, 47
    Signal at end of D-Day, 102
    Optimism, 141
    Pessimism, 154–155
    Evacuation plans, 154–155, 173
    Decision to relieve Dawley, 193
Clarke, Capt, 135
Clifford, Alexander, 194
Connolly, Rear-Adm. L., 38, 65, 84
Cooper, James, 29, 185, 226
Corbett, Capt. H. Astley, 110
CORPS
    VI (U.S.), 38, 56, 135, 142, 171, 173,
    178, 193, 195, 213

251

Index